# THE EVANGELICAL ALLIANCE FOR THE UNITED STATES OF AMERICA, 1847-1900: ECUMENISM, IDENTITY AND THE RELIGION OF THE REPUBLIC

# THE EVANGELICAL ALLIANCE FOR THE UNITED STATES OF AMERICA, 1847-1900: ECUMENISM, IDENTITY AND THE RELIGION OF THE REPUBLIC

Philip D. Jordan

Studies in American Religion
Volume 7

The Edwin Mellen Press
New York and Toronto

Library of Congress Cataloging in Publication Data

Jordan, Philip D., 1940
   The Evangelical Alliance for the United States of
America, 1847-1900.

   (Studies in American religion ; v. 7)
   Bibliography: p.
   Includes index.
   1. Evangelical Alliance for the United States of
America.   2. Christian union--United States--History--
19th century.   3. Evangelicalism--United States--History
--19th century.   4. United States--Religion--19th century.
I. Title.   II. Series.
BX4.J67 1982          277.3'081          82-24953
ISBN 0-88946-650-5

Studies in American Religion   ISBN 0-88946-992-X

    The Edwin Mellen Press
    P.O. Box 450
    Lewiston, New York    14092

Printed in the United States of America

TO MY PARENTS

ARTHUR AND EMILY JORDAN

# ACKNOWLEDGEMENTS

I wish to thank the many persons and institutions which made this book possible. Mr. Keith A. Rageth of the University of Iowa Library and Mrs. Geneva Williams of Western State College Savage Library provided invaluable aid by obtaining hard to find literature and documents. Their efforts supplemented my research in the archives and collections of the New York Public Library, Newberry Library and the Library of Congress. The staff of Union Theological Seminary deserves special mention for its generous help concerning lodging and research on numerous occasions during the last one and one-half decades—Union has the most complete collection of Alliance documents and official manuscripts.

Although their technical aid made this book possible, I would never have started the task were it not for the encouragement and advice of two scholars resident until recently at the University of Iowa, Sidney E. Mead and Stow Persons. These two men represent all that is best among historians as to teaching, research, and scholarly activity. Yet the person over the years who suffered intimately my agony and ecstasy, who proved goad and inspiration to further endeavors, is my wife Kay. Thank you Kay for providing such intellectual and emotional light to my life.

Kay also deserves thanks for the massive job of typing this book only to suffer the shared agony of its loss in the mail and consequent need to retype it. That has been handled admirably by Una Crist of Fredericksburg, Virginia.

The help tendered me by all of these people and institutions cannot be overstressed. Still, all errors of commission and omission, of statement and text are mine.

                                    Philip D. Jordan
                                    Western State College
                                    Gunnison, Colorado

1981

# CONTENTS

CHAPTER ONE

# INTRODUCTION

The time worn adage that those who are ignorant of their past are condemned to repeat it seems as appropriate as ever when we reflect on the importance to ecumenism and to modern culture of both the World Evangelical Alliance (1846-1951) and the Evangelical Alliance for the United States of America (1847-1944). I shall often refer to the latter organization as the American Alliance. By ecumenism I mean the desire to unite with other Christians in a spirit of fellowship as the one universal church and to dialogue when possible with those persons of other faiths.

Most scholars assume ecumenism arose among Protestants and Christians during the twentieth century. This contemporary bias arises from a rather Whiggish tendency to look at a modern ecumenical institution or movement and search in linear fashion back to its immediate rather than essential predecessors. Charles Clayton Morrison and William Nicholls both illustrate this point in that they trace the World Council of Churches only as far back as the 1910 Edinburgh World Missionary Conference. They do see the importance of the missions movement to ecumenism and Nicholls also realizes the Edinburgh Conference itself arose from the confluence of the nineteenth century missionary movement with the World Student Christian Federation (1895). Yet neither appreciates the existence of that ecumenical movement central to the nineteenth century, the Evangelical Alliance.[1]

Many of the scholars who try to cope with nineteenth century Christendom's yearning for unity attribute ecumenical contributions to all sorts of diverse voluntary societies such as the American Sunday School Union (1817), Bible societies, missionary societies, and confederations of denominations belonging to the same theological family like the Presbyterian (1875) or Methodist Alliances (1881) Works by Gaius Jackson Slosser and John T. McNeill clearly illustrate this generalization. Their approaches fail to distinguish between conscious goals and incidental side effects. Most voluntary societies were designed to distribute Bibles or tracts, sponsor missions, or foster some other common good. With the exception of the denominational Alliances, they made neither the spirit of fellow-

1

ship nor actual unity among Protestants their primary
object. Even the denominational Alliances fell short of
such goals because they attempted to unite only those
churches of the same theological family.[2]

   Yet some scholars sincerely have tried to understand the importance of the nineteenth century World and
American Evangelical Alliances. They tend to fall into
two schools of thought: those evangelicals groping for
their theological and institutional roots and those liberal Protestants, like myself, who have extended beyond
their liberal biases towards an appreciation of the rich-
ness of historic evangelicalism. Those taking either approach may rediscover the evangelical sources of contemporary ecumenism. One of the first modern evangelical
efforts to understand the World Evangelical Alliance is
John Ewing's official but rather uncritical history of
that body. British evangelical J. B. A. Kessler, Jr.,
however, has written an excellent history of the world
movement which argues effectively that this "Alliance
blazed a trail for the twentieth century World Council of
Churches, and acted as a laboratory for many themes on
Christian unity prevalent in the nineteenth century." Of
the liberals, the best history of world ecumenism is that
edited by Ruth Rouse and Stephen Charles Neill. Rouse
especially recognizes the distinction between conscious
goals and incidental side effects. She treats the World
Alliance, with some qualification, as the sole nineteenth
century society of Christians whose purpose was Christian
unity and which became the major precursor to the World
Council of Churches.[3]

   As for the American Alliance, Conservative Baptist
historian Bruce Shelly argues persuasively that the National Association of Evangelicals (1942) was heir to
the Alliance tradition. He errs, however, in treating
the Federal Council for the Churches of Christ in America
(1908) as a break in that tradition. To the contrary,
the American Alliance contained such a wide spectrum of
evangelicalism that it intellectually fathered both. Some
of the connections between the Alliance and the Federal
Council have been established by one of the Council
founders, Elias B. Sanford, and subsequently by John A.
Hutchison. Church historian Robert T. Handy recently
took even broader ground in an excellent overview of
American history by treating that Alliance as a major
vehicle for nineteenth century Protestant efforts to attain a Christian America. Although these men participated in what Henry F. May describes as the "Recovery of
American Religious History," no one has published a book

specifically on the Evangelical Alliance for the United
States of America.[4]

   This volume attempts to erase that gap in the history of ecumenism.  It also tries to address an issue
which many think central to American society during the
1980s.  What role ought religion to play in formulating
values, goals, indeed, even the nature of American society and politics?  The American response to this question
is really quite complex but ranges along a spectrum from
an extreme secular liberalism (not to be confused with
religious liberalism), fearful of anything religious, to
a fundamentalism, be it Roman Catholic, Jewish, or Protestant, which advocates a powerful religious voice in American affairs.  Two polar examples should suffice to make
my point.  Signatories to the "Secular Humanist Manifesto"
like behavioral psychologist B. F. Skinner and political
philosopher Sidney Hook so praise science as the source
of truth and religion of ignorance that they demand religion stay out of secular affairs.  To the contrary, Jerry
Falwell and at least the conservative evangelical and
fundamentalist Protestant portion of his "Moral Majority"
consider American society bankrupt unless evangelical morality and values are reintroduced as its foundation.  The
public furor over conservative and evangelical attempts
to outlaw abortion, eradicate pornography, and restrict
the teaching of biological evolution in the public
schools merely illustrates the intensity of feelings
which a resurgent evangelicalism has aroused.  What evangelicals perceive as social reforms are often branded by
critics as attempts at a social control threatening to
personal freedom.  This difference of viewpoint, in turn,
raises additional questions.  What, if anything, distin-
guishes social reform from social control?  Are efforts
towards social control bad in themselves?  Are social control and democracy compatible?  Indeed, does evangelicalism itself pose a threat to democracy?[5]

   That none of these questions are new may be seen
in the treatment of evangelicalism in pre-Civil War America by such current historians as Charles I. Foster, John
R. Bodo and Clifford S. Griffin.  The implicit thrust of
their early 1960's publications was to reveal the dangers
which evangelical voluntary societies like the Alliance
posed ostensibly for society.  Conservative upper class
elements within America purportedly forged the voluntary
associations of the 1820s-1850s into an "Evangelical
United Front" in order to impose their Victorian values
and reassert their waning authority over an American populace attempting to create democracy.  Such men, according

to Griffin, "feared new forces in American life, worried
about political and social upheavals, deplored new moral
standards, and lamented the decline of religion in an increasingly secular age." Primarily Presbyterians and
Congregationalists, they "believed that the spread of the
Protestant gospel and the pervasive influence of Protestant morality would not only save the souls of their fellow citizens, but would restore to men and to society,
stability and order, sobriety and safety." These "Brothers' Keepers," experiencing status decline, were the
"nineteenth-century exemplars of men who throughout American history have claimed the right and alleged their
duty to tell other men how to behave."[6]

Granting that basic association methods were persuasive rather than coercive, Foster, Bodo, and Griffin
rather subtly cast evangelical social reform efforts as
conspiratorial attempts to control society. That some
evangelicals turned to the state for legal sanctions supportive of morality is made to appear invidious. Hence,
Griffin concluded that "at the end of the Civil War, morality by persuasion and morality by compulsion were permanent characteristics of American life." Such generalizations have aroused considerable scholarly criticism.
Lois Banner has provided an especially fine critique
which shows this historical school severely underrated
the humane and generous reform sentiments among antebellum evangelicals. Hence, I feel no need to provide a detailed response to its claims—this is a history of the
Alliance rather than of antebellum (pre-Civil War) reform.
What concerns me is the implication that religiously inspired social reforms are to be feared or that all efforts towards social control are bad. A democratic society in its very nature relies on voluntary bodies, whether
they be political parties or churches, to formulate majority opinion and guide the nation. Just as too many
or incorrect standards may strangle human freedom, so anarchy or absence of rules may destroy it as well. Neither position can be defended if carried to extremes.
Each effort towards reform or towards control must be
judged on its particular merit.[7]

All human institutions, indeed culture itself, peri-
odically undergo reform and constantly participate in
social control. Historian William G. McLoughlin clearly
shows this in his brilliant application of the cultural
anthropological theories of Clifford Geertz and Anthony
F. C. Wallace towards understanding American history from
its colonial beginnings. According to McLoughlin, societies undergo periods of "awakening," of great cultural

upheaval as to values, institutions and practices, only to
settle into new identity patterns which suit the needs of
the people until the gap between their ideals and experienced reality require readjustment again.  Religion proves
central to those periods of stability as well as to those
of change.  Religious renewal movements and revivalism
accordingly are both elemental to the process of change
and the ensuing revitalized worldview and reorganized culture. [8]

    McLoughlin argues that "awakenings have been the
shaping power of American culture from its inception."
The English Puritans settling New England laid "the basic
beliefs and values that provided the original core of our
culture."  Historians call the first revitalization movement the "Great Awakening" (1730-1760).  Many would agree
with McLoughlin that it helped to foster a "sense of
unique nationality, and had inspired them with the belief
that they were, 'and of right ought to be,' a free and independent people."  Consolidation ensued during the Revo-
lutionary War and Constitutional era, capped by creation
of the United States of America during the last decade of
the eighteenth century.  Then the Cane Ridge Revival (Kentucky, 1801) precipitated a "Second Great Awakening" lasting until the 1830s.  As McLoughlin suggests, this [9]

> second era of religious revivals created the
> definitions of what it meant to be 'an Ameri-
> can' and what the manifest destiny of the new
> nation was.  After the Civil War had cemented
> our sense of the Union ('One nation, indivis-
> ible under God, with liberty and justice for
> all'), the Third Great Awakening helped us to
> understand the meaning of evolutionary science
> and industrial progress and led us into the
> crusades 'to make the world safe for democ-
> racy' in 1917 and 1941. [10]

We are now undergoing another such awakening and evangelicals again are helping to discern its meaning.

    Undergirding this theory is the notion that Ameri-
can culture revolved around a common core of beliefs from
its Puritan and, I might add, Anglican roots until now.
These beliefs altered as to emphasis and nuance but remained much the same throughout American history.  Americans have always believed themselves, in McLoughlin's
words,

        A chosen people; that they have a manifest

(or latent) destiny to lead the world to the
millennium; that their democratic-republican
institutions, their bountiful natural resources, and their concept of the free and
morally responsible individual operate under
a body of higher moral laws (to transgress
which is to threaten our destiny); and that
the Judeo-Christian personal and social ethic
(especially in the formulation described by
Max Weber as 'the Protestant ethic' and
called by recent generations 'the success
myth,' 'the work ethic,' and 'the American
dream') causes the general welfare to thrive
by allowing the greatest possible free play
and equal opportunity to each individual to
fulfill his or her potential.[11]

Do note, contrary to the impression given by McLoughlin's
statement about "democratic-republican institutions," that
democracy has not always been with us—it emerged in the
nineteenth century.

I cannot stress too much the creative role played
by evangelicals in replacing the collapsing aristocratic
order of our colonial era with an individualistic but
democratic social order and governmental system.  They
were not conservative aristocrats conspiring to suppress
the masses.  This book will show that those evangelicals
interested in one voluntary association, the Evangelical
Alliance for the United States of America, may have been
conservative in some of their ideas (for to be conservative involves retention of those past ideas and behavior
patterns thought relevant to the present), and may have
been mistaken in some of their actions, but definitely
supported democracy in a world characterized by monarchy.
Indeed, the very voluntaryist method of their societies
was elemental to that democracy which developed in America after 1800 but institutionalized during the Jacksonian
Era (1820-1840).  In aggregate, they fostered women's
rights, abolition, and all manner of individual and social perfection thought appropriate to a democratic society and free wheeling, bourgeois, capitalist economy.
From the European perspective, such radicalism was compounded by evangelical commitment to separation of church
and state, religious and civil liberty, and the notion
that ordinary man is important.  American evangelicals
sponsored such ideas at a time when most European mon-
archs and ruling classes feared democracy, thought the
American experiment destined to destruction, and believed
religious liberty based on separation of religion from

civil authority (no established church) an invitation to
civil disorder. American evangelicals knew this hostility
existed and spent much time explaining and justifying the
nature of democracy and of evangelicalism.

Another problem with the conspiratorial interpretation of these voluntary societies is the assumption that
the evangelical leadership understood their culture and
its problems so completely that a mere handful of persons
in Boston, New York, and Philadelphia could manipulate a
powerful "Evangelical Empire" of voluntary societies for
their own ends. Although the societies did overlap, and
relied considerably on Congregationalists, Presbyterians
and Reformed for support, the Empire was monolithic neither in structure nor goals, and its diverse leaders were
often confused about the trends and forces of their own
culture. A major point of this study is to show that
evangelical spokesmen, like the nation as a whole, spent
the early years of the nineteenth century as participants
in a rather chaotic awakening which ultimately may have
transformed their aristocratic and republican America into an  egalitarian and democratic nation but was initially unclear as to direction and outcome. They spent much
of these years determining who they were and where they
were going, and the remainder of the century attempting
to get there. Only slowly did they realize the implications of democracy then evolving in America, the nature
of the role of religion in a free society, and the proper
attitude of evangelicals toward each other, as well as
those of different religion, and the nation.

This intellectual history therefore treats the
Evangelical Alliance for the United States of America as
the vehicle of nineteenth century attempts to articulate
an evangelical and American identity conducive to religious unity. I use identity in Erik H. Erickson's least
complicated sense, as "a maintenance of an inner *solidar-
ity* with a group's ideals," while realizing that people
historically might only gradually attain this state of
being and might be slow to realize their emergent per-
ceptual and conceptual agreement. As an anonymous evangelical early in the century said concerning the "common
identity" of his peers, "to a greater extent than they
themselves are aware of, they harmonize with one another."
The term identity consequently refers to that group self-
definition of highly motivating religious and secular
beliefs inherent in the American Protestant worldview
and typical of most individual evangelicals irrespective
of their denominational affiliation.[12]

The Alliance was evangelical because it responded

to such essential characteristics of American religious
identity during the nineteenth century as individualism
rooted in pietistic perfectionism and a millennial worldview.  Its members were leaders of the mainline evangelical denominations and of evangelical parties within the
other churches.  Primarily, they came from the Presbyterian, Methodist, Congregationalist, Dutch Reformed, German
Reformed, Episcopalian, Moravian, Lutheran and to a lesser
extent Baptist and Disciple of Christ folds.  This highly
educated group (mostly college graduates) comprised clergymen, bishops and moderators, educators and newspaper
editors, and major business figures of the day.  Quite
often in advance of its time, the Alliance centered in
the cities where it aided its middle and upper class constituency, businessmen and professionals, in coping with
contemporary religious and secular problems.

The factors contributing to the religious dimen-
sions of evangelical identity are diverse.  It seems that
many Americans were self-conscious about the vast number
of religious bodies which comprised the Christian Church
in their nation.  The First Amendment prohibition of an
established church impelled adherents of any religion to
rely on persuasion to win the support of citizens.  This
voluntaryism inevitably led to an increase in the number
of denominations competing for the faithful, that is, to
religious pluralism, and even allowed abhorrent philoso-
phies, such as infidelity and materialism, and immigrant-
fed Roman Catholicism to flourish in the nation.  Although American evangelicals believed the voluntary nature of their religious experience appropriate for a democratic people, critics claimed the consequent pluralism
betrayed the unitary fabric which Christ intended for His
Church.[13]

As if all this were not complex enough, evangelical
self-definition evolved during a Jacksonian and antebellum period of growing sectional conflict, bitter dispute
over slavery, forebodings that irresponsible capitalists
and emergent industrialization would recreate the social
traumas of Europe in America, and deep tensions with
Europe.  The hypernationalist Jacksonian Americans were
sensitive to European criticism of their lively experiment in democracy while they were quick to angry remem-
brance that the "tyrannical" enemy of the American revolution and War of 1812, Britain, still held the fate of
much of continental America in its "bloody" hands.  "Manifest Destiny," the watchword, and westward folk migration,
the reality, meant bitter disputes arose again and again
with Britain during the 1830s over the location of U.S.-

Canadian boundaries (settled in 1842) and over title to
Oregon, Washington and present British Columbia (settled
in 1846). By the Mexican War (1846-1848), hostility to
American democracy undergirded European prediction of
Mexican triumph and subsequent European dismay over
American victory and the Mexican Cession.

Rapid conversion of the American masses enabled
evangelicals to react to these pre-Civil War experiences
with the growing conviction that America had a Christian
civilization resting on an evangelical foundation whose
pillars were religious and civil liberty. As suggested
by the dean of historians of religion in America, Sidney
Mead, this involved the "theological merging of evangelical Protestantism with the religion of the Republic" to
the point where everything but the American legal and
federal constitutional structure was christianized. I
would also agree that "the Republic's neutral civil authority," if properly understood and given enough time,
"set limits on the absolutistic tendencies inherent in
every religious sect, preventing any one of them, or any
combination of them, from gaining, or regaining, a monopoly on the definition of truth, and imposing its particular forms on all the people." A neutral civil authority,
in this sense, meant a constitutional separation of any
religion from the civil authority. But I must add that
nineteenth century evangelicals believed the Constitution
prohibited the European pattern of some Church being the
arm of the State, hence their commitment to the separation of church and state. Yet they incorrectly assumed
the Constitution permitted connections between American
civil authority and that evangelical religious consensus
held in common by most American churches. An essentially
evangelical American public opinion accordingly overrode
the civil authority's legal neutrality by reinterpreting
as *Christian* and *democratic* the essentially *deistic* and
*republican* constitutional basis of that structure. Evangelicalism thereby became the established 'religion'
(rather than established 'Church') of mid-nineteenth century America.[14]

By republican I mean the Founding Father's authori-
zation in 1789 of a national government based on the best
elements of monarchy (President), aristocracy (Senate),
and democracy (House) whose divisions of power and checks
and balances were designed to prevent tyranny of person,
group or mob. Americans had transformed their structure,
by the 1820s, into a *democratic* Republic, separated officially from the churches although watched over by a
trinitarian Godhead rather than deistic Creator, whose

Constitution, Bill of Rights and Declaration of Independence, in Ralph Henry Gabriel's terms, were thought to
reflect the divinely inspired concepts of the fundamental
law, free and responsible individual and the American
mission.  Such concepts involve a constellation of ideas
and historical precedent.[15]

     The parallel emergence of evangelicalism and democ-
racy in the early nineteenth century led the originators
of our democratic ideology to think the universe rested
on a fundamental law which comprised two overlapping
parts, natural and moral law.  The Founding Fathers of
1789 made natural law theory the basis of the American
Republic.  Turn of the century Americans, however, increasingly interpreted it to mean that only a democratic
government allowed man the full exercise of his rights.
With evangelical ascendency over American culture, the
Fathers' stress on man's natural right to life, liberty
and the pursuit of happiness was supplemented by a moral
law, recorded in Christian scripture, which obliged man
to obey divine precepts for humane living and to respect
the rights of others.  Hence, man could be a free and
responsible individual only if he obeyed the dual elements of the fundamental law and committed himself to its
implementation in society by means of the voluntaryistic
method of persuasion.  These ideas engendered so much
enthusiasm that antebellum democrats believed America
had a mission to create such a perfect example of a democratic and Christian nation that the world would follow
suit.  Most evangelicals, in good 'postmillennial' fashion, hoped such an event would introduce that 1000 year
era, the millennium, leading to Christ's final return and
the Last Judgment.

     This nineteenth century Religion of the Republic
reflected the essentials of evangelical religious identity to the point where, at the end of the Civil War, evangelicals thought them united.  Wesleyan University President and future Methodist Bishop Cyrus D. Foss said just
this in 1870: "The August Ruler of all the nations designed the United States of America as the grand repository and evangelist of civil liberty and of pure religious
faith.  And these two are one."  Such Jacksonian Era success at home inspired evangelical ambitions of spiritual
world conquest, which, together, made evangelicals gradually mindful of the myth of Christian unity and the reality of evangelical consensus.  As stated by a leader of
Methodist perfectionism, Bishop Matthew Simpson, "it is
very plainly taught that the world will never fully believe in the mission of Christ until Christians become
one."[16]

Chapters One and Two accordingly show the American ecumenical movement before the Civil War responded to pluralism by trying to articulate a group definition and to sponsor public fellowship and comity among evangelicals without consolidating the denominations into an organic union, although some hoped for denominational federation. Chapter Three emphasizes that 'theological' consensus was set forth by the 1846 London Conference of the Evangelical Alliance but the Americans who founded the Evangelical Alliance for the United States of America (1847) were unable to convince their countrymen of its accuracy. This meant death to their Alliance at home, given other factors hindering ecumenism. Evangelical comity and cooperation during the Civil War however enabled the revived American Alliance (1866) to assume that 1846 consensus valid. The War also helped eradicate such problems as sectionalism and slavery but left the threat of religious pluralism intact. The growth of a hedonistic materialism spawned by American prosperity and scientific evolutionary hypotheses, epitomized by the Darwinian theory of evolution, meant evangelicals operated in a postwar era of increasing confusion and danger to their faith.

Victory euphoria and confidence in themselves, however, enabled evangelicals enthusiastically to confront their world during the 1870s. The American Alliance after the War became far more energetic and successful than its predecessor. It attempted to increase evangelical comity worldwide through defense of religious and civil liberty, as well as separation of church and state, exportation of American democratic standards and, paradoxically enough, defense of an established religion at home. It became a bastion of the evangelical Religion of the Republic, the subject of Chapters Four and Five. By 1883, however, Alliance spokesmen began to realize their program at home was ill-equipped to solve the urban unrest, poverty and mass alienation from the churches which threatened their evangelical Republic. Convinced that transformation of the social environment was essential to save urban man, thereby conserving evangelical democracy, and turning from international to national ecumenism, the Alliance reorganized its structure, rewrote its program, hired Josiah Strong as General Secretary, and launched into its most energetic and successful period of activity. Chapter Six therefore explains how, from 1883 to 1898, the Alliance preached the social gospel and encouraged pragmatic denominational cooperation both to solve national and Protestant problems and to foster a spirit conducive to federation of the churches. Implicitly, the Alliance aspired to such federation-at-the-top since the early 1870s. Now, in

the 1880s, Josiah Strong got it to sponsor federation-at-
the-bottom by encouraging local congregations to cooperate in an Alliance structure pyramiding from local, to
state, and thence to national levels.  Once the implications of this approach became clear, however, Alliancemen
jettisoned both General Secretary and program and reaf-
firmed unofficially such federation as would preserve denominational independence.  Whatever the case, Alliance
activities throughout the nineteenth century laid the
basis for the twentieth century Federal Council, subsequent National Council of the Churches of Christ in America, and even the National Association of Evangelicals,
while simultaneously attempting to foster a national evangelical and democratic faith.

CHAPTER TWO

# "PLURALISM," THE SEEDBED OF EVANGELICAL
# IDENTITY, 1730-1839

The period of 1730-1839 witnessed two successive
Great Awakenings and massive European immigration to
America.  The warp and woof of our culture underwent dramatic stretching consequent of both the internal dynamics
of colonial society and of the addition by the immigrants
of a vast new variety of cultural and religious baggage.
Americans found such pluralism so uncomfortable they gradually but unwittingly formulated a new common ground of
values and practices, evangelicalism, to undergird their
continued diversity.  The core of this evangelical identity rests on the intellectual and emotional underpinnings of evangelical piety.  The roots of nineteenth century Protestantism obviously extend back to the Lutheran
and Calvinist Reformations as mediated by the English experience.  Augustinian monk Martin Luther undercut Roman
Catholic formalism during the early 1500s when he insisted that salvation occurred by faith alone rather than
through good works and officiation of the Church.  His
unleashing of a radical, individualist pietism, with its
priesthood of all believers, offered hope for all men and
women to attain that level of personal spirituality and
Christian perfection heretofore the property of only
those who took holy orders as priest or monastic.  Such
Lutheran pietism flowed through different European religious channels, be it the more logically rational and
legalist Calvinism, with its rule by committees of saints,
or the Lutheran/Calvinist influenced but home-grown English Reformation.  Luther's reforms therefore unleashed
an explosion which shattered Christendom into an extra-
ordinary variety of cults, sects and churches, which replaced unity with pluralism.  Yet his pietism undergirded
them all to a varying degree.

England experienced this explosion while eventually
settling into a hierarchy of its own.  King, government,
and nation were legally blanketed by an "established"
(Anglican) Church of England whose boundaries were those
of the realm and whose constituency all Englishmen.  Essentially a compromise as to form and doctrine, Anglican-

ism proved unable to satisfy the needs of many.  Approxi-
mately one-third still remained Roman Catholic while many
more sought after truth in reform minded groups like the
Puritans, Pilgrims, Seekers and Ranters.  Frustrated by
the overly Roman Catholic theology and forms of Anglicanism, and inspired by personal pietism requiring the faithful to organize both Church and State according to essentially Calvinist but biblically based divine precepts, a
portion of the English Puritans left the hard times of
their inflation-wracked and overly worldly England, crossed
three thousand miles of watery desert, and tried to complete the Protestant Reformation in New England.  Of course
other Englishmen and Europeans assayed similar trips for
equally complex economic, social and religious reasons,
thereby giving colonial America a colorful variety of cultures and religions despite the attempts by colonial authorities legally to "establish" Puritanism in New England
and Anglicanism in the South.[1]

     Pious hopes to the contrary, by 1700 nearly all re-
ligious groups believed they were sliding from their original piety into a lackluster pattern of formalism.  This
belief appeared as well among the religious in the British
Isles and Protestant areas of Europe until a rather spon-
taneous religious revival overwhelmed most Protestant
peoples bordering the Atlantic Ocean.  If one understands
the theory of "Awakenings," felt religious decline was a
symptom of larger social strains.  For example, the single
factor of population explosion, due to high birth rates
and immigration, required dramatic change, whether in town
or on the frontier, in the original churches, governments
and family institutions of colonial America.  A similar
radical transformation of English culture resulted from
the Agricultural Revolution, consequent population explosion and dislocation, and other trends wending their way
towards an Industrial Revolution emergent in the late
eighteenth century.  These social strains may be perceived
but dimly and yet predispose the people psychologically
for that religious reorientation and renewal which enables
many of them to master their new environments and lead
once again rich and rewarding lives.  Religious revival,
in this context, is both real and meaningful.

     That eighteenth century Awakening was spontaneous in
that the John and Charles Wesleys who fathered English
Methodism (1730s), the Theodore Frelinghuysen who revived
New York and New Jersey Dutch Reformed (1720s), and the
brilliant Massachusetts theologian-scholar Jonathan Edwards
who overwhelmed the now cold Puritan-become-Congregational-
ism of New England (1730s), to name a few, confronted

similar declines and inspired similar revivals unaware of
the others. Religious isolation did not last long. Methodist convert and charismatic Calvinist George Whitefield
sailed into the new world (1739) with such fiery passion
and stentorian, almost hypnotic, voice that he wielded the
individual revivals flaring throughout the various colonies
into a North American conflagration. [2]

The Atlantic world revival had become a united fact
with its own itinerant clergy, literature, and revival theology. Still, national variations abounded. In the words
of historian Sydney Ahlstrom, "only through that compulsive
outburst of piety did 'American Evangelical Protestantism'
become aware of itself as a national reality and alive to
its culture-shaping power." It especially undercut both
contemporary colonial religious authority as well as the
relatively complex theologies and forms of the day by
introducing an increasingly simplified sense of polity and
theology. [3]

This nascent "evangelical" theology stressed that the
truly repentant sinner must depend utterly on Christ's
saving grace for his redemption. Careful study of God's
Word, the Bible, clearly would reveal to the individual the
divine plan for the world. The fall of Adam imputed original sin to all mankind but God mercifully sent his only Son
to take upon himself their sins. Inspired by the Holy
Spirit, man need only believe in Christ to be saved. To
Edwards, Frelinghuysen and most awakened Americans of the
eighteenth century, this meant complete dependence on God
for such saving grace (but the nineteenth century faithful
wandered increasingly from such Calvinism to an Arminian
stress on human ability to choose or to reject disciple-
ship). Personal redemption in turn provides a more complete understanding of scriptural truth and makes possible
a priesthood of all believers. Yet the notion that some
are called to specific roles in life, coupled with the
pragmatic difficulties of finding time for true scriptural
mastery, encouraged most of the awakened to rely on the
"divine" institution of the Christian ministry, aided by
spiritual blessings from the ordinances of baptism and the
Lord's Supper, to light the pathway towards eternal life.
Membership in the invisible Church prepares the immortal
soul for the time when the Son of God will finally judge
all mankind, to the eternal blessedness of the righteous
and the eternal punishment of the wicked.

Such a theology obviously re-emphasized human sin and
responsibility, individual need for redemption and God's
loving kindness. Redemption in turn only occurred in those

individuals who underwent a drastic personal reorientation
towards God, the conversion experience.  During the colonial Awakening, this meant many members of the then mainline churches were suspect as Christians because they
lacked the requisite emotional underpinnings to their faith.
As the Great Awakening swept eighteenth century Protestantism, ever larger numbers of Christians came to accept revivalism as a primary channel of saving grace.  This evangelical institution exacerbated the ill will felt by the
more orthodox, churchly and/or Calvinistic members of the
older religious bodies who believed true piety was rooted
in proper doctrinal education rather than emotion.

Disagreement over standards of membership and forms
of worship contributed schism to the established churches
and spawned a new series of distinctly evangelical movements.  The American Revolution and subsequent disestab-
lishment of the bulk of the state churches, a process completed by 1833, Massachusetts finally giving way at that
date, contributed further confusion to the religious scene
of the early 1800s by forcing all religious groups out of
the "churchly" and into the "denominational" mode wherein
they learned to rely on persuasion, rather than state coercion, to attain voluntary adherence of the faithful.  The
"denomination," as Sidney Mead explains, is a "voluntary
association of like-hearted and like-minded individuals,
who are united on the basis of common beliefs for the purpose of accomplishing tangible and defined objectives."
Hence, the early nineteenth century was a period of flux
and adjustment for all religious groups in America.[4]

Only gradually did a tenuous order arise among the
inchoate groups of the early years.  Such order resulted
from two incompatible tendencies which emerged then but
are still with us in the 1980s.  The first witnessed to a
growing sense of unity among evangelical individuals
wherein like-minded people banded together in voluntary
associations designed to  contribute some needed service
or reform to society be it new types of prisons or im-
proved education for the blind.  They also cooperated in
such organizations as the American Board of Foreign Missions (1806) and the American and Foreign Christian Union
(an 1849 consolidation of three older societies) to carry
the gospel to the world in preparation for the millennium.
The Protestant missionaries in turn became major advocates
for union when they realized that un-Christian denominational rivalries hindered winning the heathen by mocking
the very doctrines of Christian love and forgiveness they
sought to impress on potential converts.  This sense of
brotherhood gave currency to the ageless Christian ideal

that the faithful, both the living and dead, made up the
body of "the" Church of which Christ was the Head.  It
encouraged the notion that Christians could be found in
most denominations and that the bulk of those bodies were
part of the true Church, thereby spawning the ecumenical
movement.  At the same time, the opposing tendency appeared when the more churchly minded of the day attempted
to rechannel evangelical enthusiasm for cooperation into
specific denominational programs designed to aid society
and at the same time assure the survival of their particular religious perspective.  These conservative types assumed their denomination alone the true Church of Christ
and consequently shunned association with members of other
denominations, particularly during worship, both to avoid
error and to convince others of that error.

     Paradoxically, these two schools of thought coexist-
ed in nearly every Protestant denomination until at least
the 1830s.  Each groups' sense of theological heritage
encouraged the schools to work out their internal differences while projecting an image of denominational unity to
the outside world.  The felt need for religious unity even
led Americans to exaggerate, especially to Europeans, the
evangelical orthodoxy of most American denominations.  As
the very ecumenical but nonetheless "Old School" Presbyterian Robert Baird said in *Religion in America* (1844),

> ...it is not difficult to draw a line be-
> tween the various unevangelical sects on
> the one hand, and those that may be classed
> together as evangelical denominations on the
> other.  The chief of the former, as we have
> said, are the Roman Catholics, Unitarians,
> Christ-ians,Universalists, Hicksite Quakers,
> Swedenborgians, Tunkers or Dunkers, Jews,
> Shakers, and so on down to the Mormons, be-
> ginning with the sect that has buried the
> truth amid a heap of corruptions of heathen-
> ish origin, and ending with the grossest of
> of all the delusions that Satanic malignity
> or human ambition ever sought to propagate.[5]

     Baird's generalizations, like those of other evan-
gelical leaders, oversimplified American realities.  Not
only were some religious bodies outside the evangelical
pale, but commitment to the evangelical perspective varied
among the acceptable Protestant churches.  Variation even
existed within the more correctly evangelical bodies according to the relative attachment of the differing parties to evangelical beliefs and goals.  In turn, party

spirit increased as these bodies solidified into denominational forms of polity during the early nineteenth century.
Presbyterian history provides an excellent example of this
point.  Both evangelical and more Calvinist elements of
Presbyterianism, arising respectively from New England
Puritan stock and more recent Scottish immigrants, participated originally in pandenominational voluntary socieites
dedicated to such ends as the furtherance of education and
missions.  When the Calvinist "Old School" realized these
cooperative ventures diffused Presbyterian energies, it
attempted to neutralize them by encouraging Presbyterians
to unite more fully.  Their efforts were successful to the
extent that Presbyterians did denominationalize, did assert
a sense of uniqueness and purposiveness which contributed
to greater wealth, stability and organizational coherence.
The Old School then used the growing Presbyterian resources
to create denominationally affiliated missionary, Bible and
educational societies to compete with the interdenominational societies.[6]

    As Elwyn Smith suggests, this very denominationa-
lizing process was a prime source of the Calvinist "Old
School"-liberal "New School" split of 1837-1838.  Increasing dedication of Old School leaders, like Archibald Alexander and Samuel Miller, to particularity in the form of
Presbyterian boards of education and missions conflicted
with such adherents of the evangelical New School as Lyman
Beecher and Albert Barnes over their involvement in interdenominational cooperation.  New School commitment to the
Plan of Union (1801)—which encouraged joint Presbyterian
and Congregationalist founding of churches on the New York
and Ohio Frontiers—in turn undercut Old School theological
and ecclesiastical forms by allowing a steady stream of
liberal New England doctrine and churchmanship into Presbyterianism.  New School liberalism also overflowed into
social reform and support for abolition, much to the dismay of more conservative Presbyterians.  Ultimately, the
Old School attained purity of doctrine and membership in
time worn fashion by thrusting New School evangelicals out
of the church.  This event, coupled with the subsequent
transformation of the New School into a rival church, meant
the Old School lost any ability to temper its opposition's
stance.[7]

    Division within Presbyterianism paralleled growing
tension and schism within the other developing denominations of the same period.  Internal dissension often arose
over evangelical support for superdenominational voluntary
associations dedicated to missions and other worthy ends.
These activities led evangelicals into collision with those

parties of the same religious affiliation who were attempting to stress the unique and distinct qualities of their
church. The latter group could never develop strong denominational ties if a large portion of the potential membership were expending resources on causes which did not
recruit new members or accrue specific benefits to that
denomination. The health of a denomination often depended
on its ability to divert the attentions of these people
away from the voluntary societies to support of the denomination's programs. Desire for such diversion increased
especially among those orthodox elements which became more
ritualist or confessional. Although similar in many re-
spects, ritualism applied to the Anglican and Episcopalian
folds and stressed the clerical role in more elaborate and
colorful worship services while confessionalism related to
the Reformed and Lutheran bodies and focused more fully on
restoration of what were thought to be historic creeds and
traditions of the church. Both enhanced the authority of
clergy and, potentially, hierarchy, over the laity. Each
of these churchly forms and related evangelical response
will be discussed in turn.[8]

The progress of the Oxford or Puseyite Movement
(1833-) within the Church of England, and the growth of
similar ritualism in continental Protestantism proved upsetting to Americans. Evangelicals disliked ritualism because it tended toward a Roman Catholicism teaching erroneous religious forms and beliefs. Hence, an anonymous article in the *Biblical Repository and Princeton Review*
warned that close fraternal ties between British and American religion, ties engendered by a common culture and trans-
Atlantic nature of evangelicalism, meant European ritualism
endangered faith at home. "We are not, therefore, uninter-
ested spectators of the struggle now in progress between
the two conflicting systems of doctrine and theories of the
church, the Evangelical and Ritual. The spiritual welfare
of our children and of the country is deeply concerned in
the issue."[9]

The Oxford Movement fanned into flame the long
smouldering "evangelical"-"High-church" division of the
Protestant Episcopal Church of America. The essential difference between the two camps was that the evangelical or
Low-churchman like Ohio Bishop Charles P. McIlvaine
stressed individual reception of grace while a High-church-
man such as New York Bishop John H. Hobart focused on the
institutional administration of grace. These presuppositions crystallized into distinct conceptions of the form,
liturgy, polity and goals of the church. The Low-church
emphasis on conversion experience engendered such a strong

sense of unity with other evangelicals that public affiliation to express the common faith became a duty and a privi-
lege.  As noted by late century Episcopal scholar Charles
Tiffany, "cooperative action with all denominations in
Bible and tract and temperance societies marked the men of
this mold."[10]

The High-church party did not share these sentiments.
It wanted to restore a very real sense of the uniqueness of
Episcopalian claims to comprise the only true Church of
Christ.  It could not bear to allow erroneous evangelical
doctrine and ecclesiastical views to corrupt the new denominational societies that the two camps were building together.   Both sides therefore began to compete to build
Episcopalian societies adhering to their own views during
the 1820s and 1830s.  As another nineteenth century Episcopalian, S. D. McConnell, put it,

> When High Churchmen took up the Sunday-school
> Union, the Evangelicals, disturbed at Bishop
> Hobart's Catechism, and scandalized by the
> mutilation of Mrs. Sherwood's books, started
> an Evangelical Knowledge Society as an offset.
> When this grew influential, the other side set
> up the Churchman's Library.  They worked and
> planned together to organize the new machinery
> of missions; but when the Evangelicals began
> to suspect that they had been outmaneuvered,
> they set up a rival volunteer society....[11]

The same division appeared within the small German
Reformed Church.  John Williamson Nevin and Philip Schaff,
both professors at the denomination's Mercersburg Seminary,
led the return to a more churchly view of liturgy, theology, and psychology which reflected a blend of American
sources and those deriving from a romantic and churchly
revival among the Lutheran and various Reformed faiths of
Europe.  Their "Mercersburg Theology" (1835-) precipitated
bitter warfare with the evangelicals among the German Reformed and even alienated the Dutch Reformed Church, with
which it had nearly united a few years before.[12]

Confessionalism, on the other hand, precipitated a
grave crisis within American Lutheranism during the same
period.  Samuel Simon Schmucker, clergyman and seminary
professor, had risen to leadership in the Lutheran fold by
helping to crush the residue of Enlightenment rationalism
which plagued its ranks.  He also helped to organize a number of independent ministeriums and synods into the largest
American Lutheran church of his day, the Evangelical

Lutheran General Synod of North America (1820). His commitment to American evangelical unity however conflicted
with a confessionalism inherent in the traditions of the
American church but made explicit by a heavy influx of
Lutheran immigrants from Germany and Scandinavia. Those
coming for religious reasons tended to be pietists who
fled their worldly fatherlands and rationalistic state
churches, such as the Prussian Union, with the hope of re-
turning to what they thought was Reformation orthodoxy.
Although some founded new denominations, like the Missouri
Synod (1847), others joined already existent bodies. The
net effect over the ensuing years was that confessionalism
so permeated the General Synod that evangelicals like
Schmucker became quite rare and unrepresentative; Schmucker, however, managed to retain leadership of the General Synod until the 1850s.[13]

These evangelical-churchly disputes shook American
religion at the very time when the accumulation of cooperative experience helped some evangelical leaders to realize what few evangelicals understood, they held the same
religious model of reality, or worldview. As one anonymous evangelical stated about the faithful, "born of God,
they all belong to one family; and as they are joint heirs
of the same future inheritance, *their features even now
bespeak their common identity.* Taught by the same word,
led by the same Spirit, having 'one faith, one hope,' as
well as one 'baptism,' *it must follow that to a greater
extent than they themselves are aware of, they harmonize
with one another.*" No wonder that men like Samuel Simon
Schmucker and Robert Baird pressed the faithful to recognize and express their common identity. Only then would
evangelicals attain sufficient unity to carry out the divine (and American millennial) mission: unite all Christians under the evangelical banner and convert the world
to the true faith. This very possibility aroused an ecstatic response by Rev. Thomas E. Bond, editor of the
powerful Methodist *Christian Advocate,* to the creation of
the World Evangelical Alliance in 1846:[14]

> To God be all the glory! He is preparing
> the Churches for the conversion of the world.
> The Evangelical Alliance is accomplished.
> Let all the people of God say, Amen. Now we
> are ready for the battle. 'We will go up
> and possess the land, for we are well able
> to overcome. The darkness of the pagan
> night shall be illumined by the rays of Gos-
> pel light, and the superstitions of Romanism
> shall let go their hold of Christendom. The

> simple truth without the alloy of sectarian
> and metaphysical subtleties, of human in-
> vention, shall set the nations free....[15]

Attainment of unity became more pressing as evangelicals assessed the implications of growing rationalist,
which tested all truth via reason rather than via scripture, and churchly positions in American religion.  Rationalist critiques of Christian belief plagued eighteenth century faithful in the form of deism and the teachings of
Jean Jacques Rousseau, Voltaire and Thomas Paine.  Now
they appeared under the religious guise of Unitarianism
and Universalism.  To make matters worse, the German Biblical scholar David Friedrich Strauss used the most up-to-
date research methods to raise the standard of infidelity
in his *Life of Jesus* (1835).  Although he verified the actual existence of Jesus of Nazareth, Strauss denied the
veracity of the Gospels or the divinity of Christ.  Church-
liness, on the other hand, was paving the way for ultimate
Roman Catholic absorption of Protestantism in America.
What other meaning was there to the transfer to Roman
Catholicism of English Puseyite leaders like future Cardinal John Henry Newman (1845)?  What other conclusion could
be drawn from the massive increase of votaries of the
Catholic Church in America due to immigration?  (Over
1,300,000 Irish, mostly Catholics, immigrated between 1845
and 1855 to a United States which grew in population from
20 to 27 million in the same decade).  Momentum towards
Protestant unity escalated when it became apparent that
rationalism and Roman Catholicism endangered Protestant
predominance in the nation and the Protestant world mission.[16]

Tensions between Roman Catholicism and Protestantism
existed in American culture from its colonial beginnings
and dated back to the sixteenth century Reformation.  These
tensions might be understood best within the context of
nineteenth century Protestant responses to religious
pluralism.  Despite the controversies over evangelicalism,
early nineteenth century Protestant denominations adhered
to the same elemental Christian doctrines and to scripture
as the prime authority in these matters, but were unable
publicly to admit it.  Instead, they often developed varied conclusions from similar doctrinal assumptions to
justify separate denominational existence.  The latter was
especially true of the confessionalists and ritualists
within Protestantism.[17]

Nevertheless, heavy immigration of the Irish and
some German Roman Catholics and proliferation of Mormon

(1830), Unitarian (1825) and Universalist (1793) churches,
religious groups which diverged too far from the Protestant character of America, forced evangelicals to realize
their nation was becoming unacceptably pluralistic.  Recognition of this pluralism, however, did not mean the denominations admitted immediately their mutual Protestant character.  Such admission appeared gradually as the nineteenth
century aged towards its midpoint.  It arose, in good part,
from the increasing doctrinal and stylistic similarity
which the evangelical revivals induced in the bulk of the
churches, a concomitant to the contemporary emergence of a
more unified and democratic character among Americans.  In
effect, the Second Great Awakening and subsequent revivalism equated Protestantism with evangelicalism.[18]

    This strengthening of a common "American" Protestant-
ism had two general effects.  On the one hand, it increased
the number of evangelicals and thereby made Protestant cooperation more possible.  On the other, it narrowed the
range of acceptable pluralism thereby increasing estrangement from non-Protestant perspectives.  To borrow from
sociologists Charles Glock and Rodney Stark, "religion...
is a particular kind of *perspective*" which in turn

        '...is an ordered view of one's world—
        what is taken for granted about the at-
        tributes of various objects, events, and
        about human nature.'

        Once perspectives reach the point of ad-
        dressing reality in general, of becoming,
        in effect, all-embracing *Weltanschauungen*,
        then alternative perspectives of this same
        order can no longer be accommodated.  The
        commitment to one perspective at this more
        general level virtually prohibits commit-
        ment to another.[19]

Religion still provided that all-embracing worldview for
many during the nineteenth century.  Evangelical recognition of other perspectives did not imply their acceptance.
Evangelicals generally agreed that the growth of Roman
Catholicism in America, for example, threatened evangelical cultural dominance and any modern observer reflecting
on their ecumenical movement can see its heavy anti-Catholic bias.  Does this bias mean that the principal sources
of evangelical unity were fear or irrational nativist reaction against the foreigner?  Or, does it indicate something about the psychology of Protestantism itself which
is much more complex and involves combination of impulses

from positive commitments to defensive reactions?

As Ray Allen Billington so ably shows, American religious history reveals numerous examples of bigotry, that
is, unreasoning and unjustified dislike of other religious
groups.  Still, his references to nativism and bigotry provide insufficient explanation of Protestant actions.  Ever
since the Reformation, both Roman Catholicism and Protestantism utilized their opponent's position to help define
what was not their own (witness the anti-Protestant character of pronouncements by the Catholic Council of Trent,
1545-1563).  All identity involves idealized portraits of
what the group represents as well as portraits of what it
does not.  Anti-Catholicism had to be part of Protestant
self-definition so long as Roman Catholicism was thought
to endanger the souls of men.  Indeed, the appearance of
Roman Catholicism, ritualism and other religious forms in
American culture helped evangelicals to understand their
common identity.  Hence, Robert Baird effectually equated
evangelicalism with Protestantism and, for this reason,
judged the bulk of the American religious bodies as acceptable "denominations."  Those bodies which diverged too far
from the evangelical perspective, such as the Unitarian,
Roman Catholic, Universalist and Mormon were considered
unacceptable "sects."  Even evangelical bodies such as the
relatively new Disciples of Christ (1809-) were often
thought of as sects.  The Disciples claimed to be the only
church truly based on Apostolic principle and consequently
espoused an ecumenism—it called on all the faithful to
leave the other denominations and join it—which seemed
no better than that posed by the self-styled "true church"
assertions of High-church Episcopalianism or Roman Catholicism.[20]

The actual response of American Protestant leaders
to the pre-Civil War swelling of the Roman Catholic fold
reflected both hostility and paternalism.  Protestant
spokesmen often described the Roman Catholic Church and
much of its hierarchy and clergy as instruments of the
devil.  The Roman Catholic laity, to the contrary, were
misguided beings who needed to be freed from their bonds
by the Protestant gospel.  This mixture of Protestant hostility toward the Roman Catholic Church and paternalism
towards its members was met in kind.  The majority of Roman Catholics in antebellum America were Irish immigrants
who fled a fatherland dominated by hated English Protestants.  The cultural and religious gap between Irish and
Americans therefore was enormous.  Harvard historian Oscar
Handlin's astute generalizations about the Irish in Boston
apply to the situation in America as a whole.  As Handlin

suggests, the Boston Irish brought over a distinctly different worldview and culture from that of the American natives:
"Resting on basically different premises, developed in entirely different environments, two distinct cultures flourished in Boston with no more contact than if 3,000 miles of
ocean rather than a wall of ideas stood between them." Cultural conflict inspired the Boston Irish to attack Protestantism and defend Catholicism without moderation. As Handlin stated,[21]

> ...these theological battles waged *fortitur*
> *in modo* as well as in *re*, wounded suscepti-
> bilities and stored up rancorous bitterness
> on all sides. Whatever the ultimate justice
> of the matter, defenses of the inquisition
> and Saint Bartholomew's massacre, and con-
> tinued attacks upon Luther, Calvin, and Henry
> VIII, the 'infernal triumverate' of Protes-
> tantism, and upon other propagators of 'mon-
> strous doctrines,' scarcely drew the Irish
> closer to their neighbors who held completely
> different views.[22]

Hence Protestants may have denied that Roman Catholicism
was Christian, but they found themselves treated similarly.
Former communalist and Unitarian minister become Roman
Catholic, Orestes Brownson insisted that "'a *Christian*
Protestant, is to the Catholic mind simply a contradiction
in terms.'"[23]

The gap between Protestant and Catholic became pain-
fully obvious given the actions each camp said it might
take toward the other. Public statements of one convinced
the other that it faced a massive conspiracy against its
survival. For example, in 1850, New York Roman Catholic
Archbishop John Hughes preached a fiery sermon which substantiated Protestant fears that Catholicism intended to
convert the Mississippi Valley as the first step in winning the nation.

> 'There is [he said] no secret about this.
> The object we hope to accomplish in time, is
> to convert all Pagan nations, and all Protes-
> tant nations, even England with her proud
> Parliament and imperial sovereign. There is
> no secrecy in all this. It is the commission
> of God to his church, and not a human project
> ....Protestantism startles our eastern bor-
> ders occasionally on the intention of the
> Pope with regard to this Valley of the
> Mississippi, and dreams that it has made a

wonderful discovery. Not at all. Everybody should know it. Everybody should
know that we have for our mission to convert the world—including the inhabitants
of the United States,—the people of the
cities, and the people of the country, the
officers of the navy and the marines, com-
manders of the army, the Legislatures, the
Senate, the Cabinet, the President, and all!'[24]

Such pronouncements appeared to be declarations of war to
Protestant leaders like Lyman Beecher, Horace Bushnell and
Robert Baird. Believing the Mississippi Valley would dominate the nation of the future in population, wealth and
political power, these evangelicals responded by marshall-
ing the faithful behind home missionary and educational
society efforts to save the American West. This spiritual
crusade countered the evil trinity, Roman Catholicism, infidelity and barbarism (including Mormonism), from the
1830s to the Civil War.[25]

Catholics, on the other hand, often saw real and
imagined threats in the words and actions of Protestant
leaders and their denominations. For example, in 1848,
revolution swept through most continental European nations
in an effort to transform autocratic governments into liberal constitutional monarchies respectful of middle class
values and rights. Some of the Catholic hierarchy and
newspapers in America thought these revolts consequent of
an atheistic conspiracy by international Protestantism to
destroy Catholic civilization. One such Catholic claim
charged that the Protestants "'saw the Church gathering
America to her bosom...they saw themselves losing ground
everywhere, and, as they gnashed their teeth with rage and
pined away, ministers in white choakers formed in England
and America an Alliance, and resolved to carry the war into Italy,—to revolutionize the country. It would be a
great triumph to them, and to their father, the devil, if
they could match Catholic progress in Protestant countries
....They fermented the revolutions of 1848'" by creating
"'a grand conspiracy, with its central government...in
London, and its ramifications extending even to this country...armed not merely against monarchy, but against all
legitimate authority, against all religion except an idolatrous worship of...the *God-People*..., against all morality,...law,...and society itself.'"[26]

These charges appear to be quite preposterous when
it is realized that the World Evangelical Alliance, formed
in London in 1846 and dedicated to a symbolic form of unity

is probably this supposed perpetrator of liberal revolts
against the established European order. Yet, from the Roman Catholic perspective, any Protestant movement dedicated
to the conversion of European Catholics would be conspiring
to overthrow that institution which alone was the channel
of divine power, grace and truth to man, the Roman Catholic
Church. Conspiratorial fears commonly reflect the insecurity of the people who have them. Unsure of their position
and future in America, Roman Catholics sensed that the successful conversion of Europe to Protestantism would destroy
a basic anchor of their identity.

Robert D. Cross, one of the foremost students of American Catholic "liberalism," even suggests that insecurity
wracked all of Roman Catholicism as it entered the nineteenth century. The unsettling events of the French Revolution (1789) proved to be merely a prelude to the deva-
stating problems posed for the Catholic conceptual order.
In reaction to this modern world, the Society of Jesus
(Jesuits) spearheaded a powerful conservative movement
which persuaded the Papacy to centralize church power in
its hands and to intensify devotionalism among the faithful. Rome became the center of Church life to the point
that English and American hierarchies, and even individual
bishops, delegated resident agents to watch over their
interests.[27]

Growth of these authoritarian and devotional tendencies increased the gap between the Church and the liberal
spirit of the times. Conservative churchmen opposed contemporary European tendencies towards both democracy, described in the American Catholic statement quoted above as
"an idolatrous worship of...the *God-People*," and separation of church and state as evil fruit of the French Revolution. Reaction developed to the point that, in 1864,
Pope Pius IX issued a *Syllabus of Errors* which condemned
liberalism, progress and modern civilization. Paradoxically, the Roman Catholic hierarchy in democratic America
responded favorably to these liberal currents at the very
time when unpleasant experiences reinforced immigrant
alienation from U.S. culture thereby sending many of the
Catholic laity into the conservative camp of the Church.
In Robert Cross's words, "hostile to the Protestant majority, suspicious of governmental enterprise, and averse to
the active, melioristic spirit of the times, these Catholics met secular culture so far as possible in their own
terms. Their Catholicism was the symbol as well as the
seal of their separation from the culture."[28]

Modern social psychology may explain cultural aliena-

tion but Protestants of the nineteenth century lacked this
insight and could only interpret Catholic aloofness from
democratic American culture as a prelude to destroying it.
Such a view was reasonable in the light of Papal hostility
towards liberalism at a time when the Roman hierarchy was
expanding its authority over the Church worldwide.  As Rev.
Thomas E. Bond explained in 1851, the Protestant and democratic belief in the rights of individual conscience, limited by the laws of God and legitimate demands of society
(Gabriel's free individual obeying responsibly the fundamental law), separated sharply from the Roman Church claim
that it alone understood matters of conscience and rightly
expected governments to suppress all but Catholic worship.
Bond makes the difference clear when he says,

> We take it that the rights of conscience
> are universal, and that both civil and re-
> ligious liberty are only bounded and re-
> strained by the law of God and the rights
> of society—that they are as much the boon
> of one class of men as another—of one nation
> as another.  The idea that liberty—civil or
> religious—is subjected to the arbitrary con-
> trol of a corporation—or an institution—
> called 'the Church,' throughout Protestant
> Christendom, is a paradox.  The doctrine
> taught by the great lights—and the *small*
> lights—of the Roman Catholic Church is,
> that true liberty—both civil and religious—
> consists in *obedience to the voice of the*
> *Church;* and any sort of liberty which does
> not rest upon this basis, but accords to the
> state separate and independent functions, and
> to individuals and communities the right of
> election as to what form of religion they will
> adopt, is *license,* and not liberty, and tends
> to infidelity.[29]

American Protestant leaders and publications therefore
carefully scrutinized European and American Catholic activities to warn the faithful of the dangers which they
sincerely thought a strong international Catholic Church
posed for their nation.  Even some prominent Catholics
like Rev. Augustus Thebaud, S. J., testified to the emergence of that threat during the late Jacksonian era.  He,
of course, applauded it.  Jesuit Father Thebaud recognized
America had traditionally welcomed immigration because the
immigrant helped to conquer the American wilderness.

But when the Americans perceived that they

> were being overwhelmed by a flood, that in
> New York City alone the newcomers were
> counted by more than a thousand a day, that
> the great majority of them was composed of
> Irish Catholics, and that when landed their
> first thought was to become citizens and
> take out their naturalization papers, mat-
> ters looked serious. Reflecting men saw
> the enormous social, political, and reli-
> gious change that could be the consequence
> of this new kind of invasion.[30]

By the 1840s, evangelicals could no longer ignore
growing Catholic power, religious pluralism, dominational
provincialism, and the churchly critique of evangelicalism
because they appeared to threaten the very core of American civilization. These dangers encouraged many evangelicals to discover ways of expressing visibly their fundamental agreement about what it meant to be an American
Christian. Successful cooperation of individuals in ameliorative, religious, and reform associations indicated
some basis for a united evangelical front. The more ad-
venturous clergy even supported mutual expressions of fellowship, much to the bemusement of Catholics and many
Protestants. To some observers, only a decline in piety
and religious vitality could induce men of different denominations to participate in each other's religious services. Father Thebaud assumed this when he wrote about
the "catholic" or "unsectarian" spirit sweeping evangelicalism,

> It showed itself, first, in frequent inter-
> change of pulpits or in the strange custom
> of several clergymen preaching at the same
> time, though they belonged to very different
> creeds....It is indeed difficult to imagine
> how such an idea had become not only possible,
> but usual, at the very end of a period when
> controversies had been remarkable for their
> acrimony and rudeness. A sort of courtesy
> had suddenly been introduced into social in-
> tercourse between the disputants, so as to
> induce a Presbyterian or Methodist preacher
> to invite an Episcopalian minister or even an
> uncompromising Catholic priest to walk up
> with him to his pulpit on Sunday and address
> a congregation wholly unused to the tenets of
> the visitor.[31]

To Thebaud, Protestant ecumenism rooted in declining

vitality; formation of the Evangelical Alliance was really
a hopeless attempt to avoid destruction![32]

    To the contrary, such behavior reflected a growing
sense of American and Protestant community which bolstered
the desire to amalgamate individual evangelical identities
into a common group identity by means of visible fellowship and organized ecumenism.  The dangers posed by religious and cultural pluralism of course enhanced that desire, while international tensions over territory on the
American continent gave their hope for world evangelical
comity practical urgency.  The 1840s were a period of ex-
ceptionally intense American nationalism.  "Manifest Destiny," a slogan coined by Irish-American newspaper editor
John L. O'Sullivan, captivated the American mind and inspired an incredible lusting after new territories, be
they part of New Brunswick in the Aroostook War of 1839,
tensions in general over the boundaries between British
Canada and the United States (settled in 1842), controversy
with the British over Oregon and Washington (settled in
1846), or war with Mexico over Texas and the southwest
(1846-1848).

    Part of these tensions rooted in American thirst for
more and more land.  Yet, as Albert K. Weinberg points out,
European hostility to their republic was also a source of
American belligerence:

        The view that European interference in
    America menaced American democracy apparent-
    ly rested on three principal grounds.  The
    first was the belief that whatever threatened
    American security was a danger to the politi-
    cal principle which the nation embodied.  The
    second was the supposition that, irrespective
    of strategic menace, European absolutism would
    'pollute' American democracy by its very con-
    tiguity.  The third and perhaps most influ-
    ential of all was the recognition that ad-
    jacent European power threatened the exten-
    sion of American democracy—an ideal which
    was made more precious by this menace.[33]

That Britain was our chief antagonist encouraged many evangelicals to believe ecumenical hands across the sea might
transform tension into friendship and peace.  History would
prove them correct.  Friendly contacts, shared cultural
roots, common interests and often common dangers guided
Anglo-American relations, from the 1830s until today, along
the bumpy but peaceful path of negotiated settlement of
disputes.

To varying degrees, much the same complex motivation
seems to have inspired the yearning for greater unity by
European evangelicals, particularly the British.  The
British ecumenical movement started in the 1820s in the
Liverpool rectory of Anglican but very evangelical clergyman James H. Stewart and grew in breadth and appeal over
the ensuing years, especially among adherents of the voluntary associations.  Success was hindered by the connection of part of evangelicalism to the "established" Church
of England, a connection which fostered among Churchmen a
sense of superiority vis-a-vis the other evangelicals and
also complicated relations by interjection of the notion
that some belonged to the only true church.  Non-Anglican
evangelicals were just as certain that the religious establishment was leading many a soul to hell with the additional indignity of taxing his pocketbook along the way.
This barrier to ecumenism diminished however when massive
immigration of Irish Roman Catholics into England and Scotland, during the 1830s and 1840s, precipitated cultural
conflict with, and an identity crisis among, evangelicals.
Growth of the Oxford Movement made establishment evangelicals more aware of their peers outside the Church while
controversy within the Conservative Party over the Fac-
tories Education Bill (1844) and subsequent Maynooth Bill
(1845) precipitated a rush from all sides to the ecumenical
standard.  The proposed endowment of a Roman Catholic seminary at Maynooth, Ireland, augured massive alteration of
Britain's (Protestant) Constitution towards a dual religious establishment of Anglicanism and Roman Catholicism.[34]

As E. R. Normon's fine study of anti-Catholicism in
Victorian England reveals, both Churchman and evangelical
dissenter rushed to the banners of political cooperation
raised by Anglican evangelical Sir Culling Eardley Smith.
Radical evangelicals like anti-slavery leader Rev. J. H.
Hinton and his fellow Baptist Dr. Edward Steane, however,
could not accept Churchmen's defense of "establishment,"
either in principle or in fact.  Committed to voluntaryism
as the only way to church organization, they broke subsequently from Smith's Central Anti-Maynooth Committee to
form their own anti-Maynooth pressure group.  Successful
passage of the Maynooth subsidy made it clear to all the
consequences of Protestant division——an organized Catholic
minority seemed to attain favorable legislation despite
massive Protestant opposition because the latter was not
an *organized* majority.  The rise of infidelity (or rationalism) among the upper educated classes, and infidel ex-
ploitation of Protestant disunity to win converts, merely
highlighted further the necessity of ecumenism.  As Rev.
John Angell James stated to the Congregational Union in

1842, "'The idea discussed at that time was that a union
should be formed amongst churches holding the voluntary
principle (i.e., Nonconformist churches) with the object
of combating infidelity and (three interesting p's) Popery,
Puseyism and Plymouth Brethrenism.'"[35]

The more radical evangelical (Nonconformist) elements
of Britain were so disenchanted with establishment per se,
however, that most would not consider participation in an
ecumenical movement involving evangelical Churchmen.  The
moderates, led by Sir Culling Eardley Smith, responded enthusiastically to a group of leading Scottish ministers of
all denominations who called for a congress to further
Protestant union, the Liverpool Conference of 1845.  Smith's
letter of reply, the official endorsement of the conference
by the Central Anti-Maynooth Committee, represented a large
portion of subsequent Alliancemen when he hoped the union
movement would be directed pre-eminently against Popery.
Instead, a powerful minority of moderate British evangelicals, the Americans, and the continental brethren partially
overcame their nationalisms to sustain ecumenism and identity formation as the dominant focus of the subsequent Alliance, although Roman Catholicism of necessity, as the
polar opposite, occupied much evangelical attention.[36]

The same general forces and a common cultural base
therefore encouraged both British and Americans to realize
they held an identity in common.  Ever since the 1820s,
they borrowed each other's voluntary society techniques,
attended each other's society anniversaries, and cooperated already in Bible distribution and other good causes
on the world level.  Local issues peculiar to each people
colored their desires for ecumenism, but both found the
impulse to go beyond denominational and national particularity overpowering when Roman Catholic immigration, and
growth of ritualism, confessionalism and infidelity threatened the potential evangelical hegemony of their respective
nations.  Consequently, evangelicals from both sides of the
Atlantic desired to express their common evangelical identity and sustain some form of visible unity on the national and international level.  Their efforts led to formation of the World Evangelical Alliance in 1846.

CHAPTER THREE

# THE FRATERNAL APPEAL OF WORLDWIDE

# ECUMENISM, 1839-1865

The idea of an international association of evangelicals had a number of sources. Evangelicals in both Europe and America sought to convene a world congress to organize an alliance expressive of their common identity. Among the European originators of this ecumenical movement were the great Swiss theologian and church historian Jean Henri Merle D'Aubigne; the French evangelical preacher Adolphe Monod; the theologian, preacher and leader of the newly formed Free Church of Scotland, Thomas Chalmers; and Rev. E. Kuntze, a major figure in the United Protestant Church of Prussia.[1]

As far as the American proponents of an alliance were concerned, four clergymen played prominent roles: Leonard Bacon, Robert Baird, William Patton and Samuel Simon Schmucker. Influential Congregationalist, Leonard Bacon gained wide public esteem as life-long minister to the First Church of New Haven, Connecticut, and a founder of two of the pre-eminent journals of opinion in the nineteenth century, the *New Englander* (1843) and the New York *Independent* (1848). He was the first in Baird's circle to suggest such a general conference. He induced Baird to write to Merle D'Aubigne and Patton to correspond with the British Congregationalist John Angell James in the hope that these two European leaders could popularize the idea. Baird, of course, had wide contacts in Europe due to years of residence there as an agent of the American Sunday School Union and, later, the American and Foreign Christian Union. Rev. William Patton exercised considerable influence in the American evangelical community as a minister, an editor (1867-1872) of a weekly denominational journal, the Chicago *Advance,* and finally as President (1877-1889) of the now famous school designed to educate Blacks, Howard University. Patton informed James that evangelicals worldwide would respond to an international ecumenical movement only if a call came from the leading Protestant power of the day, Britain. The conference should be publicized by an appropriate document which set "forth the object of the Convention, *as lifting up a standard against Papal and*

*Prelatical arrogance and assumption, and imbodying the*
*great essential doctrines which are held in common by all*
*consistent Protestants.*" James and other British evangelicals, in turn, initiated the first steps aimed specifically
toward an alliance in Britain by sponsoring a successful
series of large interdenominational meetings which culmi-
nated in the Liverpool Conference of October 1845—this
gathering planned the massive World Evangelical Alliance
Conference held in London in 1846.  Their efforts were
strengthened by the impact which Samuel Simon Schmucker's
*Fraternal Appeal to the American Churches,* and other literature on evangelical unity, had on the British and American Christian publics.  Men no longer responded the way
the secretary of the British Baptist Missionary Society
Andrew Fuller did to the suggestion of a similar conference earlier in the century:  "'in a meeting of all denominations, there would be no unity, without which we had
better stay home.'"[2]

    Americans were interested in union well before the
London ecumenical conference of 1846.  They created the
Society for the Promotion of Christian Union, in 1839, to
promote "'Christian Union on apostolical principles, according to the general plan proposed in the *Fraternal Ap-*
*peal to the American Churches.*'"  Well aware of the hostility that would arise among the American churches, the
Society stated in its constitution that it intended the
founding of no new sect but only to "'establish more amicable relations between the several orthodox Christian denominations.'"  It proposed to raise funds for the distribution of the *Fraternal Appeal* and to sponsor other measures designed to win the churches over to the idea of
union.[3]

    Samuel Simon Schmucker led this movement.  His cre-
dentials were well established in ecumenical circles as a
member of various evangelical voluntary societies, a major
founder of the first ecumenical body among American Lutherans, the General Synod, and as an evangelical President of
its Gettysburg Seminary from 1826-1864.  As he stated in
the *Fraternal Appeal,* apostolic principles dictated con-
federate cooperation of churches rather than organic union.
Confederation allowed each denomination to retain its own
government, organization, discipline and mode of worship
under the umbrella of a weak central government.  They
could gather together on the basis of mutual toleration
and recognition without fear of compromising their separate existence.  Schmucker also advocated full sacramental,
ministerial, and ecclesiastical communion among the participating bodies whereby each churchmember or clergyman of

good standing in one denomination could partake of the
sacraments or receive full membership in another.  If a
clergyman changed religious affiliation, he also had the
right to membership among the ranks of the clergy of his
newly adopted church.[4]

Schmucker's version of evangelical rights failed to
win the support of the churches.  Many denominational
leaders applauded his plea for confederation based on doctrinal agreement, but rejected his creed as an unacceptable gathering of discordant elements from the Apostle's
Creed and historic Protestant confessions.  Swiss-born
historian and professor at the nearby German Reformed Mer-
cerburg Seminary, Philip Schaff, for example, judged his
list dangerously ahistorical: "a church is not to be fab-
ricated in the study, by simply extracting, and putting
together in an outward way, some propositions of apparently like sound, out of different symbolical books."  Despite such criticism, Schmucker remained convinced of the
validity of his new confession but was flexible enough to
approve publicly the doctrines adopted ultimately by the
Evangelical Alliance.  After all, the Alliance did assert
those truths fundamental to evangelicalism.[5]

Schmucker's prominence in the early phases of American ecumenicity arose from the response which his public
statements evinced from others.  Bacon, Baird, Patton and
many other religious leaders gathered with him in the Society for the Promotion of Christian Union out of agreement on the apostolic core of evangelical truth and a postmillennial conviction that proper action, could speed up
the coming of the kingdom of Christ to earth.  But, their
efforts towards union faltered despite a confederative concession to the American belief in a governmental system of
checks and balances.  Denominational allegiances were too
strong to allow even this weak church affiliation; that is
why the Alliance organized subsequently around individual
rather than denominational membership.  The Society's ecumenism suffered as well from the breakdown of several
leading denominations.  The New School-Old School Presbyterian split (1837-1838) coupled with growing schism within the Methodist (1844) and Baptist (1830s) folds, due to
slavery and doctrinal issues, and the beginnings of the
American Lutheran-Old Lutheran controversy within Schmucker's own denomination, undercut its impetus.  Despite
these difficulties, the Society and its leaders did not
give up.  Schmucker even managed to obtain the Lutheran
General Synod's endorsement of his plan of union in 1839
and again received synodical support in the form of a
special Committee of Conference on Christian Union, in 1845.[6]

     During 1845, Schmucker also published his views on
union in a circular letter signed by 44 leading Lutherans,
German Reformed, Congregationalists, Methodists, New and
Old School Presbyterians, and Baptists.  The letter announced a preliminary conference on Christian union sched-
uled for May of 1846.  Among the signatories were Methodist College president Robert Emory; Old School Presbyterian and pastor of the Brick Presbyterian Church of New
York City, Gardiner Spring; Baptist clergyman and one of
the founders of the University of Rochester and Rochester
Divinity School, Pharcellus Church; and Samuel H. Cox, a
founder of New York University and Moderator of the New
School Presbyterian General Assembly of 1846 (he is also
the father of a later Episcopalian bishop, A. Cleveland
Coxe).  The adherence of men of this stature was significant.  By 1845, many of the more liberal and reform minded
evangelicals among the Presbyterian, Methodist, Congregationalist, Reformed, and even Lutheran and Baptist folds
realized that tensions with nations abroad and schism,
churchly-evangelical strife and the growth of Roman Catholicism at home required an evangelical coalition.  These
evangelicals therefore responded warmly to Schmucker's
call for union.  All, including Schmucker, were ecstatic
when the British announced an imminent convocation to create a World Evangelical Alliance.[7]

     The Americans took immediate advantage of the Brit-
ish invitation by raising funds and planning extended
travel through Europe.  Enthusiasm was such that over 80
Americans hazarded the Atlantic to attend the first major
international conference of Protestants in recent times.
As Schmucker realized, Americans could not pass up such a
great opportunity for world Christian cooperation: "it
might be more profitable for the common cause, that American Christians should unite in counsel, and therefore cooperate in action as parts of a great whole in our proper
sphere."  The bulk of participants, Schmucker included,
left for Europe almost immediately after receipt of the
invitation.[8]

     The New York Conference appeared cancelled by default
until a few decided to delay departure long enough to con-
fer together.  President Justin Edwards of Andover Seminary
chaired the sessions.  Desirous of enunciating a common
identity, the New York gathering amended the doctrinal
statement proposed for the World Alliance by the Liverpool
Conference.  Successful amendment forged a united front
which enabled the Americans to exercise a leverage at London disproportionate to their number.  The New York Report
added to the spirit of congeniality at the London Confer-

ence by applauding the tendency toward mutual recognition
and cooperation among evangelicals irrespective of church
or nationality.  And, the Americans proved so persuasive
that the London Conference of the World Evangelical Alliance finally accepted their version of doctrine as its
platform. [9]

Leading European and American evangelicals came to
order under the gavel of Sir Culling Eardley Smith to
form the great London Conference, convened from August 19
until September 2, 1846.  Its central purpose was to express evangelical identity in unity, or so the Americans
thought.  It convened to explain who the evangelicals
were and where they were going, to provide a public forum
for their conceptual order as well as a practical program of action designed to meet what they considered to
be their life problems.

As reflected in the American report, evangelicals
adhered to the ideal of unity in Spirit.  This conception
of unity, then and now, is a theological assertion elemental to the Christian tradition, and when believed, quite
motivating in practical terms.  It is part of the Protestant mythos brooding over the reality of pluralism and
sectarianism.  It inspires many to attempt to go beyond
apparent divisions towards an expression of common identity.

The London Conference passed a resolution made by
Glasgow Congregationalist Rev. Ralph Wardlaw which captured the intent of the gathering in this regard.

'That this Conference, composed of professing Christians of many different
Denominations, all exercising the right
of private judgment, and, through common
infirmity, differing in the views they
severally entertain on some points, both
of Christian doctrine and ecclesiastical
Polity, and gathered together from many
and remote parts of the World, for the
purpose of promoting Christian Union, re-
joice in making their unanimous avowal of
the glorious truth, that the Church of the
living God, while it admits of growth is
one Church, never having lost, and being
incapable of losing, its essential unity,
but to confess it, is the design of their
assembling together.  One in reality,they desire also,as far as they may be able to attain

           it, to be visibly one; and thus, both to
           realize in themselves, and to exhibit to
           others, that a living and everlasting union
           binds them all true believers together in
           the fellowship of the Church of Christ,
           "which is His body,..."'[10]

From the theological perspective, then, evangelicals conceived of unity as grounded in a spiritual union in Christ
which relegated denominational division to the state of
"common infirmity" among men.   Rev. Edward Norris Kirk,
New School Presbyterian from Boston, cited the cause of
Protestant particularity as due specifically to the infirmity of intellects arising from the fall of man in Adam.
The Conference agreed that church division arose from human sin but was not yet prepared to suggest, as some evangelicals would later in the century, that a particular denominational affiliation depended on one's aesthetic pro-
pensities.   Rather, certain religious bodies adhered more
to divine truth than the rest (and, the attending British
Anglicans tended to believe theirs *the* only true Church).
The Conference also affirmed fulfillment of Jesus Christ's
commandment to love one another as a key goal of the Alliance and absolutely essential to the inherent unity of
the Church.   Members followed this principle in practice
by avoiding discussion of such divisive issues as the Established Church, temperance and slavery, so true focus
would rest on their common faith——the moderate stance that
Sir Culling Eardley Smith and other British Alliance organizers had taken on these issues led most radical dissenters
to shun the Conference.   Further division had to be avoided.[11]

     Consensus held that the Church of God is, was, and
always will be one, despite incomplete agreement on the
corpus of scriptural truth.   Delegates cited the Conference
itself as symbolic of that unity.   Rev. Stephen Olin,
President of the American Methodist Wesleyan University,
declared that "I never felt anything more strongly, than
that our Denominational names and peculiarities are the hay
and stubble; whilst God has another way of marking His dear
children, and bringing them out as a visible Church——visible in our day, and hereafter to be so——though not so formerly."   To Olin, this assemblage witnessed to the visible
unity of all those "who in sincerity love our Lord and
Saviour Jesus Christ."   He assured his colleagues that
American Methodism agreed with the purported intentions of
their meeting to the point of sending delegates pledged to
cooperation "so long as you pursue the things which make
for peace and the glory of the Saviour."   (Please note that

some churches sent official representatives but the Alliance recognized them only as individuals representing themselves.  It could not afford to alienate the many churches
fearful of losing their autonomy in a new world church.)
A similar millennial impulse informed the preceding New
York Conference belief that the "deliberations of the [Lon-
don] convention respecting the condition of Evangelical
Christianity throughout the world...may lead to more combined and vigorous, and to more wisely directed efforts for
the conversion of the world to Christ."  May the Holy Spirit inspire the Conference to answer Christ's prayer "'that
they all may be one, as thou Father are in me, and I in
thee, that they also may be one *in us*.'"  Hence, Rev.
William Patton described the London convention as a "grand
alliance for the peace of the world; and, in the peace of
the world, the conquest of the world by the preaching of
the everlasting Gospel of Jesus Christ."[12]

One of the questions plaguing both friends and critics of the Conference revolved around this image of unity
in Christ.  Did the Alliance intend to amalgamate the denominations or to create another church?  As early as October 1845, British Christians in the Liverpool Conference
stated clearly that membership in the proposed alliance
still allowed doctrinal differences and that they were proposing "an alliance of individual Christians, and not of
the denominations or branches of the church."  The subsequent London Conference also answered both parts of the
question with a decided no.  Its very constituency made
this necessary.  The Conference represented heavily almost
every form of dissenter in Britain, contained a generous
contingent of American varieties, a sprinkling from the
continent, and a large number of Low-churchmen from the
Established Church of England.  The contradiction between
increasing belief in a universal church and the fact of
religious and secular pluralism *might* have encouraged some
evangelicals to aspire to a world or superchurch.  The
presence of Anglicans however placed limits to ecumenical
expression at the outset by defining as unacceptable all
procedures or goals which challenged the legal position
of the Anglican Church.[13]

Even those in full support of unity needed to assuage
fear of the Conference and subsequent Alliance within their
own denominations.  Hence, British Baptist F. A. Cox introduced a resolution from the powerful platform committee
designed to allay fears that the Alliance might evolve into
a denomination.  The Conference promptly voted "'that the
Alliance is not to be considered as an Alliance of Denominations, or Branches of the Church; but of individual

Christians, each acting on his own responsibility.'"  Individual connection gave the Alliance strength by avoiding
divisive sectarianism.  Although Cox hoped that the divisions among the religious bodies might be eliminated by the
Alliance in some future period, he thought only a union of
individuals possible at this time.  Clearly each denominational delegate "comes with all his pledges to maintain
that system about him; but, when he comes as an individual,
he does not abandon his Denomination; he only moves out for
a moment into this vast fraternity and brotherhood, in
order that he may investigate and consider his own misap-
prehensions."  The Conference also testified that the Alliance did not ascribe to itself the functions and authority of a church.  The delegates intended a "confederation,
on the basis of great Evangelical principles held in common by them" to "afford opportunity to Members of the
Church of Christ of cultivating brotherly love, enjoying
Christian intercourse," and promoting other useful objects.[14]

     The obvious defensiveness concerning Alliance poten-
tial to become a church sprang directly from the ability
of over 800 American, British and continental leaders to
agree on a doctrinal definition of what it meant to be an
evangelical.  As Thomas Chalmers said later,

>          ...let it further be recollected as a
>          serious difficulty in the way of the
>          Evangelical Alliance, that notwithstand-
>          ing the marvelous harmony which obtains
>          in Protestant Confessions, they form the
>          insignia of the different Churches which
>          have respectively adopted them; and to
>          make surrender of these, either to the
>          already existing standard of some one of
>          the Churches, which like Aaron's rod shall
>          swallow up all the rest, or even to the
>          new and common standard of an OEcumenical
>          Confession into which all the actual Con-
>          fessions shall be amalgamated, carries in
>          it somewhat like the humiliation of striking
>          one's colours...It is therefore well in the
>          meantime that the members of this Alliance
>          are admitted in their individual capacity,
>          and not as the representatives of, or as in
>          any way committing the Churches to which
>          they belong.  Even this wise regulation has
>          not prevented outbreakings of jealousy and
>          alarm.[15]

        Conference delegates realized that statements of
faith separated churches from other kinds of religious
organizations.  Anglican Rector Edward Bickersteth believed the Alliance doctrinal position a creedal statement
but as an organizer and leader of the Conference made it
clear that he would never allow an Alliance church to
arise upon it.  Samuel H. Cox typified the American stance
by categorizing that statement as a test of admission and
a visible bond of union.  It was designed, as he said, to
"let the World see, that we can stand here together on our
grand platform as to things in which we agree, and we have
less regard, in our social relation, to the things in
which we differ.  Now, in that sense, and in no other, it
is a Creed." Methodist President Emory also denied its
creedal importance in any ecclesiastical sense but affirmed it as a confession of faith.[16]

        The Conference did not pretend that only those ad-
hering to Alliance doctrine were members of the Church:

> ...this brief Summary is not to be regarded
> in any formal or Ecclesiastical sense, as a
> Creed or Confession, nor the adoption of it
> as involving an assumption of the right au-
> thoritatively to define the limits of Chris-
> tian Brotherhood; but simply as an indica-
> tion of the class of persons whom it is
> desirable to embrace within the Alliance;—
> Second, that the selection of certain tenets,
> with the omission of others, is not to be
> held as implying, that the former constitute
> the whole body of important Truth, or that
> the latter are unimportant.[17]

Disclaimers aside, the delegates thought the doctrines
which distinguished evangelicals from other Christians
were universal in their validity.  They gave evangelicals
everywhere a common religious identity despite association
of those beliefs with the problems and qualities peculiar
to each national and regional grouping of believers.  The
credibility of evangelical unity appeared to require public agreement on doctrine, because the nineteenth century
faithful were still too theologically oriented to accept
the subsequent early twentieth century solution to particularity, active cooperation without reference to theological position.[18]

        Doctrinal agreement also helped to ward off repeated
charges that the London Conference movement arose from no-
popery and desire for moral and social control. The ability
to agree on a doctrinal position testified to the sincerity

of faith and purpose of the delegates.  Nevertheless, Roman
Catholicism did pose a threat to evangelical identity.  According to Robert Baird, the London Conference purpose was
to diffuse true religion at home and abroad "by impulse and
excitement."  "And, if it be not a result of this great Alliance, that the Protestant Evangelical Churches shall
awake to the importance of carrying the Gospel into Papal
lands, and thus make the Reformation to commence its tri-
umphs, we shall fail in accomplishing one great object."
That the Conference often considered the implications of
its work in reference to Catholicism and infidelity is suggested by the resolve "to exert a beneficial influence on
the advancement of Evangelical Protestantism, and on the
counteraction of Infidelity, of Romanism, and of such other
forms of Superstition, Error, and Profaneness as are most
prominently opposed to it, especially the desecration of
the Lord's day."  It obviously cared about the quality of
society's spiritual life and called for organized persuasion to improve it.  In this sense, it was committed as
well to a benevolent social control.[19]

Religious truth, as the London Conference understood
it, was set forth in a nine point document, derived from
the Liverpool propositions after several days of intense
and generally amiable discussion.  Nearly everyone agreed
with the Americans that nothing less than statement of
evangelical consensus would do.  The Alliance founders assumed that freedom of interpretation would enable all evangelical Protestants to accept "The Basis" as representative
of the *essential beliefs* of their faith:

'1. The Divine Inspiration, Authority, and Suffi-
    ciency of the Holy Scriptures.
2. The Right and Duty of Private Judgment in the
   Interpretation of the Holy Scriptures.
3. The Unity of the Godhead, and the Trinity of
   Persons therein.
4. The utter Depravity of Human Nature, in consequence of the Fall.
5. The incarnation of the Son of God, His work of
   Atonement for sinners of mankind, and His
   Mediatorial Intercession and Reign.
6. The Justification of the sinner by Faith alone.
7. The work of the Holy Spirit in the Conversion
   and Sanctification of the sinner.
8. The Immortality of the Soul, the Resurrection of
   the Body, the Judgment of the World by our Lord
   Jesus Christ, with the Eternal Blessedness of the
   Righteous, and the Eternal Punishment of the wicked
9. The Divine institution of the Christian Ministry,
   and the obligation and perpetuity of the ordinance
   of Baptism and the Lord's Supper.'[20]

Although freedom of interpretation allowed delegates to adjust the Basis to their individual perspectives, the doctrines were explicit enough to exclude from the movement
those of doubtful evangelical status.  The document also
avoided certain divisive notions which might have prevented
consensus.

        Articles four and six accordingly contain significant
omissions.   Evangelicals of all types could agree on these
statements because they avoided entirely the issue of election and free will.  The doctrine of utter depravity might
allow Presbyterians and Congregationalists to envision
election while Methodists and freewill Baptists could ignore its implications and assume that each man freely chose
to be saved from his sin.  All could agree on the doctrine
of justification by faith alone as long as they were allowed these silent qualifications.  This was so obviously
true that articles four and six were not issues in the
several day debate over the Basis.  Discussion centered
instead around articles eight and nine.  The British did
not think these statements necessary but allowed them to
make the Americans happy.

        The Americans thought, in line with the New York Confer-
ence, that this document must affirm the great Christian
truths concerning the Trinity of Persons, immortality of
the soul, resurrection of the body, and a last judgment involving eternal rewards and punishments.  They allowed no
quarter to the Universalist belief in universal salvation
or the Unitarian notion that Christ was only a man.  Rev.
William Patton of New York warned his London colleagues
that Unitarianism is the "form under which all the enemies
of God and Jesus Christ are gathering as a mighty host, and
preparing for the great battle against spiritual religion."
This broad claim hardly equated with the rather small size
of the Unitarian movement in America but did capture the
relationship between Unitarianism and growing rationalism
among the educated and sections of the American upper class.
Hence it was logical that Americans proposed article nine
as a remedy.  Patton warned they would form their own alliance if the London gathering failed to include it in the
Basis.[21]

        Presbyterian theologian, revivalist, and President of
the New School's Lane Theological Seminary, Lyman Beecher
demurred to the extent that the Americans might have approved a Basis lacking this provision but, "since it had
been introduced, it could not now be rejected, without implying, as the public mind would feel, a depreciation of
the Doctrine."  Failure to believe this doctrine eliminated

the whole power by which the Holy Spirit restrained, awakened, convicted and converted men, for "knowing the terror
of the Lord, we persuade men." The purpose of the London
gathering was not to settle on the lowest common denomina-
tor of doctrines. Instead it should include so very much
of the evangelical system of belief that the Alliance would
stand strengthened in the power of the Holy Spirit. Beecher
believed this would never come to pass if the ninth article
were omitted. A high standard was necessary to elevate the
human heart.[22]

    Several British delegates attacked articles eight and
nine as repulsive to Quakers and many other Christians. The
Quakers could not accept a statement implying an institution of the ministry separated from the congregation—any
one of the faithful might be inspired by the Holy Spirit to
instruct the rest concerning God's will. Doctrinal exclusion of others would prevent the creation of real Protestant unity at a time when the Alliance intended forming a
countervailing force to the boasted Roman Catholic solidar-
ity. Anyway, such provisions contradicted the right of
individual interpretation of scripture set forth in article
two. Implicitly, these critics asked whether the rights of
conscience could be limited by consensus. Their question
highlighted a paradox of evangelical ecumenism. How does
one assert a common identity and yet allow for variation of
belief and practice? Too much freedom of interpretation
could destroy the very consensus which the Alliance was
formed to express. As far as the Conference was concerned,
proper understanding of the Bible set the boundary, but
this position raises numerous issues which must be explained carefully.[23]

    Protestants were quick to point out that nineteenth
century Catholicism was moving toward pronouncement of papal infallibility as well as making the whole corpus of
the church and its teachings the ultimate standard of
truth. They believed this an anti-democratic trend which
endangered that personal freedom of thought essential to
individual Christian responsibility and ultimate salvation.
Paradoxically, the evangelicals held the Bible alone, and
the King James Version in particular, as *their* infallible
source of divine truth. They too set limits to individual
religious belief but never understood that fact in its full
implications. Hence, the New York Report stressed "The
Divine Inspiration, authority, and sufficiency of Holy
Scriptures" as article one of the proposed Basis, followed
by "the right and duty of Private Judgment in the Interpretation of Holy Scripture."[24]

    The Americans opposed Catholicism's stress on the

priest as mediator between the individual and God.  Priestly control over the interpretation of scripture and holy
sacraments seemed to limit the transmission of divine grace
to the sinner.  To the evangelical, personal recourse to
the Bible aided salvation far more than priestly intercession.  The New York Report asserted clearly the "right and
duty of every individual man, throughout the world, to possess the Word of God, as revealed in the Holy Scriptures,
and to read and obey that Word for himself, under his responsibility to God, who has given him that Revelation to
be a lamp to his feet, and a light to his path."  Scripture,
to the Protestant, has almost sacramental significance as
did the proper observance of the sabbath.  It was the duty
of every man to possess, read and interpret the Bible.  God
has set aside a day of rest just for that purpose.  Accordingly, the New York Report affirmed the right and duty of
every man to use "the rest of the Sabbath" by avoiding secular activity, "freely worshipping God, and hearing the
Gospel, and deliberately searching the Scriptures, to ascertain whether what he hears is according to the Word of
God."  Economy of resources might require the laity to rely on a learned clergy to instruct them concerning God's
will but all men must themselves pass final judgment as to
the truth of what they hear.  The principles of individual
liberty and Christian union set forth by Apostle Paul required believers in Christ to institute those forms of
worship and ordinances which they thought teachings of the
Word, Spirit and providence warranted.  The reciprocal relationship between the learned clergy and lay judgment cannot be stressed too much because it implies that conflict
over interpretation might best be resolved by consensus.[25]

The American conception of the Basis proved that of
the majority of the Conference.  The very influential
British Anglican Edward Bickersteth captured this collec-
tive opinion when he presented the Basis.  He tried to ward
off the very criticism which arose in the ensuing debate by
arguing that the Quakers were not excluded merely by article eight (which was article nine in the original unap-
proved version) but by a number of others as well.  Protestant unity against Roman Catholicism must not be sacrificed
by emasculation of essential doctrine merely to please
Quakers.  The fact that some of the brethren are kept outside the Alliance does not imply that they are outside the
Church.  Rev. Bickersteth made it clear previously that the
Alliance doctrinal statement intended only to indicate that
class of persons thought desirable as members—it never intended to define the limits of Christian brotherhood.  Adherence to the Basis would not and should not eliminate all
differences among Protestants.

That liberty in Christ from which those differences arose
was far too precious to allow the uniformity imposed under
Roman Catholicism. According to Bickersteth, the latter
presented superficial conformity before the world while
differences still reigned within. As for the Alliance, although some Christians might be excluded, all nine doctrinal statements represented such essential elements of evangelical Protestantism that none could be sacrificed safely.

> Take the 'right and duty of Private Judgment.'
> I feel that, in these days, when the Papacy
> has, by a fresh Encyclical letter, denied the
> Scripture to the laity, as injurious to them,—
> and when Human Traditions are urged,as having
> an equal claim with the Scriptures to our
> obedience,—it becomes us to bear witness to
> the solemn, great responsible duty of all
> Christians, to search the Scriptures for them-
> selves, according to the means, and with all
> the help, which God may have afforded them,
> and to form for themselves a conscientious
> judgment of their meaning and application, to
> guide their principles of faith and their
> daily conduct.[26]

The London Conference approved the Basis as amended by the
Americans.[27]

The Conference spent the first days coming to doctrinal agreement and showing the Alliance had no intention of
becoming a denomination. It then deliberated on the scheme
of organization proposed by the business committee (this
body controlled conference programming). A number of Americans of international stature belonged to this powerful
body and exercised formative influence on its decisions.
The Committee reflected this by choosing Samuel Simon
Schmucker, one of the designers, to present its organizational formula to the general conference.

The formula proposed an Alliance of all Christians
who affirmed as individuals the principles and objects set
forth by the 1846 Conference. The World Evangelical Alliance comprised delegates from the national branches and
their auxiliaries who met in general conference every
seven years. Each conference elected its own officers and
laid its own ground rules. Alterations in the Alliance
constitution became valid when endorsed by a three-fourth
majority of the subsequent conference. The branch Alliances were to provide continuity between international
sessions. It was hoped that only five such subordinate
units would exist: Great Britain,the United States,France,

Germany, Southern Germany and Switzerland. Official recognition by two subordinate units admitted any new branch to
full Alliance membership. Branches were to cooperate
through correspondence and reports. Finally, the proposal
assumed members of one branch could obtain automatic membership in any other when they moved their place of residence.[28]

     This plan represents a compromise between the origi-
nal British intention to have a central English body with
foreign affiliates and the American desire for some more
universal form. Both proposals grounded somewhat in the
nationalism of their proponents. Although the British expected to control the movement, the Americans had no intention of accepting an affiliate status to an organization
dominated by members of a nation so recently the national
enemy and with whom tensions existed over the contemporary
U.S. war with Mexico. A spokesman for the British controlled business committee, Wesleyan Methodist Rev. Jabez
Bunting, told the delegates that the Americans fortunately
persuaded it to drop its more restricted plan of organization for their "OEcumenical" stance. He changed his mind
to one of acceptance of the American approach because
Christian union would be far stronger with the addition of
a powerful American contingent. It would also have the
happy effect of helping to preserve the peace between the
two countries.[29]

     The committee decision mirrored the views of conti-
nental Protestants as well. They favored the American
system of independent branches related to a central body
according to a confederation system of power distribution.
The American confederative ideal rested on the wisdom inherent in the federalism of their own nation's political
system and congregational tradition. It also reflected
the apprehension that too strong an international organization might alienate Americans already distrustful of Roman
Catholic claims to universality. Dr. Schmucker presented
the American view when he said a properly shaped Alliance
should rely on universality and safety as its watchwords.
In terms of universality, the Alliance "should be comprehensive, capable of embracing the World." Nevertheless,
"history teaches us, that in all institutions, Ecclesiastical as well as political, there is a tendency to accumulation and concentration of power; and, therefore, the rights
of individuals and minor Bodies ought to be secured, as far
as possible, against the aggressions of those which are
more central and powerful." According to his rule of safety, the Alliance should be strong enough to hold the world

movement together but weak enough to allow national Alliances to fulfill their particular roles.[30]

    The compromise plan, however, precipitated a crisis
which nearly destroyed the Alliance.  The key issue revolved around the American stipulation that individual
membership in a branch guaranteed full rights in the World
Evangelical Alliance and its conferences.  Innocent enough
in intention, this clause angered delegates from British
antislavery circles who feared it meant extension of fellowship to slaveholders.  The British favored increasingly
William Lloyd Garrison's radical wing of the American antislavery movement which demanded instant abolition of slavery and questioned the Christian character of any American
who failed to oppose slavery—many northern evangelicals
like Leonard Bacon and Joseph P. Thompson were antislavery
but felt abolitionist invective unfair to the Christian
slaveholder and dangerous to national unity.  Introduction
of this attitude into London Conference proceedings clearly created a volatile situation.

    American delegates disliked raising the slavery is-
sue at a time when the social and institutional fabric of
the United States began to shred from internal discord
over slavery and other sectional issues.  Northerners, for
example, tended to favor: (1) high tariffs (to protect in-
dustry); (2) internal improvements at national expense
(roads, canals, railroads); (3) cheap or even free western
land for ordinary citizens; (4) strengthening democracy
and the expansion of the rights of the average citizen.
The South, to the contrary, wanted: (1) low tariffs and
preferred free trade (important to an agrarian area importing most manufactured goods); (2) high prices for western land (to keep it out of the hands of the masses); (3)
small government and therefore opposed the bureaucracy required by expensive programs of internal improvements (which
would have to be paid for by higher tariffs and might benefit the commercial North and West the most); and (4)
feared the democratic and demographic trends of the North
wherein the immigrant-swelled northern population augured
northern dominance of the House of Representatives and the
Presidency.  The agrarian, aristocratic South felt so be-
leagured by the commercial-industrial North and free western farmers that retention of southern control in the
Senate appeared essential to protect southern culture and
the peculiar institution.  This required either the addition of new southern culture states to the Union or the
extension of the slave system to the entire nation, or
possibly both.

Given these tensions, the American War with Mexico
raging at home escalated the slavery controversy because
abolitionists like Garrison, or the more evangelical
Arthur and Lewis Tappan, and Theodore Weld, feared American victory would result in extension and survival of
slavery through territorial accession. Denominational
leaders knew that controversial issues like this could
shatter their voluntary associations. They managed during
the 1830s to protect the denominations by preventing public discussion and decisions concerning slavery within
their folds. External forces ultimately proved too strong
for long-term success of this policy. In addition to the
factors mentioned above, Garrison's journal, the *Liberator*
(1831), the New England (1831) and American (1834) Anti-
Slavery Societies and numerous other voluntary societies
simply would not let die the controversy over an institution, slavery, which many evangelicals, like revivalists
Charles G. Finney and Theodore Weld, thought sinful. That
the Nat Turner Revolt (1831) sent Virginia and the rest of
the South reeling into fearful suppression of Blacks, be
they slave or free, merely exacerbated growing alienation
by many northern evangelicals against the "peculiar institution." As popularized much later in Harriet Beecher
Stowe's *Uncle Tom's Cabin* (1851), a book which carried
whole portions of the North into antislavery, they came to
believe slavery endangered the souls of Black and slaveholder alike. Slavery was sinful! Evangelicals knew that
sin must be eradicated whatever the cost. By the 1840s,
then, the Methodist and Baptist ranks, among others, split
into northern and southern factions when perfectionists
convinced a large northern minority that slavery was so
sinful it had to be rooted out. Denominational schism in
turn augured badly for future national unity. The brunt
of division fell upon the evangelical bodies and evangelicalism, the very core of the national identity and unity,
and so alienated the northern and southern faithful from
each other that emotional religion added to that sectional
and cultural strain leading to the Civil War. Sensing
these dangerous possibilities, many Americans understand-
ably resented foreign meddling with slavery at such a
critical juncture in their nation's history.[31]

The Alliance suffered under this resentment from the
start. The British antislavery movement had begun in
earnest during the 1820s and attained full Parliamentary
emancipation of all slaves in the British West Indies in
1833, much to the consternation of the American South and
inspiration of northern antislavery forces. Not satisfied,
the British reformers turned their attention to eradicat-
ing slavery in Africa, on the high seas, and, by encourage-

ment and example, in the United States.  Quite logically,
therefore, the British meetings preliminary to the 1846
London Conference made it clear that slaveholders were un-
welcome.  As Robert Baird told a later World Alliance
gathering, this pronouncement angered many American evangelicals.  Even Dr. Leonard Bacon swore that he would shun
the movement.  Baird concluded, "if such was the effect on
Dr. Bacon's mind, who was, I firmly believe, the first to
propose the holding [of] such a General Conference...,
what was likely to be its influence upon other men in
America.  It alienated very many at its outset."[32]

Like Bacon, the reaction among some of the strongest
supporters of the Alliance idea was such that they stayed
away from the London Conference entirely.  Those of slave-
holding connection who tried to attend found themselves
barred from admission.  This issue did not really capture
full Conference attention, however, until the question of
Alliance organization arose.  At this juncture, the English antislavery Baptist Rev. J. Howard Hinton attacked
the American ecumenical provisions.  He could neither recognize slaveowners as Christian nor grant them fellowship,
yet the proposed character of the Alliance implied just
such a frightful relationship.  It made accredited members
of one branch potential members of another and of the
World Alliance as well.  The very ecumenical character of
the world body would bring British Christians into unacceptable contact with slaveowners belonging, inevitably,
to the American branch.[33]

Hinton felt no qualms about raising this issue because meetings preliminary to the London Conference prohibited extension of membership to slaveowners.  His amendment to the organization plan merely repeated that prohibition.  No credence ought to be given to American claims
of its divisive nature because, quoting American abolitionist James Gillespie Birney, the United States was already
divided into "Abolitionist" and "Anti-abolitionist" camps.
Our antislavery brethren show clearly that American churches and clergy support a slave system which would col-
lapse if they forthrightly condemned it.  Hinton thought
Alliance exclusion of Christian slaveowners might encourage the Americans to rethink their position, with the resultant destruction of slavery.  The Alliance must side
with abolition.[34]

The Americans bitterly attacked Hinton's argument.
Rev. William Patton stated they traveled to London not to
godfather a British child but to found a World Alliance on
the previously circulated Basis.  Most left for Europe

before receipt of the Birmingham ban on slaveholders. But
for recognition that the Conference determined membership
criteria, none would have attended at all. They believed
the Conference dedicated to Christian union, not antislavery. Slavery was as political a question in America as
the Anglican Establishment or temperance in England and
must be left to the respective peoples for their solution.
Patton warned that passage of this resolution would shatter the Alliance and harm Christian union.[35]

His prophecy was fulfilled when debate focused on
the slavery issue alone during the next few days. A special Anglo-American committee ultimately reported back a
compromise resolution acceptable to the Conference which
condemned the evils of intemperance, dueling, profanation
of the Lord's day, and the sin of slavery. The resolution
compromised by using a shotgun critique of the aggregate
faults of international evangelicalism rather than condemning the sins of a particular nation. Each branch Alliance was expected to treat those problems peculiar to
its region. None were to extend membership to slaveholders who willingly continued in such situation.[36]

The British thought this resolution saved the Alliance, but the Americans knew otherwise. The sabbath rest
intervened between this Saturday evening decision and the
resultant whirlwind. On Monday morning, Rev. Gorham D.
Abbott announced that an ad hoc American committee thought
the compromise essential to a successful world movement
but warned that American Christians could participate no
longer. As Dr. Olin suggested, "all the low feelings of
the Country will be raised against us. Its patriotism,
its nationalism, will be regarded as assailed." Robert
Baird protested that under the circumstances only an independent Alliance could succeed in America. He refused to
vote for the compromise resolution, even though he had
done all he possibly could to make it acceptable. "What
were we to do? We all stood in amazement. We did not
wish to be the means of preventing the formation of the
Alliance——even if, after it was formed, we could not go
with it." Baird concluded that three-fourths of American
Christians would not support the Alliance.[37]

The upshot of the whole controversy was that both
the Hinton and compromise resolutions were rescinded, but
at high cost. The plan of organization introduced by
Schmucker was dropped. The international and ecumenical
character of the movement dissipated temporarily. Creation of a centrally organized international Alliance was
left in abeyance until some unknown future date. The

British did not want fellowship with slaveholders and preferred to defer completion of a World Alliance rather than
precipitate an outright split with the Americans.  The
latter concurred because their constituencies might interpret an antislavery plank as proof of an international conspiracy to control the United States.[38]

        Ironically, the rejected plan of organization at-
tained de facto reality in subsequent history.  Given
British world power, the British Alliance tended to assume
leadership of the world movement and added to subsequent
historical confusion at times by calling their organization the World Evangelical Alliance.  Despite the confusion of names, a real World Evangelical Alliance did exist
under the guise of independent national bodies which cooperated enough to meet various international crises and
to hold a series of world religious congresses.  These
conferences gave 'the' Alliance some substance but without
authoritative structure or power to bind the world movement to definite programs.  The conferences were creatures
designed by the national Alliances to provide mutual edi-
fication, support, and leverage over church opinion. Eleven
such gatherings occurred at intervals during the remainder
of the century: London (1851), Paris (1855), Berlin (1857),
Geneva (1861), Amsterdam (1867), New York (1873), Basle
(1879), Copenhagen (1884), Florence (1891), Chicago (1893),
and London (1907).  The fact that they occurred at all reflects a compromise between the evangelical need for an
international expression of common identity and the demands of peculiarly national problems which prevented the
formation of a stronger, more lasting, international organization.[39]

        The American delegates to the London Conference of
1846 returned home quite disheartened about the fate of
Christian union.  Yet some of the more intrepid clerical
supporters of union—such as George Peck, S. S. Schmucker,
Thomas DeWitt, Nathan Bangs, Lyman Beecher, Alonzo Wheel-
ock, Pharcellus Church, Samuel H. Cox and Gorham D. Abbott
—organized sufficient support in the ensuing months to
found an Evangelical Alliance for the United States of
America, during May 5-11, 1847.  The five-day meeting affirmed the London conception of faith and order as relevant to America by adopting its resolutions and Basis in
toto.  The New York gathering defined desirable union
while also testifying to the long-term ecumenical experience of their evangelical countrymen:

            We recognize Christian union as con-
        sisting in the professed and actual unity

of the disciples of Christ in fundamental doctrinal views; in love to God and
in sympathy of feeling and mutual love
to each other; and in public reciprocal
acknowledgement of each others' Christian
character, and in cooperation, more or
less close, in the advancement of objects
of common interest; and we accordingly
recognize Christian union as having existed to a considerable extent in the
American Church, both in spirit and external manifestation, long before the
organization of the Alliance in London.[40]

Union among the disciples of Christ would show "the Father
had sent him" so the world might believe. As the Alliance
Board of Counselors rhetorically asked America, "is not a
more full, complete manifestation of the union of Christians contemplated by our Saviour, and by him made a means
of the world's conversion?" John 17:21 provides the mandate while infidel and "Romanist" critiques of evangelical
"feuds and jealousies" provide the necessity. The world
groans for the blessings bestowed by "'the gospel of
peace.'" We must show that "we have one common Lord, a
common hope, and like precious faith." These are the Alliance goals.[41]

The American body echoed the London Conference by
eschewing anything which might arouse denominational jeal-
ousy and thereby lead to its destruction. No one need
"surrender what he believes to be revealed in the word of
God." The only required rule of behavior is that members
treat each other in the spirit of love when differences of
interpretation or approach arise. Such self-conscious
disclaimers reflected the bitter opposition which greeted
the Alliance in America. The Counselors conceded the sincerity of evangelicals without its folds, but may not have
comprehended the full nature of opposition when they suggested that objections to the Alliance centered on its
practicality rather than its principles.[42]

To understand that opposition in its broadly conceived form, we might benefit from a review of the arguments made by two major religious figures: Thomas Chalmers
and Horace Bushnell. The great Scottish preacher and theologian Thomas Chalmers tried to forewarn the London Conference to broaden its proposed base. Although an "Evangelical" Alliance would lack strength due to limited constituency, Chalmers was willing to accept the name if the
movement created "Protestant" unity based on his

assumptions.  Fellowship with nonevangelical Protestants
would facilitate cooperation as long as the Alliance fore-
stalled verbal warfare by abstaining from confessional
statements.  Chalmers thought common action alone, rather
than attempts to agree on doctrine, the key to attaining
real purpose, understanding and doctrinal unity among
Protestants.  In fact, only cooperative action which ignored doctrinal differences could solve the two problems
facing the Alliance; the challenge of Popery and the practical measures which signify to the world the unity that
ought to exist among true Christians.  Assent to these two
propositions should be the only qualifications for membership in the Alliance.[43]

     Chalmers also suggested that the Protestant Alliance
approach would have the further advantage of avoiding the
divisions and controversies that the Birmingham stand on
slavery posed—slavery was not the fault of the American
clergy.  They should not be stigmatized and alienated for
something that was beyond their control.[44]

     Despite all of Dr. Chalmers' efforts, the Alliance
ignored his plea.  Just as Chalmers wrote to win over the
London Conference, Rev. Horace Bushnell—a main force in
liberal theology leading to the social gospel—expanded on
Chalmers' argument to attain American adherence to his
position before creation of the United States branch of
the Evangelical Alliance.  Both men criticized a movement
close to their hearts.  Chalmers however depended on fore-
sight into problems the Birmingham meeting posed for the
London Conference, while Bushnell benefited from hindsight
as to London Conference justification of Chalmers' fears.

     To Bushnell, the Alliance approach erred in basic as-
sumptions.  Thomas Chalmers called for a great Protestant
Alliance designed to function in the practical arena rather
than an Evangelical Alliance whose Basis divided Protestants and crippled proposed attempts to combat Roman Catholicism.  Bushnell thought even this too narrow a vision.
The felt need of the moment was worldwide expansion of religious liberty and worldwide separation of religion and
civil authority.  A Christian Alliance dedicated to these
ends could enlist most Christians, even some Roman Catholics, while avoiding those Alliance weaknesses which divided the faithful.[45]

     First, Bushnell argued that the Alliance idea pro-
duced baleful results when it drew a large number of Americans, English dissenters and members of the Established
Church together in a "sentimental but impractical unity."
By participating, the Americans unwittingly sanctioned the

tying of many British dissenters to the Established Church
by bonds of sympathetic fellowship and a social prestige
accrued through association with Anglicans.  This undercut
a potentially victorious campaign of dissenting bodies to
disestablish the Anglican Church in the name of "spiritual
religion," thereby alienating most antiestablishment dissenters from the Alliance.  American opponents of established religion, ironically, contributed thereby to Anglican support.[46]

   Second, Bushnell judged the Alliance erred enormously when it adopted the Basis.  Doctrinal agreement meant
little unless it arose from cooperative action aimed at
practical goals: "The church of God can never reach a
solid and established unity, until it goes into some grand
practical struggle, and girds on its armor for some enterprise large enough and perilous enough to absorb, as tri-
fles and fatuities, the oppositions gendered by idle theory and adverse effort."  The Basis placed the Alliance in
the absurd position of trying to exclude religious men
thought undesirable while denying the Basis operated as a
test of membership.  Such "bigotry" divided further a
movement already depleted.  Many Christians could not accept that superficiality of doctrinal agreement upon which
the Alliance rested.  Nothing was more dangerous, thought
Bushnell, than a body committed to unity alone.  If it did
not prosper, its commitment to arbitrarily selected doctrines mocked Alliance claims to spiritual unity by further dividing the Protestants.[47]

   Avoidance of these pitfalls required all Christians
to cooperate for such pragmatic ends as expansion of religious liberty worldwide, testifying to spiritual authority
in matters of "religious opinions," and creating that combined prayer and action requisite to the growth of fellowship.  Bushnell assumed that this breadth of focus could
free Americans from the dilemma posed by the slavery controversy.  Under present circumstances, they could earn
British recognition but alienate most countrymen by forming a branch Alliance that denied membership to slaveholders (the British having already organized their national
branch with such a provision).  On the other hand, they
could allow sincere Christians to join despite their slavery connections, thereby alienating the British.  A broadly conceived Christian Alliance dedicated to the furtherance of true Christian liberty, however, would solve both
the slavery issue and the proper stance toward Roman Catholicism.  Bushnell was certain that the "whole weight of
the society here and throughout the world will fall upon
slavery not less than upon the Papacy; inasmuch as they

agree, in the destruction of Christian liberty."[48]

The scope of these criticisms brought into question
nearly every aspect of the Evangelical Alliance as it was
constituted in Europe and the United States. The aggregate testimony of Alliance supporters shows that it faced
a fairly general mistrust both of its principles and
methods within the evangelical community. It also reveals
that critics often overlooked the need of many evangelicals to set forth their similarity of perspective as witness to a common identity.[49]

Rev. Thomas H. Skinner, a founder of Union Theological Seminary in New York and member of the American Alliance Board of Counselors, connected this issue with the
corollary that unity based on doctrinal agreement was impractical because impossible. On the contrary, Skinner
believed that conditions among Christians in the world
were such that no association designed to manifest unity
could possibly win the approval of all Christians. Hence,
the next best and most practical approach was to design an
organization which would please as many as possible. At
this point, however, one should note that Chalmers and
Bushnell both denied the necessity of doctrinal agreement
at all and asserted that attempts at such agreement were
needlessly divisive. Dr. George Peck, prominent Methodist
clergyman and Corresponding Secretary of the American Alliance, responded that division exists already and only
the Alliance approach can remedy it. In an article published on the first day of the May Conference, Peck reminded evangelicals that they agreed on essential morality,
but differed and would continue to differ in matters of
opinion. "Our great error has been, not in *maintaining*
our *peculiarities*, but in making them the *basis of union*.
Instead of *meeting* upon *the things in which we agree,* we
have *decided upon the things in which we differ.* We have,
in practice at least, made the things in which we differ
the basis of Christian union and fellowship. And hence
each denomination has practiced a kind of *exclusiveness*
which has infringed upon the unity of the Church." Yet
Peck hastened to add that all denominations stressed the
necessity of union upon a doctrinal basis. The Alliance
hence takes correct position on this issue, especially in
its warning against making nonscriptural doctrines central
to a basis of union.[50]

Peck also dealt with the corollary charge when he
questioned whether the Basis might be so narrow as to exclude legitimate Christians. Granted that some true evangelicals might find aspects of the Basis objectionable,

like the Baptist opposition to the clause endorsing infant
baptism, but others such as the Unitarians and Universalists are rightly excluded by its operation: "Their peculiar doctrinal basis consists in negations, and each negative proposition the contrary of some doctrine which we
deem essential to Christianity. Orthodox Christians consequently cannot unite with them without denying some great
essential doctrine of the Gospel." Others, such as members
of the Society of Friends, might find the doctrinal provisions for baptism, the ministry and the Lord's Supper objectionable but they would also be kept out by the decidedly evangelical and necessary Alliance practice of group
prayer and song, the very activity which gives its meetings
such power and unity. If we rewrite the Basis broadly
enough to include all presumably sincere professors of
Christianity, what type of union would result? Rev. Peck
assured his readers "it must be as broad as the universe,
and consequently practically powerless. If we take our
position upon the widest generalities, where shall we find
our bounds? Where is the principle of concentration?
Where is the *union*?" (Or, in the modern sense, how may we
define our identity?)[51]

> Suppose the London Conference had adopted
> a basis which would have embraced Unitar-
> ians, Universalists, Neologists, Roman
> Catholics, etc., what would have been
> gained? Could these errorists have been
> brought into contact or proximity with
> orthodox Christians by such means? Not
> at all. But if this could be effected by
> conceding that the difference by which we
> are separated from them is small and im-
> material, what good would be done to them?
> They would be confirmed in their errors.
> And what is still worse, truth would be
> sacrificed by a compromise with essential
> error, and orthodox Christianity would be
> a laughing stock before the infidel and
> heathen of the world. We have made the
> basis as wide as we possibly could, with-
> out so diminishing its strength as to
> render it worthless.[52]

Hence evangelicals like Peck thought Christian unity
impossible without precedent consensus on doctrine. Dr.
Skinner assumed this when he claimed no other Basis could
please the majority of evangelicals as much as that of the
Alliance. He implicitly repudiated Bushnell's reduction
of the nine doctrines to one. The Basis had to go beyond

a "simple acknowledgement of the scriptures as the alone
directory of faith and practice." The existence of much
greater interevangelical agreement and evangelical-nonevan-
gelical disagreement than critics admitted may be seen in
Skinner's assertion that "few Christians, of the Evangelical Denominations, would have been willing to combine together on a platform, where the friends of truth and its
greatest enemies could be equally in place, and undistin-
guishable from one another." Evangelicals were too much
true believers to accept the kind of tolerance the Bush-
nellian cooperative approach required towards men of other
religious perspectives. This was particularly true if
that approach *implied* ultimately the possibility of organic union rather than formation of just one more voluntary
association aimed at another practical end.[53]

A related issue raised numerous times by more conservative evangelicals, and not by either Chalmers or
Bushnell, attracted a reply from George Peck. As Dr. Peck
stated, "the Plan of the Evangelical Alliance is objected
to by some, because *it proposes to unite Christians upon a
DOCTRINAL BASIS, while it makes no provision for a separation between real Christians and those who are only nomi-
nally such.*" Selectivity, said Peck, would require a code
of morals and enforcement tribunals which could only anger
the churches by excluding from the Alliance some in good
denominational standing. Since the Alliance does not aspire to the functions and status of a church, it must
leave policing of Christians to the denominations.[54]

The Bushnell-Chalmers type of criticism charged the
Alliance sponsored a false sense of unity by ignoring some
doctrinal differences—avoidance of doctrine entirely, by
implication, prevented this hypocrisy—while successful
growth of such a doctrinally oriented movement threatened
denominational independence. Rev. Peck dealt with this
argument in an article bemoaning that penchant for religious controversy which continued to divide the evangelical camp. To Peck, the only acceptable type of controversy involved candid discussion intended to reveal truth,
not party spirit designed to vanquish. For "candid manly
discussion, is never injurious to truth or genuine Christian unity." Unity, in turn, can never rely on forced
submission for coherence. It is the "result of central
attraction, and not of outward pressure." "The former is
Christian Unity—the latter *Church conformity*—sometimes
miscalled '*Catholic unity*.'"[55]

According to Peck, the Evangelical Alliance was
rooted in Christian unity. There were barriers neither

to honest differences of opinion in theology nor to open
discussion of those differences—remarks quite germane,
given the letters to the editor of the *Christian Advocate
and Journal* critical of Peck's "ecumenical" rather than
"Methodist" stance at the London Conference. Peck assured
his readers "it is a grand mistake to suppose that members
of this association are either about to abandon their respective denominational associations, or that they stand
pledged to close their lips upon those subjects of difference which have given them their position in different
Christian communions." Men of such high visibility within
their own respective religious bodies would neither leave
those bodies nor give up their principles. What the Alliance hoped was modification of open discussion in tone
and quality as men of different perspectives gathered under its auspices. Differences might continue, but asperi-
ty would diminish. Peck, in effect, equated unity with
fellowship.[56]

Rev. Thomas DeWitt similarly claimed the Alliance
neither avoided religious differences nor compelled compromise on them. The only requirement was that members
advocate their particular beliefs "'with due forbearance
and brotherly love.'" In fact, DeWitt knew evangelicals
actually agreed on basics. They differed only in "minor
points, not affecting the vitality of truth," points
"which have given rise to distinct denominational organizations." Thus the great evil of the Christian Church was
not denominational particularity, but the spirit of party
and self which imbued denominational relations. The Alliance proposed to make evangelicals aware of their common
identity by the promotion of brotherly love, the essence
of unity.[57]

Christian union, said Rev. Thomas Skinner, cannot be
based on uniformity of doctrine or discipline. It cannot
be equated with the unity of all Christians in one single
visible church; such a notion is sectarian and schismatic.
"Christian Union" can only "consist in oneness of Fellowship, or Communion, notwithstanding diversities in form
and social organization." Fellowship involves recognition
that evangelicals, irrespective of religious affiliation,
are fellow members of the Christian Church obliged to holy
conduct toward one another.

> Fellowship, as now defined, assumes, that
> claims to Churchship are not invalidated
> by diversities of form or government. It
> rests upon agreement in other and weightier
> matters: such an agreement as is comprised

> in union with Christ: agreement in the
> faith of the gospel, in the spirit of
> Christianity, in Christian experience,
> in the great elements of Christian life
> and character. Fellowship concedes, that
> there may be union with Christ, or agree-
> ment in all the respects now mentioned,
> where there is diversity in other respects;
> and it supposes that a society possessing
> this union, and agreement with others also
> possessing it, may be, and is, a true
> Church, or part of the true Church of
> Christ, however peculiarly organized.[58]

Only unity of Spirit could persuade the world of the validity of Christianity.[59]

Both Bushnell and Chalmers predicted failure for Alliance ecumenism given the absence of goals practical
enough to wield the faithful into cooperative action.
Evangelicals like DeWitt, Peck, and Skinner thought engendering fellowship alone a sufficiently practical goal.
They conceived of the Alliance as a symbolic refuge from
the bitter sectarian rivalries of the Protestant camp and
a practical example of the potential unity among the
faithful.[60]

Much of the dispute between the critics and the de-
fenders of the Alliance, then, was not merely one of means
but of principle as well. Many evangelicals thought the
Alliance above all should articulate an identity which
would unify the true believers. Others, like Bushnell,
grew away from this type of evangelicalism and thereby
lacked the same need for identity: they were more interested in such practical activities as forming a great anti-
Popery association (Chalmers) and sending missionaries to
Rome (Bushnell) in the first step toward converting the
world. But as George Peck observed, either approach by
the London Conference would have kept out all of the
French and most of the Germans and Swiss for fear of
arousing their governments and established Roman Catholic
churches against them. And, it would have totally failed
in the Papal States where the Church had full control of
the government and tolerated no Protestants. He could not
understand why the Alliance might be "practical" only when
taking negative stances. The positive commitment to evangelical unity was the chief and most effective means of
dealing with worldly problems. Peck admitted, however,
that desired unity would facilitate a specific practical
end: "Union as a means is arrayed against *sectarianism* and

*schism,* and does in fact thus assume an *anti* character,
and wage war against one of the greatest evils in the
Church, and will have *enough to do* until that evil is
eradicated." The Alliance must not fall into the critics'
assumption of endorsing a definite object already carried
out by other voluntary associations. Union is the unique
Alliance contribution.[61]

   This dichotomy between stress on unity in-and-of-it-
self, in conjunction with doctrinal agreement, and the
call of others for cooperative action designed to meet immediate Christian needs proved characteristic of American
evangelical ecumenism during the nineteenth century. Un-
fortunately for the Evangelical Alliance for the United
States, Bushnell correctly assessed one of its weaknesses.
It suffered during the pre-Civil War period for lack of a
continuous practical program. Fellowship meetings offered
no compelling objects of long-run interest and occurred
too infrequently to hold public attention. The Alliance
world annual week of prayer was an exciting evangelical
ritual but of itself could not support unity. The American body tried from the beginning to avoid this potential
difficulty by hiring a general agent to popularize the
movement, obtain subscriptions to its supportive journal,
the *Christian Union and Religious Memorial,* and build
auxiliary Alliances. His efforts attained limited success
but apparent lack of funds and general apathy seem to explain the disappearance of his name and office from the
Alliance public record.[62]

   An analysis of denominational affiliation among the
44 signatories to Schmucker's "Overture for Christian
Union" and subsequent participants in the May 1846 New
York Conference, 80 delegates to London and 46 officers of
the American Alliance provides additional insight into the
pre-Civil War failure of this American ecumenical movement.
The following list gives the most heavily represented denomination first place and ranks the rest accordingly: (1)
Presbyterian (primarily New School); (2) Methodist (primarily Methodist Episcopal); (3) Congregationalist; (4)
Evangelical Lutheran; (5) Dutch Reformed, German Reformed,
Baptist; and (6) Episcopalian. The small number of men
involved suggests the limits of the movement's contemporary popularity, although it must be pointed out that they
were among the most prominent members of their churches.
The fact that over fifty percent were Presbyterian, Congregationalist and Reformed reflects that stream of ecumenism
flowing into the Alliance movement from the essentially
Calvinist Benevolent Empire. The more Arminian bodies
found the Alliance slightly less satisfactory although

heavy increases in Methodist, Episcopalian and Baptist membership after the war made the later Alliance even more
ecumenical.  The bulk of antebellum denominations and individual Protestants obviously refused to cooperate in any
actual efforts toward ending disunity.  Alliance evangelicals attributed this to lack of sufficient piety.[63]

     Yet both the critics and defenders of the Alliance
agreed it most debilitating weakness revolved around the
slavery controversy.  Rev. George Peck wrote from London,
on October 15, 1846, to the Methodist *Christian Advocate
and Journal* explaining the problem.  According to Peck, the
Americans persuaded their Continental brethren and the bulk
of the British to accept their reasons for keeping statements on slavery out of Conference documents.  Unfortunate-
ly, some immediately interpreted Alliance rejection of a
slavery provision for membership as implying that the Alliance was proslavery.  Peck assured his audience that "*no
American took proslavery ground in the convention,* and no
one said what he would do, or what he would not, when we
came to act in our own country.  What principles are to
enter into our American organization will in due time be
settled among ourselves."  Peck prayed the Alliance would
succeed in the United States.[64]

     Rev. Thomas E. Bond, editor of this Methodist journal,
assured his readers with respect to the slavery issue that
the Alliance was not a denomination and did not pretend to
prescribe the proper form of the Church, hence, the absence
of any moral code or discipline in the Alliance record.
Discipline would undercut its purpose of union without uniformity.  The Conference correctly rejected a membership
principle condemning slavery as a sin because adoption of
such a principle would have created a code of discipline,
and, thereby, a new church.  Consequently, the "Evangelical
Alliance has done all it was expected to do—all it was the
purpose to accomplish by the 'convention.'  They have settled the basis of union on elementary Christian doctrines,
leaving it to the several Churches to exercise Christian
discipline over their  members."[65]

     Although the United States Alliance was not yet or-
ganized formally, the first meeting of this branch occurred
at the Green Street Methodist Church, New York City, on
December 14, 1846.  Dr. George Peck, Chairman of the Provisional Committee, presided over a program designed to introduce the Alliance through talks by London participants.
In retrospect, this would be the only antebellum Alliance
function so popular that even standing room was taken.  The
Provisional Committee sponsored a series of subsequent

meetings during the winter months to assess the feasibili-
ty of forming an American branch.  All inevitably involved
reference to the slavery controversy because the American
and Foreign Anti-Slavery Society and other abolitionist
bodies heavily supported by evangelicals conducted an effective propaganda war against formation of an American
entity.  Amazingly, the public meetings operated in a
cordial atmosphere despite that issue.  This apparently
derived from abolitionist boycott as well as from continu-
ation of the London Conference precedent of one-half hour
of devotions at the beginning of each session.  Prayer was
a most sacred religious exercise to the evangelical, and
group prayer, facilitating group feeling, was a trademark
of the Alliance throughout the nineteenth century.[66]

The March fourth meeting, held in New York City issued a call for a five-day organizational conference in
May, the anniversary month for the other benevolent associations and therefore the best occasion for gathering members.  It set the tone for the subsequent May Congress by
calling on the Alliance to allow membership only to those
slaveowners holding slaves without malice or selfish goals.
Dr. Peck expanded on this position the following month. He
believed the American movement obliged to take a stand on
slavery for a complex of reasons.  Just as British Alliancemen discovered after the London Conference, Peck argued slavery had become the issue of the day which no new
organization could ignore.  Indeed, northern sentiment was
such that "silence looks like treason to the causes of
liberty and humanity, and will not be pardoned."  Failure
to take a stand, in turn, would alienate the South.  That
section distrusts any body which does not *affirm* slavery.
An attempt to gain southern support therefore requires
concession to the peculiar institution of that region.
Hence, it is our duty to indicate that class of slaveholders acceptable to the American Alliance: those connected
to slavery by necessity who mitigate its circumstances as
best they can.  Moreover, Peck now thought it clear that
American testimony of hatred for slavery at London implied
a promise to the British of some limit to slaveowner membership.  The Alliance must stand against slavery.[67]

The Alliance congress met in Dr. Skinner's Merchant
Street Presbyterian Church on the fifth of May and lasted
until the eleventh.  During the preceding February, the
Preliminary Committee publicized an Alliance constitutional
and goal package in anticipation of the May gathering.  The
package repeated the London Conference preambles, Basis
and constitutional provisions in their entirety, coupled
with five articles specifically relating to the proposed

American Brnach.  The 200 participants of the May gathering adopted almost the entire package without debate.  Concern arose that article four might prevent Seventh Day Ad-
ventists from becoming members until it was decided that
the statement concerning Alliance opposition to desecration of the Sabbath did not intend their exclusion.  Article five, however, precipitated debate which occupied
the bulk of the time:

> '5.  Inasmuch as the peculiar circum-
> stances of this country seem to demand an
> expression of sentiment on the subject of
> slavery, this Alliance declares that a
> discrimination is to be made between those
> who hold slaves, not by their own fault,
> or for the sake of their own advantage,
> but from motives entirely benevolent, and
> those who hold their fellow-creatures in
> bondage for the sake of gain; and that the
> former are to be regarded as entitled to
> fellowship, while the latter cannot be
> received as members of this Alliance.'[68]

Several members encouraged complete exclusion of
slaveowners.  Samuel Simon Schmucker preferred only endorsement of all contemporary American benevolent movements, including the abolitionists.  Others suggested a
shotgun critique of evils including slavery while some
countered with a call for complete silence on the issue.
Finally, the conference dropped this proposal in favor
of what became article seven of the Alliance organizational criterion:

> That while the Evangelical Alliance
> admits into its bosom such persons only
> as are reputable members of Evangelical
> churches, we are nevertheless persuaded
> that the great object of the Association,
> the promotion of a larger Christian union,
> may be furthered by a frank expression of
> our sentiments on the subject of slavery:
> we therefore declare our deep, unalterable
> opposition to this stupendous evil, and we
> hold it to be the duty of all men, by all
> wise and Christian means, to seek its en-
> tire extirpation and removal from the land.
> Still, the one object of the Alliance shall
> be steadily kept in view, which is the pro-
> motion of Christian union and brotherly
> love.[69]

This compromise provision proved acceptable to all
but one of those attending. Even Vice-President of the
Alliance Rev. Thomas E. Bond approved. The past several
months debate convinced him that inherent moral obligations and implied delegate pledges to the London Conference required an American Alliance stand against this evil.
Although the Alliance did not forbid admission of slaveowners, none joined, given Alliance antipathy to the peculiar institution.[70]

Compromise or not, the infant Alliance expired within three years and slavery was chief of the five deadly
poisons. As Robert Baird suggested, the Americans went to
the ecumenical conference in London hoping to "set forth a
brief statement of doctrine, a symbol of faith, in which
all evangelical Protestants could unite." They wanted to
provide the means for keeping each other informed about
the progress of the "kingdom of our Lord" in all nations,
for promoting Christian fellowship, and for uniting all
true Protestants against the "Man of Sin," the Pope. They
expected open reception as members of reputable evangelical churches and irrespective of their national and religious faults; the national and regional bodies alone were
competent to deal with those faults. Horrified by the in-
temperate clergy attending the Conference, the Americans
kept quiet about their views concerning alcoholic bever-
ages and the sin of connecting church to state rather than
endanger the unanimity of the movement. To their amazement, they found themselves condemned for the institution
of slavery which they opposed but could not easily eliminate.[71]

Baird judged correctly that the resultant American
antislavery resolution hampered their Alliance to the
point of destroying it. The delegates from the United
States kept their pledge by writing an article which repudiated slavery, thereby alienating the South from the
movement while their subsequent silence on the issue angered the abolitionist forces of the North. Of course
such a statement irritated northern church leaders still
trying to avoid the slavery issue——they knew that the Old-
New School Presbyterian schism of 1837-1838 to some extent,
defections from the Methodist and Baptist orders in the
late 1830s and early 1840s, and the splintering of the
Methodist General Conference of 1844 into northern and
southern bodies arose in large part over slavery. Even
after schism, some leaders in northern churches continued
to hinder concern with slavery. Indeed, the General Assembly of the Presbyterian Church of the United States
(Old School) retained a national base up to the Civil War

by refusing to judge slavery.  Hence, in 1844, this body
told the Free Church of Scotland

> 'That the petitions that ask the Assembly
> to make the holding of slaves in itself a
> matter of discipline, do virtually require
> this judicatory to dissolve itself and
> abandon the organization under which, by
> the divine blessing, it has so long pros-
> pered.  The tendency is evidently to
> separate the northern from the southern
> portion of the church; a result which
> every good citizen must deplore as tend-
> ing to the dissolution of the union of
> our beloved country, and which every en-
> lightened Christian will oppose as bring-
> ing about a ruinous and unnecessary schism
> between brethren who maintain a common
> faith.'[72]

Many northern church leaders therefore wanted nothing to
do with what appeared to be an abolitionist body, in this
case, the American Evangelical Alliance.  Indeed, English
injection of the slavery issue into ecumenism infuriated
those who thought this slavery regulation symbolic of
British interference in a purely American matter, a situation not to be tolerated by a patriot.

    Second, the denominations ranged from indifference
to hostility towards the Alliance because they thought
this voluntary association of individuals might attempt to
become a superchurch.  Third, many persons remained aloof
from the Alliance because they thought their church alone
the true way to salvation.  They refused to associate with
an ecumenical movement which inherently attributed such a
function to all evangelical denominations.  It appeared to
this type of person that their own body's distinctive religious views and practices were so threatened that the
Alliance had to be evil.  Few listened to the disclaimers
of men like Rev. Bond that "a union with sin and Satan,
and a truce in the holy war against the world, the flesh,
and the devil are things which the members of the Alliance
never thought of."[73]

    A fourth obstacle in the way of the Alliance was in-
tradenominational feuding and schism arising primarily
over slavery, doctrine and the forms of worship.  Although
many sought ecumenical identity as a result, others refused to ally with schismatic brethren.  As Rev. Bond
noted, "Presbyterians, Baptists, and Methodists can unite;

but *Old School* and *New School* Presbyterians cannot. Nor
can members of the Methodist Episcopal Church and those of
seceding bodies unite, while each will unite with all other
evangelical denominations." This problem was exacerbated
by the tendency of evangelicals to treat brethren of
churches other than their own as martyrs if they fell under
denominational discipline—expression of such smypathy by
Alliancemen redounded to the disadvantage of an organization already suspect. Finally, as has been noted previously, the Alliance failed through lack of a practical program
sufficient to sustain active membership participation.[74]

Demise of the organized United States Alliance did
not eliminate its presence completely in the new world.
Various Alliancemen sponsored public meetings in its name
during the 1850s. One of the most important gatherings occurred in November 1858 under the auspices of Thomas DeWitt,
John McLoed, Abel Stevens, Thomas H. Skinner and Robert
Baird. These five men were sufficiently prominent in New
York City to mobilize a large confluence to protest Swed-
ish persecution of Roman Catholics. The Alliance was sincere enough in its commitment to freedom of conscience and
religious liberty even to defend members of a faith
thought to be the polar opposite of evangelical truth. Alliance spokesmen also wrote articles in its emasculated
name to explain the significance of the Civil War to the
British. Clearly, the Alliance could not weather the very
sectional, cultural and political animosities which shattered the American Union with Civil War, dividing evangelicalism for years thereafter, until that war was brought to
successful issue. Hence, their organization did not revive until 1866 when it began planning a World Evangelical
Alliance General Conference to be held in New York City.[75]

CHAPTER FOUR

# AN EVANGELICAL RELIGION OF

# THE REPUBLIC, 1866-1873

The Sixth General Conference of the World Evangelical Alliance (October 2-12, 1873) captured American attention as the major media event since the Civil War itself. National fascination led not only the religious press, but even secular newspapers like the *New York Tribune*, to print almost verbatim coverage of the conference papers and proceedings on a daily basis. Attendance exceeded expectations to such a crushing degree that four additional meeting halls had to be opened simultaneously to the central one in order to cope with the more than 15,000 laity and ordained who wished to witness the concluding exercises of this momentous gathering. No one could have predicted this would be the best attended World Evangelical Alliance conference of the century but neither did its American planners anticipate the bitter economic "Depression of 1873" nor the related American rush to the churches; the Alliance sessions occurred during a period of social trauma and religious revival. Obviously such popularity was gratifying and rewarding to U.S. members of the Evangelical Alliance who had worked so very hard to hold the first major ecumenical conference, one of worldwide proportions, that the nation had ever seen. Alliance efforts were truly ecumenical irrespective of its anti-Roman Catholic bias. Bridging nineteenth century Protestant division was difficult enough without attempting to achieve unity with religious groups beyond the Protestant pale.[1]

That the American Alliance leadership was pleased with the success of the Conference of 1873 is understandable. What is not so obvious, however, is the American body's subsequent interpretation that "the late Conference has vindicated the position which Evangelical Christianity holds in the United States of America." The statement causes one to wonder, what was the position of evangelical Christianity in America which needed vindication? And the very existence of such an Alliance inspires the questions, why and how was the American Evangelical Alliance reborn?[2]

The interrelated answer grounds in that "national
character" which emerged during the Second Great Awakening
(1800-1830), appeared threatened by the forces leading to
the Civil War, but now flourished in the postwar era.  In
William McLoughlin's words, "the Second Great Awakening
was America's coming-of-age as a subculture; if it was not
yet the equal, it was no longer the child of Europe.  The
dominant white, Protestant majority had committed the nation to developing its own human and natural resources in
its own unique way."  Postwar American Christians consequently desired to show the world their nation's voluntaryist religious system allowed the most perfect religious
freedom while sustaining underlying Christian unity.  Their
religious liberty  succored a unique compound of civil
liberty and political democracy so precious it had to be
shared.  Yet this idyllic American scenario appeared
threatened by serious postwar growth of materialism, infidelity and Roman Catholicism.  As stated in the introduction, many Americans therefore desired to explain and to
strengthen existing evangelical unity as well as the Religion of the Republic, that interrelationship of evangelical Protestantism and democracy thought necessary if religious and civil liberty were to prosper.  The rebirth of
the American Alliance in 1866 facilitated these desires.
This body showed publicly that American evangelicals were
united by common cultural and religious perspectives,
making organic union unnecessary, while Alliance existence
increased the Protestant potential to defend the status
quo.  Its rebirth also reflected American evangelical recognition of a common worldwide evangelical identity premised on essential theological agreement and millennialist
commitment to conversion of mankind, an identity symbolized by the World Evangelical Alliance.[3]

That the U.S. Alliance could be rebuilt in 1866,
again as a northern institution, was due in large part to
the eradication of the five limiting factors during and
just after the Civil War.  The destruction of slavery removed a major roadblock to an evangelical sense of unity.
The prevalence of revivalism increasingly blurred the distinctions between Protestant denominations and appealed to
Americans at all levels of society and culture be it businessmen like William E. Dodge, Sr. and Jr., popular theologian and preacher Henry Ward Beecher, or intellectual
and scholar Philip Schaff.  The bitter rancor of the prewar era was forgotten when northern denominations had to
face the same wartime conditions and problems.  Interdenominational cooperation in such efforts as the United
States Christian Commission increased the identification
of evangelicalism with the democratic Union while leaving

a heavy residue of postwar mutual goodwill which overflowed into ecumenical stirrings.  As New School Presbyterian
Henry B. Smith observed, "the progress of events has shown
that the ecclesiastical tendencies, in the midst of our
civil strife, have looked in the direction of union rather
than of increased subdivisions."  Consequently, evangelical attempts in the late 1860s to win the Protestant community over to a recognition of its common evangelical
perspective were more successful than before.[4]

This ecumenical process occurred simultaneously on
the denominational and interdenominational levels.  Methodists, Baptists, Congregationalists and other religious
groups experienced growing comity with bodies of the same
faith.  The spirit of fellowship within particular religious movements proved essential to the overall ecumenical
movement by eliminating that family bitterness which kept
them apart formerly on the broader platform.  Indeed,
these generalizations are particularly true concerning the
successful Presbyterian reunion movement because it precipitated such enthusiasm for ecumenism that Presbyterian
and Reformed provided a good share of initial Alliance
leadership during its rebirth.[5]

The original 1837-1838 Presbyterian split resulted
from a complex of factors such as tensions over the slavery issue, doctrinal differences and the desire of the Old
School to develop a tightly knit denomination at a time
when the New School still cooperated with the Congregationalists and fully supported the evangelical empire.  The
subsequent transformation of the New School into a denomination made it more aware of the validity of Old School
desires for a strong church organization.  At the same
time, revivalism and other evangelical experiences brought
Old and New School membership, if not theologians and
clergy, closer together in doctrinal views.  The removal
of the southern wing from the Old School, in 1861, eliminated the bulk of the proslavery influences which had continued to alienate the New School from the Old.  Hence, in
1862, the Old School suggested the interchange of delegates and the New School Assembly of 1863 responded by
sending such a delegation.  A subsequent reunion conference of both denominations, held during the sessions of
the Old School Assembly of 1864, confirmed the soundness
of doctrine and church order of each body.  This increasing spirit of unity enabled the New School to declare
fraternity and a desire for Presbyterian reunion to the
Old School.  Favorable replies from the Old School inspired the New School Assembly of 1865 to call for continued correspondence to establish a basis for union.  This

escalating mutual encouragement sponsored mightily by the
pious urban laity, ultimately led Old and New Schools into
organic union as the reunited Presbyterian Church in the
United States of America, in 1869.[6]

     Similarly mutual encouragement at war's end brought
together evangelicals of all types for the salvation of
the nation.  The *New York Observer,* for example, carried a
letter which called for "Evangelical Christians" to gather
in Cleveland on September 27, 1865.  Delegates were welcome whether they represented individual pastors or congregations, churches, missionary and tract societies, or
even YMCAs.  The purpose of the meeting was to "organize a
National Society for Evangelization—*a Christian Commission for the masses*—to carry the Religion of Jesus, in
all of its saving efficacy, to those not reached by effective Christian influences."  Among the signatories to this
letter were men who would become prominent in the American
Alliance and many of whom were associated formerly with
the U.S. Christian Commission: Methodist Bishop Matthew
Simpson, Presbyterian businessmen George H. Stuart and
William E. Dodge, Sr., Episcopal priest Stephen H. Tyng,
and evangelical clergymen Thomas D. Anderson and W. I.
Budington.  Their plea brought over 300 delegates who reflected the full range of evangelical parties and denominations.  Salmon P. Chase, Chief Justice of the United
States Supreme Court, acted as presiding officer.  The
conference followed the outline set forth in the public
letter when it decided that a Commission of Sixty should
collect and diffuse information and suggest the means most
suitable for the conversion of the masses.  It was not intended to replace the churches in any way because "the masses, if they get the Gospel at all, must get it *from* the
pulpit and *in* the pews.  This is simply Christ's plan."[7]

     These evangelicals were confident in general about
the outcome of their efforts.  They expected to be successful in converting that large segment of the American
people still outside the evangelical fold, thereby ensur-
ing their perspective would permeate fully American institutions, thought patterns and culture.  Nevertheless,
their efforts reveal a sense of urgency.  One of the chief
factors affecting evangelical union and even Presbyterian
reunion was the need for an evangelical front united, in
defense of true religion and American Christian civilization, against Roman Catholicism and infidelity.  These
chief perils, to the Protestant mind, always subsumed
high-church Protestantism tending to Roman Catholicism,
rationalism and materialism.  For example, in 1868, the
report of the joint Old-New School committee on reunion

made it quite clear that revitalized "anti-Christian
forces—Romanism, Ecclesiasticism, Rationalism, Infidelity,
Materialism, and Paganism itself," much of them considered
of immigrant origin, were struggling for national ascendency.  As a result, "the welfare of the whole country,
and the kingdom of our Lord in all the earth" providentially required evangelical unity.[8]

     Such concern may also be seen in the ideas of the
Rev. Henry B. Smith, one of the leading advocates of both
Presbyterian reunion and Christian union.  Smith was Professor of Church History at Union Theological Seminary of
New York City and would become Chairman of the Executive
Committee (i.e., ruling body) of the American Alliance
from 1866 to 1870.  As the retiring Moderator, Smith gave
an address on "Christian Union and Ecclesiastical Reunion"
in which he warned the New School Assembly of 1864 that
infidelity posed even greater dangers to the "citadel of
our faith" than before.  Its extreme forms of "materialism
and idealism" were organized to "ally themselves with modern civilization and modern democracy."  Indeed,

>          Each claims to be the final system for men—
>          idealism in the name of the inductive pro-
>          cess of demonstration, and materialism in
>          the name of the inductive philosophy; while
>          Christian theism attempts to hold and recon-
>          cile both these methods.  Philosophical and
>          historical criticism are at work to undermine
>          the faith.  The Essays and Reviews, the
>          Colenso controversy in England, Renan's *Life
>          of Jesus,* and Strauss's new elaboration of
>          his life of Jesus for more popular effect,
>          are but the beginnings of a contest which
>          has been long foreseen, and in which the
>          whole of historical Christianity, the Bible,
>          the church, and all the doctrines of our
>          confession of faith are at stake....And this
>          infidelity will strive for the possession of
>          our land as for no other, in the full con-
>          sciousness that thus it holds the future in
>          its grasp.[9]

Assuming that Roman Catholicism often led to infidelity,
Dr. Smith interpreted French military occupation of Mexico
(1861-1867) during the American Civil War as a threat to
the Union.  The appearance on the continent of a Roman
Catholic power sympathetic to the South frightened northern evangelical denominations because of their deep commitment to Union victory as well as their fear that the

French presence augured massive internal subversion of
American Christian and democratic institutions by Roman
Catholicism and infidelity.  Papal pronouncement of the
*Syllabus of Errors* in 1864, which seemed to attack the
principles of democracy and religious liberty, served to
increase this Protestant fear of subversion.[10]

    Just as these dangers inspired further desire for
reunion among Presbyterians, their awesome menace to the
democratic realities of the American Religion of the Republic clearly required a unity which went beyond the
Presbyterian fold to include all evangelicals.  Consequently, members of the Old School Presbyterian Assembly
and evangelicals of other affiliations gathered together
at a mass meeting, in Pittsburgh on May 23, 1865, to prepare a general program of defense.  Both Roman Catholicism
and infidelity seemed to be "arch enemies of Truth in the
midst of the professing Church of God, and arch traitors
to the civil and religious freedom throughout the world."
In response to the Pittsburgh Conference call for denominational cooperation, the New School Assembly appointed a
committee to "consider the expediency of forming a National Protestant Union, or Organization of Evangelical Denominations."  The Old School Assembly took similar action
out of a "desire for more outward  fellowship and more
vigorous co-operation for the defense of Protestant Christianity against the encroachments of Roman Catholicism and
infidelity in our land!"  The Synod of the Dutch Reformed
Church also wished to cooperate.[11]

    There is no doubt that individual Presbyterians such
as Henry B. Smith, the two largest northern Presbyterian
bodies and the Dutch Reformed synod wanted to reinforce
evangelical unity both to facilitate the more complete
conversion of America and to counter the threats posed by
infidelity and Roman Catholicism.  This, however, does not
answer a basic question: Why did many leading Presbyterians, Reformed and evangelicals of other churches decide
to revive the American Evangelical Alliance rather than to
create some entirely new body?

    In part, the answer lies in the fact that while the
American body may have died in 1850, interest in its national and international ecumenical focus did not.  Many
of the surviving members of the original American body
cherished its objects after the war to the extent that
they established the 1866 Alliance upon "The Basis" and
constitution of the 1847 American body.  Among this group
were Lutheran Samuel Simon Schmucker, Methodist John Mc-
Clintock, Methodist Daniel Curry, Baptist Pharcellus

Church, Presbyterian Robert Carter, Dutch Reformed Thomas
DeWitt, Presbyterian John Forsyth, Reformed Presbyterian
John McLoed, Presbyterian Edward N. Kirk, Presbyterian
William Patton, Presbyterian Edwin F. Hatfield and Presbyterian Alfred E. Campbell. Several new and talented re-
cruits such as Matthew Simpson, Henry B. Smith, Philip
Schaff, William E. Dodge (senior and junior), Samuel Irenaeus Prime and John Jay increased their ranks during the
1850s.

The movement which revitalized the American Alliance,
according to Samuel Irenaeus Prime, started in Philip
Schaff's New York home in 1865. This Swiss-American began
his career in the American German Reformed Church as one
of the formulators of Mercersburg Theology, eventually
moved into Presbyterianism, and became a professor at
Union Theological Seminary in New York in 1869. After a
decade of critical aloofness, Schaff began his association
with the Alliance in 1857 as a delegate to the Berlin Conference of the World Evangelical Alliance. His commitment
to ecumenicity was such that he became one of the prime
movers of the American body from its inception in 1865 until his death in 1893. Unlike most contemporaries, he
espoused a breadth of ecumenicity which even looked to the
ultimate consolidation of the Roman Catholic, Protestant,
and Greek Orthodox churches into a single evangelical and
catholic church. Although he was in no way as theologically oriented, being more inclined to perfectionism and
personal holiness, Bishop Matthew Simpson also entered the
Alliance as a delegate to the Berlin Conference and thereafter gave the American movement the support of name and
presence despite the onerous duties of his Methodist
charge.[12]

William E. Dodge, Sr., became president of the revived American Alliance in its first year of official existence, 1866. Dodge was a great merchant and financier
of New York City (he was the principal mover in the great
Phelps-Dodge mining and metal importing corporation); his
business and social influence extended throughout the nation. An active New School elder, he strongly supported
revivalism, numerous pandenominational and Presbyterian
benevolent societies and reunification of the New and Old
School churches. Despite his busy schedule, he even acted
as supply preacher for many local revivals. His financial
benevolence became legend during his lifetime because he
supported more budding theological students through seminary than can be counted and became financial angel for
many of the religious causes of the day, especially for
the Alliance. Among other things, he was lifelong Presi-

dent of the National Temperance Society, a Director and
then Vice-President of the American Board of Commissioners
for Foreign Missions, a Director of the board of foreign
missions of the Presbyterian Church, a Director and Vice-
President of the American Tract Society, and an Executive
Council member of the U.S. Christian Commission during the
war.  William E. Dodge, Sr., therefore brought enormous
prestige to the Alliance during his active presidency of
that society from 1867 to his death in 1883.  His is an
example of the rise of devout laymen to positions of great
power within the benevolent and denominational assemblies
of the postwar period.  Laymen finally fulfilled another
trend inherent in antebellum Jacksonian Democracy, despite
often bitter clerical opposition, by acquiring a share in
the government of all the churches.  The clergy no longer
ruled alone.[13]

     Another major recruit to the revived Alliance cause
was Old School Presbyterian Samuel Irenaeus Prime.  Prime
was editor and principal owner of the powerful *New York
Observer*.  He used his religious newspaper during the postwar era as a forum for Protestant ecumenical and anti-
Catholic sentiment, presented within an evangelical context.  Prime greatly influenced the policies and direction
of the American Alliance until his death in 1885 and was,
along with Dr. Schaff, largely responsible for the success
of the New York Conference of 1873.[14]

     A significant portion of the more prominent new re-
cruits, such as Smith, Schaff, and Dodge, Sr., were associated with the New School's Union Theological Seminary
either as faculty or members of the board of directors.  Of
the two largest elements of American Presbyterianism, the
New School held true to its traditions of cooperation with
other evangelicals by being the leading Presbyterian supporter of the Alliance during the 1860s.  Nevertheless,
the enthusiasm engendered by Presbyterian reunion increased
the number of former Old School men in the Alliance during
the 1870s while massive addition of leaders from other denominations made it truly ecumenical.[15]

     John Jay, Episcopalian and scion of the great Jay
family of New York, engaged actively in Alliance affairs
throughout the late nineteenth century.  He even served as
President of the Alliance in 1884-1885 and would have continued indefinitely in that office were it not for his desire to avoid compromising his position as President of
the Civil Service Commission in New York State.  This
state body was part of a controversial national reform effort, sponsored by liberal Republicans, which attempted to

eliminate that Jacksonian era democratic reform called
"rotation in office." Believing the ordinary man capable
of filling well any office of government, the Jacksonians
thought their political victory meant a public mandate to
place Jacksonians in most appointive offices. A classic
example of one generation's reform souring into another
generation's nightmare, this "spoils system" degenerated
into rewarding party hacks with positions for which they
were unqualified. By the 1860s, corruption pervaded state
and federal bureaucracies, particularly the U.S. Customs
Houses (tariff). Reformers gained little headway until a
staunch supporter of the patronage system, President James
A. Garfield, was assassinated by a frustrated and mad office seeker. Vice-President-become-President Chester A.
Arthur swung with the groundswell of public outrage to
help the reformers attain the Pendleton Act (1883). Civil
Service had dawned on the national bureaucracy and some of
the more liberal states as well.

Active in national and New York political reform, as
were many other Alliancemen (most were liberal Republicans), John Jay found himself in an embarrassing position.
The Alliance made enemies among Roman Catholics by blocking legislation proposed to obtain public funds for parochial schools and denominationally controlled institutions. Jay could not afford to remain President of the
Alliance at the very time when he needed as much nonparti-
san support as possible for civil service reform. His
resignation opened the way to another prominent layman,
William E. Dodge, Jr. The younger Dodge lived under the
business and philanthropic shadow of his father until the
latter's death allowed greater public recognition of his
merit and activities. William E. Dodge, Jr., joined the
Alliance in the 1860s and became its president during the
period of its greatest national influence, from 1885 to
1898.[16]

Other significant Alliance supporters were: Bishop
Charles P. McIlvaine, leader of the evangelical party in
the Protestant Episcopal Church; the nationally famous
Methodist Episcopal scholar and President of Drew Theological Seminary, John McClintock; Rev. James McCosh, Scottish Presbyterian immigrant, theologian, and President of
Princeton College; J. C. Havemeyer, one of the sugar mag-
nates who devoted much of his life to interdenominational
religious activities and societies; R. R. McBurney, a formative genius behind the New York and national YMCA movements who helped to bring them to the peak of their success; and Rev. Cyrus D. Foss, Rev. John F. Hurst and Rev.
John H. Vincent, men who became leading Bishops of the

Methodist Episcopal Church.  It is this retention of old
and recruitment of new talent to the Alliance that provided the essential continuity of leadership as well as that
more youthful ability, prestige, and momentum which helped
to revive and sustain the Alliance as an active ecumenical
force in the postwar era.  It gained a healthy spectrum of
membership from among the evangelical elements within the
Episcopal, Methodist, Presbyterian, Dutch Reformed, Congregational, Moravian, and to a lesser extent, Lutheran
and Baptist churches.[17]

     That the bulk of the Alliance constituency derived
from New York City, Boston, Philadelphia, Washington, D.C.,
St. Louis, Cincinnati and Chicago, itself requires some
explanation.  Despite determined efforts by leaders to
broaden its following, the only viable affiliates aside
from those centering in or near New York City were urban, although  dozens of short-lived rural branches appeared now
and again.  Wherever they were, those alliances looked to
the New York City based Evangelical Alliance for the
United States of America as the national organization and
true leader.  The source of Alliance constituency related
to the very nature of the urban world itself.[18]

     The mainline denominations grew in affluence when
their urban membership rode the wave of antebellum com-
mercialization and postwar industrialization of the national economy into middle and upper class prosperity.
Despite benefits to evangelicals, industrialization created such vast wealth in the nation that it reinforced the
spirit of hedonistic materialism spawned by the Civil War.
Men like Jay Gould and Jim Fiske made a mockery of the
evangelical worldview, which stressed honesty, integrity,
hard work, and especially, deep piety, by seizing wealth
and satiating their senses at the expense of others.  Desires for immediate gain led these two men to engineer a
struggle with Cornelius Vanderbilt, shipping magnate and
founder of the New York Central Railroad, for control of
the Erie Railroad.  Nearly bankrupting the Erie (they
would proceed to do so later), and legally liable to Vanderbilt for some six or seven million dollars, they re-
gained their fortunes by cornering the New York Gold Exchange and precipitating the financial Panic of 1869, a
sharp recession which hurt many ordinary Americans.
Their's represented the less desirable activities of a new
breed of businessmen who made terms like corporation, pool,
monopoly and trust something to be feared by businessman
and ordinary citizen alike.

     If greed and economic materialism seemed to gain an

ever larger public following, materialist interpretations
of reality also gained notariety through publication of
Joseph Ernest Penan's *Life of Jesus* (1863) and the re-
printing of that by David Friedrich Strauss.  Those methods of biblical criticism intended originally to validate
Christian faith now seemed to auger growth of infidelity.
As if all this were not serious enough, the very foundations of the religious worldview shook to the point of
shattering when the mountainous handmaid of theology, science, erupted into strange new theoretical shapes and
forms.  Major American scientists like the chemist, physi-
ologist and physicist John William Draper began to espouse
materialist explanations of reality and to popularize the
notion that religion had held back scientific progress.
Since  very popular lecturers  like agnostic Robert Inger-
soll  used science to question basic Christian teachings
about creation and human purpose, these developments confronted American Protestants with a two-pronged but very
painful dilemma.  The very nature of post-Civil War America—its telegraph, steamship, railroad, and later, electric lights, telephone, sewing machine and a whole cornu-
copia of time and labor saving inventions—meant that so
much of modern hope as well as modern problems appeared to
spring in genetic series from industrialization, back to a
massive technological revolution, and finally to this scientific revolution.  What, then, ought evangelicals to
think and do about this new science?[19]

On the one hand, most evangelicals wished to retain
what appeared to be the ever-growing comforts and standards of living which science and technology offered.  Besides, technological wizardry seemed to justify the notion
that science held the key to unlocking the truths of the
universe.  Such a notion had a strong hold on the American
mind ever since the Founding Fathers stressed "the laws of
Nature and of Nature's God," affirming both the moral laws
inherent in natural rights theory and those universal laws
undergirding nature akin to Newton's law of gravity.  The
notion of a created universe operating according to universal natural laws arose, in the words of historian of
science Stephen G. Brush, from the "First Scientific Revolution:" "Dominated by the physical astronomy of Coperni-
cus, Kepler, Galileo, and Newton," it "established the
concept of a 'clockwork universe' or 'world-machine' in
which all changes are cyclic and all motions are in principle determined by causal laws."[20]

Both this notion of a rationally ordered but lawful
universe and the general Enlightenment interest in science
continued among nineteenth century evangelicals and other

Americans albeit filtered through their scriptural and
creationist perspective as well as through a scientific
ideal thought to originate with Francis Bacon.  Their
Baconian model, to quote Theodore Dwight Bozeman, required
a "strenuously empiricist approach to all forms of knowledge, a declared greed for objective *fact*, and a corresponding distrust of 'hypothesis,' of 'imagination,' and,
indeed, of reason itself."  This essentially inductive,
fact-counting and almost antitheoretical orientation allowed antebellum Americans to create "scientific" and
"Baconian" natural theology, biblical studies, geology,
biology and philology which accorded with their religious
principles and yet came to terms with such contemporary
scientific theories as catastrophism, progressivism, uni-
formitarianism, the unity of mankind, and higher criticism.[21]

        On the other hand, even though accommodation between
religion and science continued through the remainder of
the century, that rooted in Baconism collapsed by the
1860s when the volcanic uplift of the new scientific revolution began to crystallize.  According to Brush, that
second scientific revolution, "associated with the theories of Darwin, Maxwell, Planck, Einstein, Heisenberg, and
Schrodinger, substituted a world of process and change
whose ultimate philosophical meaning still remains ob-
scure."[22]

        This revolution in the theory, definition, and na-
ture of science—for science is a heavily *interpretive* approach to reality—stressed evolutionary process rather
than instant Creation, and posited massive theoretical
constructs to explain reality, "evolution" for example,
rather than staying within the severe inductive and empiricist limits of Baconian science; that Charles Darwin,
whose *Origin of the Species* (1859) first brought the new
scientific way to general public attention, relied heavily
on deduction from general theory, merely made matters
worse.  This new scientific model was also frightening because "relativism" and "open-endedness" inherent in the
theory of evolution posed materialist and potentially agnostic implications threatening to religion.  If science
be the key to truth, were those implications supported by
science or were they merely human error?  Evangelicals
distraught by the demise of Baconism, or attracted to dispensationalist theology and premillennialism, simply re-
nounced modern science and turned to fundamentalism.  The
more liberal and postmillennial evangelicals like James
McCosh, Joseph P. Thompson and Josiah Strong to the contrary, thought the new scientific model compatible with

their religion, in part because they set limits both to
its relativism and to its new form of causal explanation.
The retention of God, Providence and the millennium as the
backdrop to the natural and human drama of the universe
enabled men like Josiah Strong, Richard T. Ely and John R.
Commons to applaud physical science for giving man mastery
of his environment while they portrayed social science as
essential to the creation of a scientifically progressive
society.[23]

If economic and scientific materialism, as well as
other strains of infidelity did not pose sufficient difficulty, the wedding of American culture and evangelicalism
during this period tied the urban faithful to the dominant
cultural forms of their nation at the very time when wave
upon wave of foreigners settled in the cities. The immigrant presence greatly complicated the situation by contributing cultural diversity to an American civilization
which ostensibly had just become homogeneous. Such diversity was particularly upsetting because so many of the
new Americans were Roman Catholic.

It was in the urban area therefore that the scientific industrial complex and immigration were most clearly
adding the spirit of materialism and cultural variation,
respectively, which appeared to threaten American cultural
homogeneity. Middle class urban evangelicals naturally
responded more quickly than their rural counterparts to
the need to defend the dominant evangelical culture—this
was especially true of the college educated leaders who
built the Alliance. In turn, the concentration of so many
evangelical leaders and bureaucrats in New York City, a
city where diversity and materialism were becoming especially apparent, facilitated that cooperation and intercommunion essential for evangelical unity to be possible.
Although Alliance rolls never exceeded more than several
hundred persons, they were for the most part either leading evangelical clergymen, and were thus heard around the
nation, or they were editors of religious journals and
papers, college presidents, voluntary society and church
board presidents, directors and general secretaries, bishops or moderators of denominations and prominent laymen.
Their total number was insignificant (several hundred)
when contrasted to the millions of evangelicals around the
nation but their individual prominence was such that they
extended Alliance influence far beyond its limited constituency. They brought it into contact with that vast interlocking directorate of evangelical voluntary societies,
publications, church boards and assemblies which enabled
the Alliance to reflect the general evangelical opinions

of the time and to influence them in small but important
ways.  Growing confidence in each other at a time, when
the dominant culture appeared increasingly threatened, enabled many evangelicals therefore to seek more concrete
expression of unity and cooperation and led to the revival
of the Alliance.

It might be noted at this juncture that participation of so many religious leaders in the ecumenical movement poses the possibility that a strong motive for unity
arose from the bureaucratic impulse towards empire building, order and efficiency.  This does not appear to be
true of the Alliance until the 1880s; denominational and
creedal affiliations were far too strong to allow reasons
of power and efficiency such a central role, and then only
as a minor theme.  It will be far more true of the early
twentieth century movement when business rhetoric, procedures, and businessmen gain even greater sway over the
denominations and deeply affect the newly-formed Protestant ecumenical body, the Federal Council of Churches.[24]

The Alliance did have a disorganized rural following
who recognized less clearly these religious and cultural
dangers until late in the century and then much of the
rural world, be they transplants to the city or still in
the country, found the urban (and Alliance) solutions too
liberal; they remained conservative or turned to fundamentalism.  The Alliance centered in many urban areas of
the New England, central and midwestern states.  Just as
postwar southern churches were alienated from their northern counterparts by antebellum and wartime strife, so they
disliked the Alliance for its antislavery stance, democratic nationalism and pro-Union sympathies.  Unable to get
along with their northern sister bodies during Reconstruction, they could hardly associate with a northern based
Alliance.  Anyway, the very rural South experienced few
of the dangers posed to evangelicals by the urban world.
Only when the end of Reconstruction (1877) allowed more
amicable feelings toward the rest of the nation, and the
social and religious crises of the mid-1880s attracted
national attention, did southerners, particularly Methodists, enter the Alliance in numbers and then they came
primarily from the border states of the former Confederacy
rather than the deep south.  Those southerners active in
the Alliance before this time, like Methodist clergymen
Charles F. Deems  in the 1870s, were actually living and
working in the north.[25]

Rebirth of the Alliance also rooted in the desire of
many Protestants to form an organization that went beyond

a merely defensive position to one which clearly stood for
existing evangelical unity. As noted by Samuel Simon Schmucker, this concern led American evangelicals in two directions during the 1860s. One pandenominational ecumenical effort channeled into the revival of the American
Evangelical Alliance, in 1866, and the other led to an
abortive attempt to federate denominations in the Council
of Evangelical Denominations, in 1869. The federative
movement reflected discontent with the practical weakness
inherent in an extradenominational society of individuals
dedicated to unity, the Alliance form of organization. The
desire for a federation of denominations with enough power
and influence to preserve evangelical dominance in American culture inspired the Dutch Reformed Synod of 1868 to
plan an interdenominational conference for the next year.
The Dutch Reformed committee appointed to organize this
ecumenical conference comprised Elbert S. Porter, President
of the General Synod, David D. Demarest, Stated Clerk, and
elders Robert H. Pruyn, Sanford Cobb and Frederick T.
Frelinghuysen. All but Demarest and Cobb would become
supporters of the Alliance by late 1869, although the five
men were initially committed to organize the October 1869
convention which would hopefully found a Council of Evangelical Denominations.[26]

The circular letter announcing the convention made
clear that the proposed "Council shall have for its great
object the concerting of proper measures for promoting, *not*
organic, but fraternal union, for the maintenance of the
common doctrines and ethics of the Christian Church, whose
one head is the Lord Jesus." The Council would consist of
five representatives sent from each evangelical denomination and function as an advisory body to the denominations.
Although both Old and New School General Assemblies sent
official delegations, and numerous evangelicals of other
bodies attended, the Council failed to survive its organizational meeting because it faced three insurmountable ob-
stacles.[27]

First, Philip Schaff and his associates managed to
nurture the feeble creature reborn in Schaff's study in
1865 into a full-blown and organized Evangelical Alliance
for the United States of America of 1866. Although men of
high visibility attended the October Council meeting, as
Dr. Schmucker noted, a "large proportion of them are the
known friends of the Evangelical Alliance." They desired
to federate the denominations, but, beyond that, found
their goals and personnel varied little from that of the
already organized Alliance. This may have surprised some
of the participants but Schmucker accepted it with genial

good nature.  He decided the two movements must be united
and wrote *The True Unity of Christ's Church* to convince the
Alliance of the merit of his position.  Recognition of the
implicit duplication of effort led the bulk of the Alliancemen to withdraw their support from the Council.[28]

Second, the American Evangelical Alliance offered
the advantages of belonging to an international ecumenical
movement dedicated to the defense of evangelicalism and
religious liberty wherever and whenever needed, the World
Evangelical Alliance.  The persecution of missionaries and
converts as well as outright suppression of religious liberty by many governments around the world made the Alliance diplomatic and pressure group tactics, designed to
change those government policies, rather attractive to
many leading U.S. evangelicals.[29]

Third, the idea of federation aroused denominational
fears of losing their autonomy.  Such fear is implied in
the report of the special Old School committee which encouraged participation in the Council.  It assured the Old
School Assembly that the decisions of the Council would be
"confined to said committee *personally;* not to the denomination as such."  Commitment to the denominational system
was still so very strong that evangelicals were afraid of
anything which smacked of a superchurch but could often
approve of the Alliance because it sponsored Christian
unity among individuals rather than direct consolidation
of the churches.  Hence, the Presbyterian General Assembly
of 1870 hoped the World Evangelical Alliance conference
proposed for that fall would "greatly promote the cause of
Christian union, and the more rapid progress of the Redeemer's Kingdom in our land and over the world."  Dr.
Schmucker attempted to win the Alliance to federation but
died before he could present his "Plan" to the Conference
of 1873.  The latter was published in the Conference proceedings accompanied by an editorial comment, one typical
of evangelical reaction to federation until the 1890s,
that however "desirable it may be in itself; [it] is cer-
tainly not practicable or obtainable at the present time."[30]

By a process of elimination, then, evangelicals were
attracted to the Alliance more than to other bodies because its basis and constitutional provisions made clear
to America and to the world what they thought it meant to
be an evangelical.  Such affirmations as "belief in the
*divine-human person* and *atoning works of our Lord and Saviour Jesus Christ,* as the only sufficient source of salvation, as the heart and soul of Christianity, and as the
centre of all true Christian fellowship" purposely set the

evangelical faithful apart from Unitarians, free thinkers,
confessional or high-church advocates, sectarians, and
above all, Roman Catholics and Mormons. Agreement on the
Basis tended to elevate evangelical unity above religious
differences to the level of common identity. With due regard to "the minor differences of theological schools and
religious denominations," the Basis was interpreted as a
"summary of the *consensus* of the various evangelical Confessions of Faith." That these men could relegate the
theological and religious particularities of the evangelical denominations to the realm of "minor differences"
tells us quite a bit about the qualitative change in attitudes since before the war. Although the men of the 1840s
were not yet prepared to reduce denominational particularity to a minor aesthetic level of personal discrimination,
many evangelicals of 1866 seem to have come to just that
opinion. This change in perspective indicates how much a
sense of common national and religious identity had developed among a large segment of leading evangelicals by the
1860s.[31]

Consensus on essential doctrine and fraternal regard
among the evangelical faithful, irrespective of denomination, was seen as the only type of unity possible at that
time among the Christians of democratic America. As Episcopal Bishop Gregory T. Bedell stated at the New York Conference of 1873, general misconceptions of the meaning of
unity among both the faithful and the enemies of Christianity led to constant attacks on Protestantism for fail-
ing to overcome its diversity of "administration": "It is
time that Evangelical Christians should affirm that *unity*
*does not depend on organic* union. We have lost, immeasur-
ably by magnifying differences in form, minifying the
unity of evangelical opinion, sentiment, and practice, and
tacitly yielding to a current impression that Evangelical
Christianity is in essence, in the very nature of the case,
disintegrated." But if organic union is not the ideal,
the Bishop asked rhetorically, what "measure" and "manner
of Christian union" is needed to express the oneness of
Christ's Church? In answer, he said "'Alliance' is a
well-chosen term. It solves the question immediately by
force of definition. It expresses all union expedient or
possible among Christians who conscientiously differ in
forms of administration; while it admits full liberty of
individual opinions, within a broad range agreed upon."
To Bedell, only an Alliance allowed individuals to express
their sense of Christian unity and still retain both their
respective denominational affiliations and theological
differences.[32]

The Bishop thought such respect for personal variation essential.  The denominations themselves arose from
differences in nervous temperament, mental constitution
and in physical build as well as from religious imperfection among the faithful.  Indeed, resulting disagreements
over polity and order within the Church reflected a law of
history which advanced the pure truth of the gospel
through clash and controversy.  As a result, Bishop Bedell
believed that no organic union of evangelicals based upon
"abandonment of conscientious religious distinctions"
could survive the return of sober thought.  The only unity
possible was that which characterized the Church of Christ
through the ages: "God be praised for whatever in the
Evangelical Alliance will nurture and fortify in our souls
a sense of this spiritual unity in Christ Jesus our Lord."[33]

Given the deep attachment to denominationalism, most
evangelicals believed organic union impossible short of an
undesirable recourse, state coercion—hence their aloofness from High-church Episcopalian calls for organic union
as well as subsequent more liberal Lambeth ecumenism.  Defending the Alliance approach to unity against High-church
critiques, Mercersburg theologian John W. Nevin observed,
"the Episcopal Church—in spite of her self-distinguishing
title of '*The* Church'—is in truth at least a section only,
or sect, of the Church Catholic, and not by any means the
wholeness of its proper life."  Philip Schaff accordingly
made clear on different occasions that Christian union
must rest on liberty of opinion.  "Christian union cannot
be enforced or artificially manufactured," he wrote, but
"must grow spontaneously from the soil of Christian Freedom; it must proceed from the mighty Spirit of God...; it
must flow from a closer union of individual believers in
Christ."  Moreover, evangelicals like Schaff and James Mc-
Cosh, President of the College of New Jersey (Princeton),
believed that there was no conflict between denominational
diversity and Christian union.  Each denomination fulfilled a particular function according to God's design.
If sectarian exclusiveness was subordinated to the welfare
of the kingdom of God, individuals could be united with
their own brethren in Christ and still remain loyal to
their own church.[34]

The object of the American Alliance, then, was not
to constitute Christian unity but to manifest before the
churches of the world the national religious unity which
already existed.  Commitment to this goal proved stronger
than the numerous temptations for the Alliance to go in
other directions.  In 1870, the Christian Commission approached the Alliance with the desire to amalgamate, but

the Executive Committee of the Alliance followed Philip
Schaff's advice and continued on its ecumenical course.
Again, in 1872, the Executive Committee declared that the
"definite aim of the Alliance is to promote religious liberty and Christian union." Work so meaningful in itself
means "we must avoid all entangling alliances and ecclesiastical complications, or interference with the specific
work of church organizations and the numerous voluntary
societies of our country. The Alliance may prepare the
way for, but cannot do the work of Bible, Tract, and Missionary Societies." The Committee concluded that its
original purpose should not be lost in attempts to satisfy
numerous recent requests, both at home and abroad, to establish churches in foreign nations or aid various benevolent societies.[35]

A successful revival of the Alliance in 1866 also
depended upon the creation of a practical program designed
to engage the active participation of its members. Retaining the purpose statement of the 1847 American body,
the Alliance must promote evangelical union to increase
the success of general Christian activities, "to counteract the influence of infidelity and superstition...to as-
sist the cause of religious freedom everywhere; to hold up
the supreme authority of the Word of God; to urge the observance of the Lord's day; and to correct the immoral
habits of society" by functioning as a bureau of correspondence and information. This method appealed to the
Americans because it was congenial to their voluntaryistic
and persuasive system of religion and proven effective by
the World Alliance. The latter used it to sponsor revivals of religion, a week of worldwide annual prayer, petition to governments for an end to persecution of the faithful and the counteraction of infidelity and Romanism. To
summarize in Philip Schaff's words, the Alliance definitely opposed the principles and practices of Roman Catholicism, but the primary and practical "object of this Alliance is to exhibit and set forth the Christian unity which
all true Christians possess. It has for its object the
promotion of religious freedom. It is supposed that unity
and freedom go hand in hand, and it is supposed that Christianity itself flourishes best on the soil of freedom."[36]

The revival of the U.S. Alliance appealed to many
evangelicals because it clearly went beyond a restatement
of the goals of the old Alliance. It was revived in good
part as a vehicle for holding an international evangelical
conference in America. Such a conference would serve a
threefold purpose. In an immediate sense, the conference
was intended to reveal world Protestant unity to counter-

act the claims and attacks expected from the highly adver-
tised Roman Catholic ecumenical council planned for 1870.
More important than this symbolic stance, the exposure of
European leaders to America during the two weeks of conference would provide such practical instruction in the
merits and interrelationship of American evangelicalism and
democracy, of the Religion of the Republic, that the American system would be vindicated before the world.  Above
all, Americans hoped to show that religious unity existed
in the United States despite diversity because both American evangelicals and their European counterparts shared
the same religious elements of identity.[37]

     The Americans planned to convene the New York Con-
ference in 1870 but European unpreparedness and then the
Franco-Prussian War and its after effects delayed the Conference until 1873.  Belief in impending spiritual conflict with the forces of evil convinced many Americans, by
1869, of the truth of Episcopal Bishop Charles P. Mc-
Ilvaine's prediction: "The state of the world, so remarkable at this time, and the gathering of the two great
armies of the powers of darkness, in their joint war
against the Church of Christ and His precious Gospel, are
a loud call upon His people, essentially *one* to be *united*
in *their* warfare for their glorious Head, and the great
salvation.  The contest will be such as the Church has not
known before in its double aspect, against Popery and Infidelity."  Now, in 1870, Samuel Irenaeus Prime could see
the hand of God in the defeat of the leading Catholic
(France) by the rising Protestant (Prussia) nation—God
was preparing the way for the "furtherance of the Gospel."
Conference delay, although inconvenient enabled evangelicals around the world to digest the implications of the
Vatican Council's affirmation of both the *Syllabus of Errors* and the new doctrine of papal infallibility.  As the
Congregationalist Joseph P. Thompson told a special meeting of the Alliance, once the Vatican Council of 1870 had
taken place, evangelicals would better know their responsi-
bilities and duties to the Church of Christ.  He captured
contemporary evangelical opinion when he observed that

          The Pope has thrown down his Syllabus—as
          a challenge to modern society—denouncing
          a government untrammeled by the Church;
          denouncing a free press, civil marriage,
          secular education, and whatever tends to
          the improvement of mankind, apart from the
          traditions and sacraments of Rome; and it
          is alleged, that he has manipulated the
          composition of the council, with a view to

> secure its sanction to the usurpations
> that he has so steadily pressed in the
> interest of Papal autocracy and infalli-
> bility.[38]

From the evangelical perspective, the subsequent Vatican
Council seemed to fulfill this prediction.

Expectations as to Vatican Council actions, in turn,
strengthened American evangelical desires to justify the
evangelical and democratic orders. Some comprehension of
their view of both orders may be obtained through analysis
of the evangelical interpretation of the American Civil
War. Ever since the 1840s, the British Alliance had been
critical of American evangelicals for allowing slavery to
survive in America. The British evangelical leadership as
a whole made such a point of opposing slavery and those
associated with it that northern evangelicals like Robert
Baird, Henry B. Smith, and Matthew Simpson naturally became upset when the British failed to applaud the groundswell of northern efforts to eliminate slavery before and
during the Civil War. Northerners attributed this cool-
ness to the aristocratic (anti-democratic) view of the war
held by the British evangelical elite, but much more was
involved than this. All European powers except Russia desired southern victory, mostly for the same reasons, and
autocratic Russia favored the Union only because of contemporary problems with Britain. France took advantage of
American disunion to establish an empire in Mexico. As
far as British attitudes are concerned, the upper and middle classes feared continued success for American democracy would increase worker demands for power at home (and
this is just what began to happen when Union victory inspired Britain's lower classes to demand and get the Reform Bill of 1867). Many hoped Union defeat would destroy
democracy and thought continuance of slavery in an independent South an acceptable price to pay for such a happy
end. Given the similarities of lifestyle and aristocratic
traditions between British rulers and southern gentry,
England went beyond neutrality to actually aid (unofficially) the southern rebellion. Finally, Britain feared a
reunited American nation might become a great power by the
end of the century, thereby threatening England's world
dominance.[39]

Henry B. Smith discussed this aspect of evangelicalism in a speech which the American Alliance authorized him
to give to the World Evangelical Alliance Conference at
Amsterdam, in 1867. Dr. Smith suggested that one reason
for revitalizing the American movement was to recement the

bonds of friendship with European evangelicals which had
been shattered by misunderstanding over slavery and wid-
ened further by European hostility to the Union cause
during the Civil War. His comments implied that U.S.
evangelicals were particilarly upset about the conception
of the war which generated such hostility. Europe failed
to realize that the North was "contending for liberty under sanction of law" in its attempts to defeat secession.
"God's Providence" brought this holocaust upon America to
make it sensible of its many sins which could only be
washed away in sacrifice for the good of the nation and
humanity. The war therefore glorified God and contributed
to the "welfare of the kingdom of his Son." It taught
Americans "that the success of our nation could help on
the victory of human rights and freedom all over the
earth." The elimination of slavery removed the great road
block to the fulfillment of the "essential idea of our
Republic," the "progress of freedom."[40]

Most important of all, Smith judged that Christianity in America had been tested by the war and found true.
Like the Republic, the denominations in America had
emerged from the war stronger than ever. They aided the
state in saving the nation while upholding untarnished the
great moral issues of the conflict. The genius of American Christianity was now proven to be the "way of safety
and of growth." Relying heavily on the work of both
Robert Baird and Philip Schaff for his insights, Dr. Smith
told his European audience that the "determining characteristic" of American Christianity was the "separation of
Church and State." Such separation rested upon the principle of "religious liberty" and "upon a confidence in the
self-sustaining power of Christianity itself." Surely the
Church can survive without the support of the state, but,
just as obviously, "religious liberty is necessary to true
civil freedom" and to separation of church and state.
America may not have attained final solution of the great
"problem of the relation of the Church to the State," but
she allowed *full freedom* for the elements of solution to
work out their course in this transition stage of human
history. Rather than apologizing to the Europeans for the
large number of religious bodies in America, Smith stated
that they were signs of "the fullness of growing life" in
Christianity and "an indication that we are at work on a
problem not yet fully solved and reduced to scientific
order." That ultimate and dimly seen goal will only be
reached "when the State shall be penetrated in all its
laws and acts by the vital principles of the Christian
system."[41]

The evangelical interpretation of the Civil War
therefore rested on a whole series of assumptions.  Northern Protestants assumed that evangelical religion, which
received inspiration, content and direction from God's
Word, was the source of liberty of conscience and freedom
of worship.  They further assumed that such freedoms were
the cornerstones of civil and political liberty, in general, and of democracy and American republican institutions,
in particular.  If one takes these assumptions seriously,
and the northern evangelical did, threats to democracy and
the Republic endangered their source.  Efforts to preserve
the Union and democratic order, then, were efforts to preserve the voluntaristic form and God-given freedoms of
evangelical religion.  The New School Committee on the
State of the Country could therefore testify that divine
grace enabled the Presbyterian churches and ministry to
uphold the "rightful Government."  "Identifying the success of the Nation with the welfare of the Church," Union
victory meant that "not only has our American Christianity
been vindicated, our faith and order maintained intact,
and our Christian benevolence enhanced," but the purpose
and plans of Presbyterianism have been enlarged to meet
greater national needs.  Hence, northern churches viewed
Union victory as conclusive proof to the world of the via-
bility and vitality of the evangelical conceptual and ecclesiastical order.[42]

Wartime experience so heightened the unquestioned
commitment of northerners to the democratic ideology and
cause that some evangelicals adhered to a rampant nationalism.  Methodist Bishop Matthew Simpson, for example, participated in this more extreme version of the Religion of
the Republic when he told a crowd of cheering thousands
that "if the world is to be elevated and raised to its
proper place...God cannot afford to do without America."
Taking a more moderate position, in 1866, the New School
Presbyterian Committee on the State of the Country called
on the faithful to protect America's Protestant civilization against infidelity and "foreign priestly domination"
so that "the sacred interests of civil and religious freedom, of human rights and justice to all, of national loyalty and national unity, may be enlarged and perpetuated,
making our Christian Commonwealth a praise among the nations of the earth, exemplifying and speeding the progress
of the Kingdom of our Lord and Saviour, Jesus Christ."[43]

It is in this context, then, that Philip Schaff
thought Europeans might contribute their wisdom to America
but "the foreign delegates will learn more here, in the
few days of the Conference, on the working of our volun-

tary, self-supporting, and self-governing principle than
they could in years" on their own.  Such statements might
be explained away as merely another aspect of religious
nationalism but for the applause that they received in
some European circles.  For example, General Secretary
James Davis of the British Evangelical Alliance toured
America long enough in 1870 to gain real insight into some
aspects of evangelicalism in the United States.  Secretary
Davis reported to his Alliance brethren in Britain that
the American portion of the Church was rather unique in
the depth of its support for union: All denominations
seemed to express such support.  Although he was unsure
whether the absence of a state church, or the impact of
equalitarian  influences of social and political institutions, or the fraternal competition of several churches
throughout the nation were the reason, Davis noted that an
Evangelical Alliance was scarcely needed in America to
make Christians acknowledge, respect and love one another.
Americans had no notion of the words "Dissenter and Nonconformist," words so prolific of strife in his country.
Differences of church government, not creed, were the actual lines of demarcation between the denominations and
contributed to a rivalry after an apostolic pattern of
"'love and good works'"[44]

     Above all, the Americans wanted to sponsor a great
"Ecumenical Council" as a platform to reveal their essential unity of Protestant perspective despite formal diversity.  As Secretary Davis said to the British Alliance,
"'with little need of an Alliance, either to produce or to
manifest union at home, our Christian brethren across the
Atlantic desire intensely, for the best and noblest purposes, to be drawn into closer fellowship with all in
every land, and of every section of the One Catholic
Church who 'love the Lord Jesus Christ in sincerity.'"
The resultant Sixth General Conference of the World Evangelical Alliance met in New York City from October 2-12,
1973.  Listing 100 speakers and more than 500 delegates,
the official Conference program represented the elite of
world evangelicalism.  The topics of discussion ranged
from the state of contemporary religion to questions of the
best means of evangelizing the masses.  Although the pattern of order of World Alliance conferences located the
state of world evangelicalism as the introductory topic,
an ever-present concern among evangelicals, Christian union, held first place in the real program of interest at
this congress.[45]

     Rev. William Adams' welcoming address established an
ecumenical spirit from the start.  Pastor of Madison Square

Presbyterian Church and future President of Union Theological Seminary, both of New York, Dr. Adams made clear that
the purpose of the conference had nothing to do with forms
of church organization and government, for "we meet to
manifest and express our Christian unity." Despite the
variety of religious bodies and nations represented, "we
desire and intend to show that...there is a real unity of
faith and life; believing, according to the familiar expression of our common Christian creed, in the 'Holy Catholic Church and the Communion of Saints.'"[46]

The American evangelicals who spoke about unity before this body elaborated on various aspects of what proved
to be a general consensus. In fact, they saw the conference as symbolic of the unity which they propounded, unity
in spirit. That consensus, strangely enough, found its
most complete expression in a speech given by a man whom
his son has characterized as so temperamentally conservative
that he saw no contradiction in opposing the schism among
Presbyterians in 1837-1838 and then, in 1870, opposing successful attempts to reunify northern Presbyterianism. In
each case, Princeton theologian Charles Hodge supported the
status quo. Nevertheless, Hodge's statements in New York City
echoed the themes of dozens of Alliance speeches over the years.[47]

Although Dr. Hodge, like Adams, conceived of the
Church of Christ as an organic whole comprising all the
redeemed whether living or dead, his main concern was with
the Church in the world. Concluding that men would agree
in doctrine insofar as they were taught by the Spirit,
Hodge outlined what was substantially present in the Alliance Basis as the scriptural doctrines held by all evangelicals. Indwelling of the Spirit united the faithful by
convicting them of their sin and need for renewal. "Ador-
ation, love, confidence, and devotion" for Christ gave them
essentially the same religious experience. This in turn
provided the "congeniality" needed for a "mutual bond of
love." The bond of love also arose from relationships
with the same Master and Father and resulted in mutual
recognition as brethren. Human nature did limit complete implementation of such recognition, Hodge admitted,
but a divine command and law of history impelled the churches toward greater Christian unity: They ought to be subject to brethren in the Lord.[48]

Despite this providential requirement, Charles Hodge
knew discord existed within the Church due to circumstance,
human imperfection and conscientious difference over matters of doctrine and polity. Rejecting legally coerced
union as reprehensible, Hodge decided that "denominational

churches are therefore relatively a good." Such a judgment nevertheless left unanswered a basic question, how
may the real unity which exists be shown in the midst of
diversity? Despite frequent lapses, Hodge thought such
union evident in the "mutual recognition," "intercommunion," noninterference, and cooperation which characterized relations among denominations in America—they of
course needed to be implemented more fully.[49]

The unity which Hodge and other evangelicals claimed
existed, and of which the conference was symbolic, then,
was unity in Spirit. As Methodist editor George R. Crooks
observed, when he stood in for ailing Bishop Simpson, the
faithful comprise the body of Christ which "is made one by
the operation of the spirit." This simple insight, however, is rather of recent origin among Protestants. Crooks
believed that Protestants traditionally had tried to attain unity around a common creed while Catholics maintained unity through external organization alone. Both
methods "fail, as they deserve to fail; the fact that they
have led to bloody persecutions is *prima facie* evidence
that they are not the true principles of unity." We have
only lately come to realize "that the oneness of Christ's
Church" is not a fact to be created for it exists already.
We have finally discovered that "oneness of thinking" and
"oneness of method" are not the revealing facts of unity.
Rather, it exists solely in "spirit and life."[50]

Similarly, Episcopal Bishop Bedell denounced the
folly of seeking organic union. The purpose of the Conference, said Bedell, is boldly to affirm the truth.
"Protestantism" is not a church nor is "evangelical Christianity" an organization. Rather, "they are systems of
positive truth characterizing many churches." Yet even
these do not constitute the unity of Christianity for "it
exists as a living, active reality of spiritual communion,
consistent with, but independent of forms of organization."
If denominational differences therefore continue, Bedell
asked, how may Christian unity best be symbolized short
of an impossible organic union, but by communion or spiritual union? Only an alliance allows individual expression
of unity without transgressing on individual adherence to
different religious polities or to some variation in the
agreed upon range of acceptable opinion. Such religious
particularity reflects natural differences in nervous tem-
peraments, in mental constitutions and in physical build
as well as religious imperfection. Church history shows
these differences in polity and order advance the pure
truth of the gospel through clash and controversy. As a
result, any organic union formed upon evangelical

"abandonment of conscientious religious distinctions"
would split into a thousand fragments upon the return of
sober thought. The only unity possible is that which
characterized Christ through the ages: "God be praised for
whatever in the Evangelical Alliance will nurture and fortify in our souls a sense of this spiritual unity in Christ
Jesus our Lord!"[51]

In conclusion, the general direction of American
evangelicals in the Alliance and its 1873 General Conference reveal similarity of religious perspective and consensus regarding the relationship of religion to the democratic order. Episcopalian Noah Hunt Schenck capped this
position in the "Farewell Address" before the General Conference. In the name of the Evangelical Alliance for the
United States of America, Schenck stated "the purpose of
this Conference is not to organize a new church, or indulge vain fantasies of organic unity, or sketch utopian
pictures of unified doctrine and uniform practices in religious theory and ecclesiastical method." The Church in
the world represents diversities of gifts and administration, because it is a working rather than an ideal church.
We have gathered here neither for selfish nor secular purposes nor for the defense of Protestantism. The Protestant idea is powerful enough to defend and propagate itself.

> But this Christian Convocation has been
> summoned for fresh declarations of unity
> realized, for the interchange of the ele-
> ments of varied Christian civilizations,
> for debating and arming in defense of
> Christian liberty, for asserting the fran-
> chise of free conscience, for making full
> exposition of catholic orthodoxy in applied
> religion, proving that the Evangelical Al-
> liance holds and enforces those measures of
> truth which all Christian denominations
> confess and apply as *essential* for righteous
> rule in government, the correct ordering of
> society, and the salvation of the soul.[52]

This does not mean that American evangelicals agreed
fully on either essentials or the means to best symbolize
and advance their acclaimed unity. Alliance concern about
"union" services proposed for the conference were justified by schism in the Protestant Episcopal church. It resulted from the participation of Bishop George David
Cummins and Rev. R. Payne Smith, Dean of Canterbury, in the
*unofficial* union communion services finally designed for

the conference.  They realized the comments on Christian
communion and practical means for its implementation by
men like Charles Hodge and F. W. Conrad aroused considerable hostility among some Presbyterians, Congregationalists, Episcopalians and Baptists.  And, they were well
aware of the widespread claims to the success and the
widespread critique of the failure of their Conference in
terms of its material impact on unity.[53]

Indeed, after the evangelical euphoria and opposing
furor subsided, Alliance Councilor and Evangelical Lutheran editor James A. Brown published a careful analysis of
reaction to the Alliance according to denomination. Noting
that the World Alliance and its six world conferences
since 1846 "has shown a vitality and permanence which
place it among the marked phenomena of Protestant Christendom," Rev. Brown insisted "no one can have failed to
notice that the condemnation has been mostly by denominations or factions which represent the extremist sectarian
narrowness and exclusiveness, whilst the favoring judgment
has come from those denominations, or parts of denominations, which are among the most truly evangelical and active portions of Protestant Chrisitanity."  Hence, Protestant Episcopal Low-churchmen applauded the Alliance while
High-churchmen attacked it bitterly.  The Baptists were
somewhat cordial toward the Alliance but generally remained aloof from active participation (until the late
1880s) because of their closed communion stance—Baptists
had to shun communion with non-Baptists.  The German Reformed Church was friendly and the Presbyterian, Dutch Reformed, Methodist and Congregational groups supported it
strongly.  Daniel Curry, chief editor of the *Christian
Advocate* and Alliance supporter, discussed some Methodist
unhappiness with the organizers of the New York Conference.
Noting  that "Drs. Schaff and Prime, and Mr. William E.
Dodge, and a few others, chiefly Presbyterians, were leaders in the matter from the first," Curry reminded his
readers that the Presbyterian and Reformed revived the
movement and formulated plans for the Conference before
Methodists decided to endorse it.  Anyway, a goodly number
of leading Methodists (including Curry) held positions of
importance in the successful Alliance and its conference
programs.  Brown also located some of the deepest division
over the Alliance within the Lutheran fold.  The Evangelical General Synods, both North and South, heartily approved of the Alliance while the confessional Synodical
Conference bitterly opposed it and the confessional General Council appeared cordial, only to renounce the Alliance
in the end.  Consequently, ecumenical evangelicals knew
many Americans failed to realize their participation in

the Alliance consensus while others opposed it on principle. Their work for the remainder of the century seemed
obvious, to manifest evangelical identity and justify it
to their brethren.[54]

All of these factors—abolition of slavery, religious nationalism, the defense of democratic culture, wartime cooperation engendering denominational and interdenominational comity, victory euphoria and reaction to the
threats posed by immigration and its assumed concommitants,
materialism, infidelity, Roman Catholicism, as well as
concern over the new directions of science—contributed to
a heavy groundswell of support for a revived U.S. Alliance
and for immediate fulfillment of evangelical aspirations
in the New York General Conference of 1873. Indeed, when
properly read against the light of their Religion of the
Republic, the Conference itself was a major reason for the
revived American Alliance. It would provide a unique opportunity for a grand concourse of representative European
evangelicals to experience firsthand the actual state of
religion and democracy in the United States. It would
prove to delegates of various nationalities the superiority of American religious and democratic systems, thereby
advancing the conversion of the world to the American way.
Daniel Curry endorsed this belief:

> The foreign delegates who have been among
> us have had an opportunity to learn some-
> thing of the working of our system of
> Church life,... The best argument in favor
> of a free Church in a free State is in the
> demonstration of facts as presented in this
> country. That this Conference will have a
> decided and valuable influence on the
> pending contests about this subject, now
> going forward in the Old World, may be
> earnestly and confidently hoped.[55]

And, as the New York Synod of the Presbyterian Church subsequently made clear, evangelicals thought the fate of
America and the world rested on the kind of dedication to
Christian union which the Alliance represented: "No such
council was ever before assembled in the New World. Whether regarded as a manifestation of the reality of Christian
union, as an argument for the truth and power of the Gospel, or as a testimony of popular faith and interest in
things pertaining to the kingdom of God, it was one of the
most remarkable religious events of the age."[56]

CHAPTER FIVE

# RELIGIOUS LIBERTY ABROAD AND EVANGELICAL

# ESTABLISHMENT AT HOME, 1874-1882

Evangelical Protestantism emerged from the Civil War confident in its future.  Although organized religion soon faced challenges to its system of thought and its social program, they registered only gradually with the more astute leadership.  The twofold crisis elicited less immediate alteration of beliefs and goals among the bulk of the faithful than the ensuing theological and socioideological divisions might indicate.  As Robert Handy suggests, "the Protestantism that faced post-Civil War America was far from being a static entity continually being challenged by external forces.  Rather, it was an aggressive, dynamic form of Christianity that set out confidently to confront American life at every level, to permeate, evangelize, and Christianize it."[1]

Actually, the opposite to Christianization of culture occurred.  Postwar evangelicalism became so acculturated that it accepted the laissez faire, individualistic, free enterprise system as part of the moral order of things.  Lacking an adequate theological or ethical basis for social criticism, and assuming that conversion elicited those personal qualities of serious hard work and thrift requisite to social mobility and worldly success, indeed, the very nature of evangelicalism—its personalist moralism defined in such terms as sabbath observance, temperance and avoidance of frivolous amusement—meant it largely ignored contemporary social evils.  Hence, between the 1860s and the 1880s the urban faithful became entwined in a whole gamut of ethical problems and crises, spawned by the acquisitive socioeconomic structure of late nineteenth century America.  They found themselves, as individuals and whole churches, caught up in a new urban and industrial world wherein emerging but giant railroad, steel, oil, and all manner of other corporations were nationalizing the economy, unifying and standardizing the culture, and exercising a power beyond the control of person, city or state.  That urban evangelicals rode the corporate

crest of this industrial and immigrant-swelled sea, as
part of a new and vastly larger middle class liner, vested
them with strong attachments to those very changes threatening their beloved evangelical democracy.[2]

At first stunned by inexplicable blight of their national utopia, urban evangelicals groped toward comprehension of and accommodation to the realities of their culture through a variety of movements, the most important
being the social gospel reorientation of evangelical theology and social conscience. The focus shifted from individual moralism and preparation for the afterworld to em-
phasize those social teachings and actions of Christ which
seemed to require: (1) elimination of oppressive social
environments (slums, poor economic and working conditions,
illiteracy, etc.); (2) reorientation of the capitalist
economy (by supporting labor unions, profit-sharing, arbi-
tration between labor and capital, concerns for the natural environment, etc.); and (3) new approaches to the human intellect and spirit (through Chautauquas, Christian
physical and social sciences, institutional churches, as
well as the preached gospel) to make human worldly existence more pleasant as well as to facilitate salvation of
the urban man. Although the Evangelical Alliance was
among those organizations in the forefront of this cultural re-evaluation, the process did not get under way until
the mid-1880s. Earlier postwar prophets of religious and
social reform were ignored generally by the evangelical
rank and file. The U.S. Evangelical Alliance therefore
reflects the evangelical complacency of the 1865-1880 period and the subsequent confident but frenetic questioning
of the 1880s and 1890s. It is true that the optimistic
activism of postwar evangelicalism hid, as is the case of
the Alliance, some hesitant questioning and self-doubt,
but events never induced evangelicalism in general to rethink any of the basic elements of the Protestant perspective or the democratic and social ideologies of America
until the 1880s.[3]

The Alliance during the period from 1873 to the mid-
1880s, therefore, sought fulfillment of other goals. It
attempted to expand and defend religious liberty and the
separation of religion and civil authority both at home
and abroad. The principles involved were elaborated before the war by Robert Baird and after it by leading figures such as Philip Schaff, H. B. Smith, Samuel Irenaeus
Prime, James King and Josiah Strong. The absence of social concern does not mean the Alliance and its spokesmen
were either fundamentalist or reactionary during the pre-
1880 phase. They were no more conservative than the bulk

of the middle class during their day and often took positions which were well ahead of their contemporaries on
theological and historical issues; they participated in
"modernization" of religion and the larger culture by ac-
commodating their thought and actions to the newer intellectual, technological and scientific trends.  For example
both James McCosh and Joseph P. Thompson thought there was
less conflict between religion and science, the Bible and
scientific theory, the story of the Creation and the doctrine of development than many believed to be the case.
Both invoked a liberal rather than literalistic interpretation of the Creation story, which in their eyes showed
that scripture actually allowed qualified theories of development.  Hence, they rejected one of the tenets of what
would later be called fundamentalism, that is, biblical
literalism, and favored a modified Darwinian theory of
evolution.  Most of the other leading evangelicals in the
Alliance also were not biblical literalists.  In fact,
quite a number of Alliancemen cooperated with Philip
Schaff, Chairman of the (American) Bible Revision Committee, in revising the King James Version of the Bible according to the standards of modern Biblical research and
criticism.  Still, most were very evangelical in their
stress on both the need for a conversion experience——
Philip Schaff felt refreshed by Dwight L. Moody's revivals
of the late 1870s and early 1880s——and on the importance
of scripture to faith and worship.[4]

Alliance leaders did indulge in the general complacency of the middle class during the 1870s and therefore
may be judged socially, if not theologically, conservative.
(It should also be pointed out that many Alliance personnel supported the liberal Republican movement of the 1870s,
the "mugwump" break from the Republican Party in 1884,
Civil Service and other political reform movements at a
time when the majority of Republicans thought them radical
——the label of conservative does not fit easily men of
this mold).  Their individualistic, laissez faire economic
and social theories enabled them to overlook pressing social problems of which they were often woefully ignorant.
Nevertheless, the evangelical position on religious and
civil liberty was often admirable.  Even when it was not,
as in some of the Alliance dealings with Roman Catholicism,
its position often reflected an increasing awareness of a
massive growth of non-Protestant religious and cultural
pluralism in American society.  That pluralism forced
evangelicals to make some painful adjustment in various
aspects of their conceptual order.  As Robert Handy suggests, while the middle third of the nineteenth century
may best be described as a "Protestant Age" in America,

postwar Protestantism faced an increasingly frustrating
growth in the heterogeneity of the culture it once so
fully dominated.  Of course, Protestantism would still
dominate the culture to the end of the century but only at
the cost of concessions to non-Protestant pressure groups
and interests.[5]

     Evangelical commitment to religious liberty, after
the war, paradoxically reflects both complacency about the
cultural status quo coupled with growing comprehension as
to the untenability of certain of their assumptions about
religious liberty.  Their's is a case where the social and
political influence of a mushrooming, immigrant-fed Roman
Catholic minority forced the evangelical leadership to re-
assess the formal and informal relationships of civil authority to evangelicalism.  Reassessment obliged evangelicals to confront once again the essentially deistic origins to the democratic constitutionalism of their Religion
of the Republic as well as the First Amendment requirement
that civil authority hold neutral ground between religion
and the public.  Rediscovery, however, did not mean automatic correction of views or behavior.  Their adjustment
to the situation was more practical than theoretical, more
to the presence of circumstance and necessity than to the
conviction that adjustment was correct inherently.  An account of postwar evangelical democratic idealism and its
subsequent accommodation to new realities provide the substance of this chapter.[6]

     Much of the Alliance activity between 1874 and 1885,
then, centered on attempts to defend and expand Christian
liberty at home and abroad.  Such a focus does not conflict really with commitment to Christian unity because
evangelicals assumed a direct relationship between the
idea of Christian unity and the idea of liberty.  As early
as September 8, 1873, the Rev. Noah Hunt Schenck, Episcopalian and Honorary Corresponding Secretary, introduced
resolutions from the Program to Executive Committee concerning the future of the U.S. Alliance.  (By this time,
the Honorary Secretaries were elected during the annual
meeting of the Evangelical Alliance based upon the criteria of prominence and the need to represent each of the
major denominations.)  According to Schenck, the Alliance
exercised "offices toward religion and humanity as are not
held or administered by any other organization of Christians, viz: the defense of religious liberty and the vindication of the reality of fraternal communion as between
members of different branches of the Church of Christ."
He thought these functions, coupled with frequent discussion of the great questions relating to society and church,

made it necessary to hold an annual Christian convocation.
Such congresses would arouse public interest and make the
Alliance and its affiliates a power in the land.[7]

Alliance leadership responded to these suggestions
by forming a special planning committee which comprised
the Honorary Corresponding Secretaries, including Schenck,
Philip Schaff, and Samuel Irenaeus Prime, as well as the
Finance Committee. Presenting its report to the Executive
Committee, Prime applauded the success of the New York
General Conference (1873) because it removed "every doubt
as to the fact that the Alliance has the power of exhibit-
ing the unity and strength of concentrated evangelical
Christianity." It showed the "Alliance is a living power
in nearly every Protestant country and in distant Missionary fields." Prime expected the U.S. Alliance to carry
out a leading role in the world movement and warned that
it could only do so by retaining a flexible liberal organization: "it ought never to be allowed to become a close
corporation, or to be managed by a party, or to be per-
verted to Alien ends" such as interference in denominational affairs.[8]

It is within this context that Prime's report suggested, and the Executive Committee adopted, a very evangelical five-point program:

1.  Correspondence with the Foreign Branches
    of the Alliance, and such auxiliary Branches
    as may be formed within our own country;
2.  Arrangements for the Annual Week of United
    Prayer;
3.  Co-operation with the other Alliances in
    defending the rights of conscience wherever
    and whenever assailed;
4.  Co-operation with other Branches in Con-
    vening, from time to time, a General Con-
    ference;
5.  Arrangements for a Biennial Meeting of the
    United States Alliance in one of the Cities
    of the Union, for the discussion of reli-
    gious questions of special interest to
    American Churches.[9]

The beauty and power of Christian union and the fundamental doctrine at the core of the Alliance provided the
means to do the proposed work: "the influence of this
Union has been manifest and precious in the City of New
York, where the seat of the operations of the Alliance has
been hitherto, and the same delightful effects would be

produced in every place where the Alliance shall be practically established." That Alliancemen still assumed unity both a goal of their organization and a method of
securing other ends may be seen in the constitutional
changes suggested by Prime's report and adopted by the
body in an effort to streamline its actions. Rev. William
Adams amended the report so Article II of the constitution
would stress that "the objects of this Association shall
be to manifest and strengthen Christian Unity, and to promote religious liberty and co-operation in Christian work,
without interfering with the internal affairs of different
denominations." The amended report and constitution were
endorsed by the Annual Meeting.[10]

        Whatever its immediate activities, the Alliance
queued into an elemental evangelical assumption. In
Philip Schaff's words, Christian unity and religious freedom "go hand in hand" and "Christianity itself flourished
best on the soil of freedom." Consequently, as late as
1883, the Alliance letterhead seal contained the motto
"Christian Union and Christian Liberty, one and insepar-
able." These beliefs reflected a peculiarly evangelical
interpretation of scripture, basic Protestant doctrine,
and American democratic ideology. Since no one evangelical seems to have enunciated fully all of the implications
of their belief in freedom, freedom of conscience, liberty
of conscience and religious liberty—these terms often
were used interchangeably—we will have to piece together
statements from a number of evangelical leaders in order
to ascertain their meaning.[11]

        One traditional definition of religious liberty was
expressed by Rev. Noah Hunt Schenck before the New York
Conference of 1873. He defined it as "the liberty of the
sons of God—yea, perfect freedom in Christ, and oneness
in the Beloved." To the evangelical, this was the ultimate definition of liberty because it was the ultimate
state to which the sincere Christian ought to aspire. It
could be attained only through conversion to faith and
trust in Jesus Christ, the saviour of mankind. As Robert
Baird stated in 1848, "I proceed at once to say that it is
Christianity alone which can give the noblest freedom. In
the language of its glorious Author, this wonderful truth
was uttered: 'If the Son shall make you free, ye shall be
free indeed.'"[12]

        But religious liberty involved much more than this.
As early as 1847, Robert Baird told an audience that this
magnificent gift of divine providence gave the American
nation a special world mission by blessing Americans with

numerous rights. "And here I mean, by Religious Liberty,
the enjoyment of the right to preach Christ's Gospel where
and when men desire to have it preached—the right to hear
it—the right to believe the Gospel in what appears to be
its true meaning; and the right to profess that belief
under all circumstances, and in such modes as commend
themselves to what are, in our opinion, the requirements
of the Word of God." The greatest evil imaginable would
be the absence of such liberty and requisite obligations,
an absence typical of many nations. Although God awarded
Americans prosperity and strength to carry their spiritual
Christianity to the world, Baird concluded his countrymen
could venture into foreign missions far more than they
seemed inclined to do. God demanded the nation fulfill
its obligations.[13]

In 1848, Baird again expanded upon the implications
of the free and responsible religious individual. The
gospel (obviously rooted in scripture) frees man from condemnation to hell, death, degrading and vulgar supersti-
tions, and slavery to his senses, as well as from the
thralldom of ignorance, by revealing God's providential
actions in history. In addition, it establishes paternal
authority but denies such authority that despotism found
in pagan lands. It transforms the woman from the place of
a slave and burden bearer to the happy and virtuous help-
mate of her husband. It spreads peace, love and goodwill
among people throughout whole regions. In fact, it de-
prives slavery wherever it exists of half of its curse by
making both master and slave fully aware of their mutual
love and obligations, while preparing both for the final
dissolution which will occur inevitably to that horrible
institution.[14]

Baird concluded it is the Christian religion alone,
and evangelicalism in particular, which forbids all violence and oppression and which will rectify differences of
class by elimination of despotism and inequities. Christianity brings to the fore the inevitable question as to
the validity of oppression of person and conscience. The
Reformation itself witnesses to this fact in that reformers overthrew both ecclesiastical and civil authority
whenever they infringed upon freedom of conscience. Baird
understood removal of the government in power did not assure attainment of civil liberty or elimination of despotism. In a statement which probably had the Revolutions of
1848 most immediately in mind, he argued that the revolts
in Europe and Latin America during the last fifty years
failed to attain the scope and character of the American
example because "they have not been the fruit of the pure

Gospel; they have not been sustained by an evangelical
faith; they have not occurred in nations which had been
penetrated by a true Christianity; they have not taken
place where the Bible is in the hands of almost everyone,
and its sanctions felt in millions of hearts.  Therefore
it is, that the governments which they have given rise to
have been unstable and very imperfect."  Yet all was not
lost even for those benighted countries because "these
revolutions are opening the way for the diffusion of the
pure gospel."  Only after they "experience its renovating
influence," "will they be enabled to obtain and maintain
those free governments which they desire, but for which
they are at present so greatly unprepared."  Such allu-
sions to predominantly Roman Catholic parts of the world
were not lost on American evangelicals.[15]

     By 1870, Episcopal clergyman John Cotton Smith di-
lated upon similar notions.  Smith believed that the movement towards "Evangelical Unity" was "characteristic of
our times" and like all great movements in society generally took place on an unconscious level.  Yet Smith still
felt a number of factors were quite apparent.  First, "*the
Evangelical System is in harmony with the tendencies of
our time towards civil and religious freedom,*" although
opposed to license.  In Ralph Henry Gabriels' terms, Smith
called for the conscious exercise of individual freedom
within the moral limits of the fundamental law:

          Sacerdotal systems of religion have
          always allied themselves with exaggerated
          claims of authority and rationalistic sys-
          tems with a freedom inconsistent with the
          interests and even the maintenance of so-
          ciety.  The evangelical system, however,
          is based upon principles which necessarily
          lead to that rational liberty wherewith
          the Son maketh us free.  It dignifies the
          individual, and recognizes the supremacy
          of conscience.  At the same time it im-
          poses upon society and the individual
          great moral laws by which the social order
          is maintained.  The noblest advocates for
          this freedom have consciously or uncon-
          sciously found their most powerful argu-
          ments and influences in the principles
          of the Gospel of Christ.[16]

Quite obviously, Smith thought freedom and an ordered society mutually compatible only among an evangelical populace.  All other religious perspectives tended to tyranny

or to anarchy.

This evangelical abhorrence of civil and religious oppression even applied to nations wherein a large amount of both liberties existed but in which a state or established church still remained. Samuel Irenaeus Prime discussed just this problem in "Religious Liberty and Church Freedom" (1869). He applauded the contemporary disintegration of religious and ecclesiastical despotism in Europe, and particularly in Austria and Spain, because eclipse of Roman Catholic or other state churches opened the way to rapid spread of the true gospel. The heart of Prime's editorial centered on contemporary efforts in the British Parliament to disestablish the Anglican Church in Ireland. Applauding those efforts, he reminded Americans that "we, who do not believe in compelling the minority of any people to support the Church of a majority, nor even in compelling a minority to pay tithes for the support of the religious prejudices of the majority, can see in that contest which is going on in the British Parliament over the Irish Church the beginning of the end of Church Establishments under the authority of enlightened English men." Such sentiments rooted in wishes for the well-being rather than destruction of the Anglican Church: "we wish to see it purged of its Erastianism; we wish to see it freed from its taint of Popery; we wish to see it free from the control of worldly wicked men, such as are always likely to come into power...in the Government of England which now controls the Church." Like so many other evangelical adherents of the Religion of the Republic, Rev. Prime believed only that church independent of the state could fulfill "its destiny as the free Church of Christ, bound by no human government" and replete in piety and vigor.[17]

Reminiscent of James Madison's argument in *The Memorial and Remonstrance*, evangelicals also thought freedom of religion essential because recognition of religious truth occurred within the persuasive arena of personal opinion rather than through state coercion. The *New York Observer* pointed this out in its running battle with Catholic periodicals and newspapers. In the editorial "Faith Without Opinion," the *Observer* criticized the *New York Tablet* claim that Protestants adhered only to personal opinion rather than religious truth. The *Observer* replied "Protestants, Romanists, Greeks, Jews and Barbarians, believe what *in their opinion* is the truth; and nobody whether Protestant or Romanist, Greek, Jew or Barbarian, believes anything to be true but what *in his personal opinion* is the truth." Illustrating this point, the *Observer* noted it is a matter of personal opinion whether or not sufficient

evidence warrants faith in the infallibility of the Pope.
Because "faith is the evidence of things not seen," "we believe for ourselves" alone.

> The *Observer*'s personal opinion is that
> men make creeds and enjoin them; that
> the only rule of faith is the Bible, and
> that all creeds are of human construc-
> tion, the personal opinion of the fram-
> ers as to what is truth.  No creed is
> obligatory upon the conscience, except
> as it carries with it to the conscience
> the evidence that it expresses the mind
> of God.  And so we get back to the idea
> of personal opinion, of private judgment,
> of individual responsibility, and the
> direct accountability of every human
> soul to the soul's Author.[18]

No church or priest can come between that soul and God,
bear the responsibility of that soul's salvation and
faith.  No human agency whether it be cathedral or altar
can share Christ's saving action.  Thus no man should con-
sign to damnation those who do not adhere to his creed.
"Let him commit [himself] to the justice and mercy of God,
and be sure of his own salvation, believing that the Judge
of all earth will do."[19]

Similarly, Episcopal Bishop Gregory T. Bedell stated
"this nation is Protestant.  Its national religion is dis-
tinctively *Protestant*," not in the sense of protesting
against the dogma or practice of a particular church, "but
Protestant in principle, against a false idea in State or
Church."  In its elementary sense Protestantism "is the
protest of individual responsibility against corporate responsibility..., a discovery that quickly brought Civil
and Religious Liberty into light and life....The root idea
of both civil and religious freedom is, that each individual is responsible before God (and before his fellow men)
for his opinions and his deeds."  Many evangelicals therefore, again in the tradition of James Madison, defined religion in principle as one's personal opinion.  Such a
definition avoided that opportunistic acceptance of the
status quo aimed ultimately at imposition of conformity of
view on the people.  Rather, it rooted in the definite
conviction, as Philip Schaff stated, that "religious freedom" is "one of the fundamental and inalienable rights of
man, more sacred than civil freedom or the freedom of
thought and speech.  It is the highest kind of freedom,
and is at the same time the best protection of all other

freedom.  The dominion of conscience is inviolable.  No
power on earth has a right to interpose itself between
man and his Maker."  Interference with freedom of conscience, then, would ruin true religion, create hypocrisy
or infidelity, and destroy consequently all civil freedoms
and democracy itself.[20]

Religious freedom, according to Schaff, was quite
different from toleration.  A governmental edict of toleration presupposes a state religion and the right of the
government to control public worship.  The reasons for
permission of religious worship divergent from state forms
may range from necessity, prudence, liberality to indifference.  Such an edict might allow religious bodies dissenting from the state church to practice their own religion but one must remember the difference between religious toleration and religious liberty: "the one is a concession, the other a right; the one is a matter of expediency, the other a principle; the one is a gift of man, the
other, a gift of God."  Thus religious liberty is a fundamental and inalienable natural right of man because it is
"founded in the sacredness of conscience, which is the
voice of God in man."  It is therefore above human authority and control.  Hence, "liberty of conscience requires
liberty of worship as its manifestation."  Anything else
would cease to be religion and end up being hypocrisy or
infidelity.[21]

Like many American evangelicals, Schaff saw a direct
connection between the extent of religious freedom and the
proper relation of religion to the civil authority: "Toleration is an intermediate state between religious persecution and religious liberty.  Persecution results from
the union of Church and State; toleration, from a relaxa-
tion of that union; full religious liberty and legal quality requires a peaceful separation of the spiritual and
secular powers."  Again, Schaff captured another aspect of
the evangelical conception of the separation of church and
state in America when he denied the idea that such separation meant "a separation of the nation from religion."
Rather, "it means only the absence of an established or
national church to which all are bound to belong and to
contribute...; it means that every man is free to choose
his own creed or no creed, and that his religious opinions
and ecclesiastical connections have nothing to do with his
civil and political rights."  Schaff was certain that
America was a "Christian nation."  One only need to look
at such evidence as the vast number of churches and seminaries, the prestige of the clergy, and the government use
of chaplains to ascertain that "Christianity is an integral

part of the common law of the land, and enjoys as much
protection in the courts of justice as in any country
der the sun.  It is deeply rooted in national habits,
which are even stronger than laws, and has a mighty hold
on the respect and affections of all classes of society."
Some evangelicals such as former Yale University President
Theodore Woolsey, however, cited the same facts as proof
that America was a Christian nation insofar as the populace and public opinion was Christian but they did not say
that Christianity was part of the common law and/or law of
the land.  And a very few others, such as Methodist editor
Daniel Curry, concluded "the *unlawfulness* of Church aid
from the State, as a matter of principle, is, therefore,
not so easy of demonstration as some seem to suppose.  The
extent to which it shall be given or accepted, or whether
it should be practiced to any extent, are matters to be
determined by the law of expediency and a reference to the
highest interests of society."  The one control Curry insisted should guide all government aid to religiously
oriented schools and charities was fairness in distribution of funds.[22]

     The ambiguity of the evangelical position on reli-
gious liberty and freedom of conscience shows forth stark-
ly in Schaff's hearty approval that American common law,
culture and habits made Christianity the national religion.
Consequently, it is doubtful American evangelicals would
have remained so firmly committed to religious freedom,
and the corollary principles of persuasion and voluntaryism, if confronted by an adversary capable of persuading
the general populace and society to accept some other form
of religion or even irreligion and secularism.  The evangelicals never faced squarely this possibility because
psychologically and ideologically they were unable to believe that they, as God's faithful in the world, could be
defeated in any open debate for the voluntary adherence of
the public to their position.  They assumed that any group,
such as the Roman Catholic or the Mormon, might only pose
a threat to their dominance of American culture by means
of undemocratic and illiberal tactics.

     Despite these limits to the voluntary principle, men
like Philip Schaff believed religious liberty the "most
precious of all liberties, and the strong foundation of
all other liberty."  It was guaranteed consequently "within the limits of public peace and order" by the Federal
and most of the state constitutions in America.  "And thus
it may be regarded as the American theory, that Church and
State should be separate and distinct, each independent in
its own sphere, yet not hostile, but equally interested in

public morality and national prosperity, the State protecting the Church by law, the Church self-supporting and
self-governing, and strengthening the moral foundations
of the State. In one word, the American system is a free
Church in a free State." Although this might not be the
final solution to the proper relationship of the church
and civil authority, Schaff concluded it was the only possible solution in America under the circumstances.[23]

To evangelicals like Schaff, freedom of conscience
enabled a man to believe what he wished in the realm of
religion while religious liberty enabled him to put those
beliefs into practice. Possibly with European criticism
of the American system in the back of his mind, Schaff
wanted it clearly understood that the principles of religious liberty did not mean individuals or groups of individuals might resort to license or implement beliefs that
were socially dangerous: "a State cannot control private
opinions, but may forbid and punish overt acts of a religion which disturbs the peace of a society, and undermines
the moral foundations on which government rests." Schaff
thus felt it quite consistent with these universal American principles that the Federal Congress outlawed Mormon
polygamy (Edmunds Act, 1882). He was devoted to the principles of freedom of conscience and religious liberty,
but, like many American evangelicals, Schaff recognized
that such freedom could not exist if it were abused to the
point of endangering or destroying the social order which
insured those liberties. This position becomes quite
clear in his comparison of the true liberty exercised in
the American system with the "red-republican theory of
religious freedom" or "liberty" characteristic of the
French Revolution of 1789. "True liberty is a positive
force, regulated by law; false liberty is a negative
force, a release from restraint. True liberty is the
moral power of self-government; the liberty of infidels
and anarchists in carnal licentiousness." Implicit in
Schaff's assessment is the belief that the Christian base
of American culture defines the limits of true liberty,
both religious and civil. By definition, a vital and
free culture cannot exist without a Christian base. As a
result, the American separation of church and civil authority "rests on respect for the church" while infidel
separation rests "on indifference and hatred of the church,
and of religion itself." The French Revolution implemented the infidel theory. It started with toleration and
ended with the reign of terror and the abolition of Christianity. This "in turn prepared the way for military
despotism as the only means of saving society from anarchy
and ruin."[24]

Philip Schaff warned that American infidels and anarchists (a reference, among others to the Chicago Haymarket Conspiracy and labor riots of the mid-1880s) would
re-enact this calamity if they were allowed to gain power.
They already openly displayed their "hatred and contempt
of our Sunday-laws, and Sabbaths, our churches, and all
religious institutions and societies." He believed the
American system allowed such dissent from the evangelical
ideals and institutions but only within set bounds: "the
American system grants freedom also to irreligion and infidelity, but only within the limits of the order and
safety of society."[25]

Although such sentiments might appear to be reactionary to some twentieth century ears, they rested on a
series of assumptions held by most evangelicals and well
expressed by Schaff: "The destruction of religion would
be the destruction of morality and the ruin of the state.
Civil liberty requires for its support religious liberty,
and cannot prosper without it. Religious liberty is not
an empty sound, but an orderly exercise of religious
duties and enjoyment of all its privileges. It is freedom *in* religion, not freedom *from* religion; as true civil
liberty is freedom *in* law and not freedom *from* law."
Citing the famous French visitor to Jacksonian America,
Alexis de Tocqueville, Schaff thought "despotism...may
govern without faith, but liberty cannot." He expected
that a "self-governing democracy which does not obey the
voice of conscience, and own God as its Ruler must degen-
erate into mobocracy and anarchy." Consequently, "our
safety and ultimate success depends upon the maintenance
and spread of the Christian religion." Since Schaff believed God in His providence assigned regular roles to
each nation in history, he was certain, if America failed
to sustain and propagate its Christian institutions
("God's Church, God's Book, and God's Day"), "God will
raise up some other nation or continent to carry on his
designs." Most evangelicals accordingly could agree with
Schaff, who parallels the thinking of English contemporary
and philosopher John Stuart Mill, that "republican institutions in the hands of a virtuous and God-fearing nation
are the very best in the world, but in the hands of a corrupt and irreligious people, they are the very worst, and
the most effective weapons of destruction."[26]

The evangelicals in the United States Alliance attempted to act out the implications of these conceptions
of freedom of conscience and religious liberty on both
international and American stages. At the international
level, it exercised a protective function on behalf of

those persecuted for their religion. On the American
level, it attempted to counteract what it thought to be
conservative Roman Catholic attempts to eliminate such
core ideals and practices of the Religion of the Republic
as the separation of church and state and the principles
of freedom of conscience and religious liberty. These
shall be discussed in order.

As Ruth Rouse suggests concerning the international
Alliance movement in general, "it would be difficult to
exaggerate the services of the Alliance to the cause of
world-wide missions" both in terms of the fruitful ideas
and plans for missions spawned by the great Alliance General Conferences held during the second half of the nineteenth century as well as its advocacy of religious liberty around the world. In fact, nineteenth century missionary and ecumenical movements held a symbiotic relationship. Millennial aspirations inspired the World and national Evangelical Alliances to encourage and protect missionary activity. The 1854 Annual Meeting of the British
Evangelical Alliance, for example, discussed plans for the
first in that series of International Missionary Conferences leading to the famous 1910 Edinburgh Conference.
Field experience, in turn, taught the missionaries the
need for doctrinal agreement and practical cooperation at
a time when mother churches were trying to retain their
separateness and peculiar differences. Missionaries and
their home supporters consequently advocated ecumenism as
essential to the conversion of the world.[27]

Inspired by such millennial convictions, the U.S.
Alliance reflected this symbiotic relationship with the
mission field. Like the other national Alliances and the
international conferences, the American body often had
direct contact with missionaries. The New York General
Conference (1873), for example, inspired American missionaries in Japan to organize an Alliance of their own, and
the Alliance in America forged links with this body
through correspondence and transmission of its publications. The U.S. body often received notice of the formation of other new Alliances by missionaries who were directly aware of the strengths of unity and also hoped to
use the world influence of the Alliance to win religious
freedom in their respective mission fields. These organizations as well as individual missionaries sent numerous
requests throughout the century for help in attaining religious freedom. Indeed, the American branch received
first-hand information on the state of missions and the
progress of religious freedom in foreign lands, because
missionaries often attended its meetings when home on
leave.[28]

In 1871, the American Alliance  summarized the world
movement's relationship to religious liberty and Christian
union.  The World Evangelical Alliance was founded in 1846
"for the express purpose of promoting religious liberty
and Christian union on the basis of that liberty.  True to
this object, it has on every proper occasion interceded in
behalf of persecuted Christians, without regard to their
faith and nationality."  Such a statement characterized
just as clearly the U.S. Alliance position on religious
liberty throughout the nineteenth century.  These American
evangelicals were quite proud that they adhered to a rather successful tradition of religious liberalism as shown
by the efforts of the World Alliance on behalf of all varieties of Christians in Italy, Spain, Sweden and Turkey:

> The release of the Madiai in Tuscany, of
> Matamoros, Carrasco, and their fellow-
> prisoners in Spain, whose only crime was
> reading the Bible and holding private
> meetings for devotion, the abolition of
> the death penalty for apostasy from Moham-
> medanism in the Sultan's dominion, and the
> abrogation of the penal laws in Sweden
> against Roman Catholics and Protestants not
> belonging to the Lutheran Confession, are
> due in part to the moral influences exerted
> by the labors of the Alliance and its depu-
> tations, composed of prominent Christian
> men of different countries and denomina-
> tions, and actuated by purely philan-
> thropic and religious motives. [29]

Deep commitment therefore inspired Americans to try
every practical measure which might advance religious liberty in the world.  At times the American Alliance sent
embassies directly to the offending government, as in 1871,
when the U.S. organization cooperated with the other European bodies in a joint mission to Russia.  The American
Executive Committee instructed its delegation to obtain
abrogation of all Russian penal laws concerning dissenting
religions, in general, and to secure religious freedom for
Protestants in the Russian Baltic provinces, in particular.
The reasoning used to justify those demands finds classic
expression in the charge to the delegation and foreshadows
most arguments advanced in American petitions to offending
governments during the rest of the century.  It reflects
the basic concepts which men like Robert Baird, Henry B.
Smith and Philip Schaff helped to clarify for their fellow
evangelicals.

> 'In support of such a plea, the delega-
> tion may confidently appeal to the genius
> of Christianity, which is spiritual in its
> nature and succeeds best by spiritual means;
> to the example of Christ and the apostles,
> who would rather suffer martyrdom than re-
> sort to carnal weapons; to the inborn rights
> of conscience, which demand an outward ex-
> pression in freedom of public worship; to
> the spirit of modern civilization, which
> everywhere favors religious liberty; and to
> *our* American experience, which has abund-
> antly proved to the world that both the
> State and the Church are the gainers by the
> full recognition and enjoyment of religious
> liberty, as the most sacred and valuable of
> all liberties. Our system of a peaceful
> separation of the two powers allows each to
> manage its own affairs in its own way with-
> out interference from the other, and yet
> secures to religion the legal protection
> of the government, and to the State the in-
> calculable benefit of the moral influence
> of religion, as the main pillar of public
> and private virtue and happiness. The same
> system seems to be destined ultimately to
> prevail in the whole Christian world. The
> Evangelical Alliance intends to promote
> Christian union on the basis of religious
> liberty.'[30]

The Americans were quite certain that their form of religious and political order attuned to the genius of Christianity and to human progress, to the wave of the future.
In addition to this kind of argument, American petitions
usually praised the offending government so as to engender
that cordial atmosphere conducive to interpreting Alliance
"criticism" as "helpful suggestions" designed to improve
government policy. The U.S. petition to the Russian government was ordered in this fashion.[31]

The multinational delegation chose Philip Schaff as
chairman, in recognition of his world prominence, and with
the hope that American leadership might draw upon the post-
Civil War goodwill between the United States and Russia,
thereby gaining the embassy a more favorable audience in
Russia. The issue at hand was the Imperial laws and practices designed to force people of non-Orthodox faith and
particularly Lutherans of Livonia, Esthonia and Courland,
into the Greek Orthodox Church. The American delegation

included such major figures as Bishop Charles P. McIlvaine,
Rev. William Adams, Rev. Noah Hunt Schenck, Rev. E. A.
Washburn, Rev. Philip Schaff, and evangelical entrepre-
neurs William E. Dodge, Sr., Cyrus Field, and Nathan Bishop. The combined European-American delegation received an
audience with the Russian Foreign Minister Prince Gortschakoff. Contemporary estimations of the success of this
mission vary. It technically failed because the Russian
Minister politely refused any concessions by denying the
existence of the problem in the first place. Still, feed-
back from European correspondents to the American body
seem to indicate that persecution of non-Orthodox Christians did decline subsequently in the western provinces of
Russia. The evangelicals claimed their embassy an immediate success.[32]

An embassy was the less typical American method of
dealing with religious persecution. Wallace N. Jamison
noted correctly the U.S. Alliance received so many requests for aid that it developed a general formula of action: (1) corroboration of the claims to persecution; (2)
an appropriate resolution or memorial designed to convince
the offending government of the necessity of religious
freedom, signed by Alliance leaders and by men of affairs
who were hopefully of national and international stature;
and (3) application to the U.S. government for diplomatic
action. The Americans therefore used the popular press,
published documents, memorials and embassies to bring
moral and diplomatic pressure to bear toward achievement
of its goals. Such methods characterized British Alliance
efforts too, and, given cooperation among the national
branches as well as the great power of Britain in the
nineteenth century, evangelical use of diplomatic channels
often gained the desired policy change from the offending
nation. Although most interested in protecting Protestants, the Alliance aided Roman Catholics, Jews, and Greek
Orthodox whenever and wherever they faced persecution or
denial of religious liberty, even if by a Protestant nation. Indeed, as early as 1859, the Americans organized a
mass protest against the persecution of Roman Catholics
in Sweden.[33]

Despite the fact that the post-1885 Alliance would
become less interested in international activity and more
interested in the state of religion and society in America
—nationalism and internationalism were always balanced
uneasily within American ecumenism since the antebellum
beginnings—it still continued to protect those persecuted
for religion until the end of the century. As Henry B.
Chapin and Norman Fox stated before the Executive Committee

in 1885, the Alliance "is a nucleus around which good men
rally, when bigotry or religious persecution call for determined and combined resistance."[34]

The U.S. Alliance at home attempted to implement its
assumptions concerning religious liberty and the separation of religion and civil authority by defending the legal and institutional status quo on the state and national
level. The final portion of this chapter will highlight
implicit contradictions within this *evangelical* Religion
of the Republic. As suggested previously, their strong
sense of identity meant evangelicals rejected other religious worldviews. Assuming one's religious perspective
spilled over into all areas of life, evangelicals believed
Roman Catholicism dangerous to America because related to
an authoritarian and hierarchically organized church;
faithful Roman Catholics accordingly could not adjust to
an American democratic structure based on Protestant sources. By definition, then, the true "American Citizen"
must be evangelical and anti-Catholic because the bulk of
Roman Catholics could be neither democratic nor evangelical. Catholics, in turn, thought evangelicals too libertarian and illiberal, libertarian because they allowed
overmuch freedom and diversity in the realm of religion
and illiberal because their actions seemed to belie commitment to religious liberty and separation of church and
state. Therefore, to be Catholic involved being anti-
Protestant and suspicious of the Protestant power structure dominating American Society.

Just as conservative trends in European Catholicism
before 1865 seemed to justify evangelicals in their attitude towards Roman Catholicism, trends during the immediate post-1865 period provided new "proofs" for the accepted evangelical view. Two such proofs in evangelical eyes
were the *Syllabus of Errors* (1864) and the promulgations
of the Vatican Council (1870), especially that of Papal
Infallibility. If, as Catholic historian E. E. Y. Hales
suggests, the *Syllabus* stunned Catholics in 1864, it had
an even stronger impact on the non-Catholic world. American evangelicals were horrified because it seemed to attack the very foundation of the American experiment in religious and civil freedom. An anonymous article in the
*New York Observer,* "The Signs of Our Times," lashed out at
this "revived and ultramontane Romanism and a revived
philosophic and scientific Rationalism." The growth of
rationalism in America might be seen in the reprint of the
works of Strauss and the appearance of those of Renan. It
also thrived "under the mask" of that "liberal Christianity" symbolized by the recent Unitarian convention in New

York City—the Unitarians reduced "the Redeemer of mankind
to a level with sinful man." On the other hand, Roman
Catholicism returned to temporal power in Europe after the
defeat of Napoleon Bonaparte and tried to rehabilitate
"the ancient politico-papal and anti-liberal regime." Subsequent events lulled the foolish into believing "the
spirit of the nineteenth century had overmastered the genius of Popery; but the encyclical of Pio Nono...has disturbed the composure of their dream. It is nothing less
than the declaration of war against all civil and religious liberty."[35]

     Philip Schaff provides a far more scholarly evangeli-
cal analysis of Roman Catholicism in his *Creeds of Christendom.* Schaff believed recent trends within Roman Catholicism were foreshadowed by the doctrine of Immaculate
Conception of the Virgin Mary (1854). Quoting from an encyclical letter sent to his bishops by the Pope, Schaff
shows that Piux IX believed "'God has vested in her the
plenitude of all good, so that henceforth, if there be in
us any hope, if there be any grace, if there be any salvation...we must receive it solely from her according to the
will of him who would have us possess all through Mary.'"
Like so many evangelicals, Schaff interpreted the dogma as
lifting Mary from among "the fallen and redeemed race of
Adam" to place "her on a par with the Saviour." Schaff
voiced the question on countless evangelical lips when he
inquired as to the authority for such a revelation. He
asked rhetorically why such a revelation had been delayed
eighteen centuries rather than being revealed originally
to the Apostles. Schaff did recognize "from the Roman
point of view, the new dogma is the legitimate fruit of
the genuine spirit of modern Romanism" and its modern
modes of worship. Yet he was distressed that "her worship
overshadows even the worship of Christ" and is made the
mediator between Christ the saviour and the believer—this
contrasts sharply with the evangelical belief that the
only mediator between man and God is Christ. Dr. Schaff
thus concluded Roman Catholic doctrine crystallized an im-
passible gulf between itself and Protestantism. "Romanism
stands and falls with Mariolatry and Papal Infallibility;
while Protestantism stands and falls with the worship of
Christ as the only Mediator between God and man and the
all-sufficient advocate with the Father." Indeed, he
judged this doctrine "striking proof of Romish departure
from the truth" and recourse to a "superstitious fiction
of the dark ages, contrary alike to Scripture and to genuine Catholic tradition." To Philip Schaff, an analysis
of the proofs set forth in support of this doctrine condemned it as "*unscriptural,*" "*anti-scriptural,*" and

opposed by Catholic tradition itself for centuries before
its pronouncement.[36]

As for the *Syllabus of Errors,* the document which
aroused so much Protestant fear and ire, Dr. Schaff judged
it to be a mixture of truth and error.  In its condemnation of atheism, materialism and other forms of infidelity,
all Christians could agree.  But the key to understanding
the *Syllabus* and the source of Protestant irritation may
be seen in Schaff's recognition that the purely negative
format of the *Syllabus* "implies the assertion of doctrines
the very opposite to those which are rejected as errors."
Accordingly, "it expressly condemns religious and civil
liberty, the separation of Church and State; and indirect-
ly it asserts the Infallibility of the Pope, the exclusive
right of Romanism to recognition by the State, the unlawfulness of all non-Catholic religions, the complete independence of the Roman hierarchy from the civil government
(yet without allowing a separation), the power of the
Church to coerce and enforce, and its supreme control over
public education, science, and literature."  In the light
of the Vatican Council (1870) endorsement of portions of
the *Syllabus* and of Papal Infallibility, Schaff concluded
the *Syllabus* had become part of the Roman creed and expressed the "genuine spirit of Popery."  The logic of the
Catholic position struck evangelicals sharply.  Philip
Schaff felt convinced that "Popery accepts and utilized
[*sic*] indifferently all forms of government and all political parties, and assails and undermines them all if they
are no more serviceable to its hierarchical interests.
American Romanists must be disloyal either to the fundamental institutions of their country, or to those parts of
the Syllabus which condemn those institutions."[37]

The other proof which post-Civil War evangelicalism
adduced in support of its distrust of Roman Catholicism
was the Vatican Council itself.  Even before the Council
convened, evangelicals anticipated it would endorse the
*Syllabus* and promulgate the doctrine of Papal Infallibility.  Indeed, an editorial in the *New York Observer* hoped
the Council would do so because it would make clear to the
Protestant world that the Church of Rome was in avowed antagonism to the Bible and the age, to free education and
human liberty.  By April 28 of that year, an *Observer* editorial letter to the President of the United States
claimed the Vatican Council made the *Syllabus* (and its
condemnation of religious liberty, free public schools and
nineteenth century progress) the rule of the Catholic
Church.  Thus Philip Schaff assessed the chief object of
the Council as assertion of the supremacy and personal

infallibility of the Pope: "It settled the internal dis-
sensions between Ultramontanism and Gallicanism, which
struck at the root of the fundamental principle of authority; it destroyed the independence of the Episcopate, and
made it a tool of the Primacy; it crushed liberal Catholicism; it completed the system of Papal absolutism; it
raised the hitherto disputed opinion of Papal Infallibility to the dignity of a binding article of faith, which no
Catholic can deny without loss of salvation."  Roman Catholics applauded their forthcoming Council as ecumenical in
nature but Schaff claimed "for Protestants and Greeks the
Vatican Council is no more ecumenical than that of Trent,
and has only intensified the antagonism" with non-Catholic
perspectives.  Schaff noted "Old Catholic" protests
against the illiberal nature of Council proceedings but he
implied the subsequent submission of most recalcitrant
Bishops (those who voted against infallibility) meant one
could not discriminate between the bulk of the Catholics—
"henceforeward Romanism must stand or fall with the Vatican Council."[38]

     Like so many evangelicals, Rev. Schaff thought the
"sinlessness of the Virgin Mary and the personal infallibility of the Pope are the characteristic dogmas of modern
Romanism" and those upon which the fate of Romanism rests.
"Both rest on pious fiction and fraud; both present a re-
fined idolatry by clothing a pure humble woman and a mor-
tal sinful man with divine attributes."  Quite incredibly,
it meant Roman Catholicism held the Pope in the same respect as the Protestants did "the absolute supremacy and
infallibility of the Holy Scriptures."  All past papal
doctrines, both the good and the damnable, thereby became
the infallible truth.  Of course a scholar like Schaff
understood private opinions of Popes were fallible but
found the notion that a man could even be a heretic and
yet infallible as Pope, if *officially* pronouncing on some
problem, both repugnant and false doctrine when judged according to scripture and tradition.  Evangelicals so disliked these doctrines and the related Vatican Council that
the aftereffects of the Franco-Prussian War (1870) nearly
sent them into ecstasy.  A summary of evangelical reaction
to this event might be seen in Schaff's triumphant statement:

          It is certainly a most remarkable provi-
          dential occurrence that the last OEcumeni-
          cal Council and the proclamation of the
          dogma of Papal Infallibility was swiftly
          followed by the brilliant triumph of Protes-
          tant Prussia, by the downfall of Napoleon

> III, 'the oldest son of the Church,' the
> political pillar of Popery, by the deep
> humiliation of France, the greatest
> Catholic nation, and by the overthrow of
> the temporal power of the Pope through
> the Catholic Italians. Truly, there is
> a God in history, and the history of the
> world is a judgment of the world.[39]

Although such criticism of Romanism might lead one
to think all evangelicals were opposed implacably to Catholicism, this was not the case. Like many of his fellow
evangelicals, although for varying reasons, Philip Schaff
distinguished between Romanism and Catholicism. The former was merely a modern aberration from the truly Christian tradition of Catholicism. Schaff hoped "the destruction of the infallible and irreformable Papacy may be the
emancipation of Catholicism, and lead it from its prison-
house to the light of a new Reformation." Another type of
distinction was set forth by Rev. George Samson, an Honorary Corresponding Secretary of the national body, before
the first Biennial Conference of the Evangelical Alliance,
held in Pittsburgh in 1875. Rev. Samson claimed that "Ultramontanism" (what other evangelicals often called "Romanism") had to be distinguished from Roman Catholicism. Ultramontanism was merely a sect within the Church, but it
had such exalted political ambitions for the Church that
European Catholic statesmen found it necessary to rebuff
it severely. Ultramontanism was an "ecclesiastical power,
seated at Rome" which claimed both civil and ecclesiastical authority over nations on the part of the Roman Church
and the Pope, its infallible head. It was Ultramontanism,
rather than the Church as a whole, about which Samson
warned America to be wary. Americans must protect their
experimental but constitutional heritage of democratic
government and society—all nations of the world would
eventually accept that heritage as their own.[40]

This distinction between parties within the Roman
Church reflects considerable understanding by evangelicals.
Historian Robert Cross argues that the Roman Church in
Europe and America divided both at the hierarchical and
lay levels along a spectrum from liberal to conservative,
according to the extent that those parties were willing to
accommodate Catholicism to the modern world. In postwar
America, liberals like Cardinal James Gibbons and Archbishop John Ireland desired church acceptance of modern
liberalism and American culture. They thought accommodation to democratic ideas and culture would enable the
Church to convert America without any material loss of its

traditional values and doctrines or their efficacy.  On
the other hand, conservative Catholics such as Archbishop
Michael A. Corrigan and Bishop Bernard McQuaid thought
such accommodation would destroy the Church and the faith
of its adherents.  Each group struggled with the other for
the allegiance of Catholics in the United States.  They
wished also to implement as Church policy their respective
theories of accommodation or isolation in all areas of immediate contact with American culture, such as education
and charity.[41]

     Although evangelicals often knew of these divisions,
and some distinguished between Catholicism and abhorrent
Ultramontanism, many agreed with Josiah Strong that Catholic citizens accepting Papal authority and Infallibility
could not break from Romanism even though its principles
opposed diametrically those of the Republic.  In proof of
this belief, Strong noted that most liberal American prelates opposed strenuously the doctrine of Papal Infallibility only to capitulate in the end.  The logic of all
this seemed clear.  "In view of the fact that their opposition thus utterly collapsed, what reason have we to expect that liberal Romanists in this country, who have already assented to the infallibility of the Pope, will ever
violate their oath of obedience to him?  If the liberality
of avowed opponents of ultramontanism yielded to papal authority, what reason is there to think the liberality of
avowed ultramontanists will ever resist it?"  As Philip
Schaff, Josiah Strong and other evangelicals indicated,
the *Syllabus of Errors* and doctrine of Papal Infallibility
intensified divisions between Protestant and Roman Catholic perspectives.  It added doctrines to the Catholic position repugnant to both Protestantism as well as the liberal and democratic ideology and culture with which American Protestants were wont to associate their religion.
This is the general source of tension between devout evangelicals and devout Roman Catholics in postwar America.[42]

     There were, however, practical reasons for this ten-
sion.  Roman Catholics as a group were loyal to the democratic Union during the Civil War and emerged from it ex-
pecting to be treated as first-class citizens.  They hoped
to gain: (1) what they considered to be full religious
liberty in public institutions; (2) a portion of the public funds then being spent on non-Catholic but private
ameliorative institutions; and (3) a more representative
share of the political offices from which they were so
often barred by prejudice.  Despite their differences,
both liberal and conservative Roman Catholics were quite
upset about the existence of an established religion in

American culture and institutions.  As an anonymous article noted in Paulist Father Isaac Hecker's journal, the
*Catholic World,* "it is true that you cannot call the colorless Protestantism of these institutions peculiarly Methodist, or peculiarly Episcopalian, or peculiarly Baptist;
but it is nevertheless Protestantism.  We have a name for
it.  The late 'Evangelical Alliance' gives it to us.  The
word 'Evangelicalism' will express the Protestantism of
our incipient national and state churches."  Irrespective
of their orientation, Catholics demanded those institutions be adjusted to meet Catholic rights to freedom of
conscience and worship, rights which the evangelical nature of those institutions did not fully allow.[43]

      This Catholic confrontation of evangelical elements
in the public structure made some Protestants more aware
of the undesirable implications of their accommodation to,
and impact on, American culture.  Most Protestants nevertheless continued to defend the status quo as inherently
just and refused to judge the Catholic critique on its
merits.  Because it was more conservative Catholic statements and actions to which evangelicals so often reacted,
it might help to take a detailed look at one such position
to understand late nineteenth century religious controversies over public funds and institutions.  An anonymous article in the *Catholic World,* "Unification and Education,"
bitterly criticized the educational program which Sen.
Henry Wilson designed supposedly to wed evangelicalism to
the Republican Party and thereby give the latter control
over America.  Sen. Wilson espoused "*National Unification
and National Education,*" "the social and religious unification of the American people by means of a system of universal and uniform compulsory education" under the juris-
diction of the national government.  The article claimed
the Party concentrated much of the *civil* power at the national level before and during the war.  "The work of consolidation or unification is nearly completed, and there
remains little to do except to effect the social and religious unification of the various religions, sects, and
races that make up the vast and diversified population of
the country; and it is clear from Mr. Wilson's programme
that his party contemplate [*sic*] moulding the population...
into one homogeneous people, after what may be called the
New England Evangelical type" found in "all the denominations united in the Evangelical Alliance."  The national
system of compulsory public education was intended to
catalyze such homogeneity but far more direct circumstances than this would ensue, for homogeneity unleashes a
virulent republicanism which would reduce government to
anarchy or the "despotism of majorities."[44]

Contrary to the anonymous Catholic author's belief,
many contemporary evangelicals also feared talk of a national, rather than regional, educational system.  What
upset evangelicals was the dislike of majority rule and
notions about education found in Catholic articles like
this.  Americans used democratic ideology to justify their
educational system: proper education gave all men, irrespective of their origins, a greater chance to advance in
society and be effective citizens.  Indeed public education was often considered an inherent part of the democratic structure.  Rev. George Samson stated this idea quite
well when he said the American system of government and
society depended on education of the populace: "one hundred years ago a civil government founded on the ideal of
the ages, began to be tested in practice, having these
three features; rulers elected by the people, duty to God
distinct from duty to State, and education fitted to prepare citizens to be both rulers and subjects."  The more
conservative Catholic, to the contrary, often denied that
justification.  Quoting again from "Unification and Education,"

> We do not believe that the great bulk of the
> people of any nation can ever be so educated
> as to understand the essential political, fi-
> nancial, and economical questions of govern-
> ment for themselves, and they will always
> have to follow blindly their leaders, natural
> or artificial.  Consequently the education
> of the leaders is of far greater importance
> than the education of those who are to be
> led.  All men have equal natural rights,
> which every civil government should recog-
> nize and protect, but equality in other re-
> spects...is neither practicable nor desirable.
> Some men are born to be leaders, and the rest
> are born to be led.... Nothing could be worse
> than to try to educate all to be leaders.[45]

Given these assumptions, our anonymous author applauded
the education received by peasantry of Catholic countries
two centuries ago.  Although often unable to read or write,
they were better educated ostensibly than the great mass
of the American people now: "they had faith, they had morality, they had a sense of religion...and they had the
virtues without which wise, stable, and efficient government is impracticable."[46]

This kind of argument, and its inherent critique of
the nineteenth century American common man, made evangeli-

cals deeply distrustful of the Catholic Church and its educational and charitable programs. Again and again, Rev.
James King, powerful New York Methodist and a leading Alli-
anceman during the 1880s, quoted Orestes Brownson and *liberal* Catholics to the effect that Roman Catholic education
trained youth to live in the past rather than in the modern
world by inculcating a character foreign to American ideals
and culture. King believed this liberal Catholic critique
sufficient witness to the dangers Catholicism posed for
American institutions and democratic practices. Clearly,
the virtues cited as necessary for stable society and government, in "Unification and Education," went against the
central grain of democratic ideology and upset evangelicals
to no end: "For the great mass of the people, the education
needed is not secular education, which simply sharpens the
intellect and generates pride and presumption, but moral
and religious education, which trains up children in the
way they should go, which teaches them to be honest and
loyal, modest and unpretending, docile and respectful to
their superiors, open and submissive to rightful authority,
parental or conjugal, civil, or ecclesiastical." The logic
of this argument meant "this sort of education can be given
only by the church or under her direction and control."[47]

Such a conception of the character and role of education angered evangelicals but paralleled their own belief
that religion be taught in public schools to inculcate
these virtues necessary for good citizenship and stable
society. The Catholic view of freedom of conscience and
religious liberty as "corporate" rather than "individual"
in nature also mystified and infuriated the evangelical—
"we demand [the same] freedom of conscience and the liberty
of our church, which is our conscience, enjoyed by Evangelicals" as rights promised to us by the Constitution and
laws of the land. It was statements such as this which
convinced Rev. James King that by religious liberty the
more conservative Catholic meant liberty of the Catholic
Church to exercise authority over religion, education and
government. King, to the contrary, knew the only correct
understanding of the term was the right of the individual
to freedom of conscience, freedom of decision and freedom
of worship.[48]

Based on his corporate view of religious liberty, our
anonymous Catholic author argued (since education could be
acceptable only when religious and under control of the
Church) the state could not found merely secular schools.
Civil authority must create schools which taught religion
and a modicum of secular knowledge. Given the public ex-
penditures involved, the state had the right to inspect

all schools to ensure instruction in required secular subjects.  Of course religious pluralism in American society
posed problems for implementation of this theory, but,
like many conservative Catholics, our author knew equity
required transformation of public into denominational
schools supported by public funds.  Unhappily, evangelical
use of the public school system to secure "national, social, and religious unification" prevented equity and
threatened true religion.  Conservative Catholics believed
sincerely that the evangelically dominated public school
was a tool for "carrying out their purpose of suppressing
the church and extirpating Catholicity from American soil,"
for educating Catholic children in evangelical democracy.[49]

    Although this author might have erred somewhat in
his analysis of Wilson's goals, he was fairly insightful
as to evangelical assumptions concerning the function of
American schools, public institutions and culture.  Most
evangelicals expected them to Americanize both immigrant
and Roman Catholic to the point where they became evangelical devotees of the Religion of the Republic.  Philip
Schaff attested to this fact before the Evangelical Alliance General Conference in Basle (1879).  Discussing the
Roman Catholic Church in America, Schaff noted "many believe that in a thoroughly Protestant atmosphere, and under the moulding influence of the public schools and republican institutions, it will gradually undergo a liberal
transformation."  Schaff was not so sanguine.  The submission of America's ablest prelates and opponents of Papal
Infallibility, such as Archbishop Kenrick of St. Louis,
meant the Church could rely especially on the Irish Catholics of America.  Doubting the liberalization of the
Church, Schaff still assured his audience that massive
immigration and Protestant division would not lead to a
Roman Catholic triumph in America: "history never moves
backward, and the open Bible and Protestant freedom are
making faster and deeper progress than Romanism."  To the
contrary, evangelicals in the Alliance anticipated success
in both worldwide efforts to convert Roman Catholics and
preservation of the evangelical character of American culture.  The U.S. Alliance 1871 report applauded the destruction of Papal temporal power (of the Papal States)
and the creation of a "'free church in a free state'" when
Italy unified in 1870; destruction of the temporal power
of the Pope nullified his prohibition of free preaching
and the circulation of scripture in the vernacular tongue.
All evangelicals understood this event symbolized the
ultimate conversion of Italy.[50]

    But, how could this Protestant dream materialize if

the evangelical character of America were endangered by
the presence of an increasingly large body of Catholics?
The fact that evangelicals and Catholics both wanted goals
antagonistic to the other meant continued friction.  Evangelical Protestantism aspired to convert Roman Catholics
to evangelical truth while Catholics, and especially many
Catholic converts from Protestantism, like Orestes Brownson and Paulist Father Isaac Hecker, hoped eventually to
win the Protestant masses to their religious perspective.
Roman Catholics wanted to accommodate the culture to their
ideals and needs while the evangelicals desired to make
the culture more evangelical and expected Catholics to adjust to it.  The net result of Catholic attempts to gain
favorable cultural adjustment after the Civil War was a
revived Protestant conviction they were witnessing a concerted "politico-religious" campaign by subjects of the
Pope to subvert American ideals and institutions.  As was
true of the antebellum movement, postwar anti-Catholicism
derived most of its leaders from the clergy and religious
press, although the later movement lacked the scope and
bitterness of the earlier.  Historian Robert Lord and his
Catholic collaborators attribute the organized aspects of
this so-called new Protestant crusade, at least in part,
to the rise of the Evangelical Alliance for the United
States of America:

> The ministerial phalanx, here and else-
> where, was solidified by the formation in
> 1867 of the American branch of the British-
> born Evangelical Alliance, which took for
> one of its chief tasks to fight every legi-
> slative measure favorable to the Catholic
> Church and to champion amendments to the
> Federal and State Constitutions forbidding
> money grants in favor of 'sectarian' schools
> and charitable institutions.  For several
> decades it was to be a great power in the
> land.[51]

The motive most often offered in explanation—a revival of "inherited prejudice"—is quite an oversimplifica-
tion of Alliance anti-Catholicism.  The principle Alliance
stronghold was New York State, the very place where some
of the major controversies over the relation of religion
to public schools and publicly funded private charities
occurred.  As John Webb Pratt details in his *Religion,
Politics and Diversity: The Church-State Theme in New York
History,* so called anti-Catholicism was as much an aspect
of state reform movements and politics as it was the outcome of controversy over specific religious issues.  For

example, the attempts of New York City's Boss Tweed to win
greater immigrant support, through city and state appropriations to Roman Catholic parochial schools and benevolent institutions, caused considerable uproar among Protestants.  Superficial evidence convinced Protestants that
Catholics were responsible for urban government corruption
in general and for such boss systems as the Tweed Ring in
particular——Did not Catholics receive vast sums from the
machine?  Were not the bulk of machine supporters Catholic
immigrants?  Evangelicals were as upset about the size of
the public sums given Catholic institutions as the related
transgression against separation of religion from civil
authority (most Protestants only became concerned about
such appropriations when Catholics began to receive the
lion's share).  Protestant fears escalated further when
Catholics attempted to translate past *defacto* relationships, between Protestant institutions and government,
into *legally endorsed* connections open to Roman Catholicism as well.[52]

    Protestants effectually started to question govern-
ment funding of private nonsectarian charities and schools
only when massive immigration made Roman Catholicism powerful enough to challenge the system.  By the eve of the
Civil War, Protestants had agreed to teach what they
thought "nonsectarian" but was actually "evangelical"
Protestantism in the public schools and state-supported
institutions.  Although many of the larger Protestant
bodies at one time wished those institutions would inculcate their own doctrinal views, this compromise arose when
it became apparent that no body was strong enough to impose
its will over the other churches and the public.  Such a
compromise meant most state and national educational and
reform institutions were essentially evangelical Protestant in character by the 1850s.  Now in the post-Civil War
period, Catholics were a sufficiently large and self-con-
fident portion of American society to make felt their demands for a share in the benefits which fell formerly to
the nonsectarian and Protestant bodies alone.  One such
challenge may be seen in the anonymous article just summarized from the *Catholic World*.  The intrusion of the demands of a powerful Roman Catholic minority into what had
heretofore been a Protestant sphere of influence largely
negated the value and acceptability of the so-called nonsectarian compromise.  The Catholic perspective could not
accommodate to that evangelicalism and still remain Catholic, or so many of the adherents of both perspectives believed.

    That most evangelicals were unable conscientiously

to disassociate their religious perspective from the ideology and institutions of the democratic republic, from the
Religion of the Republic, explains further not only much
of the Alliance anti-Catholicism at this time but the
groundswell of evangelical concern about immigrants in general.  Deriving primarily from northern European stock,
evangelicals witnessed an incomprehensible gap during the
1880s between themselves and an urban poor recruited increasingly among Roman Catholic, Greek Orthodox and Jewish
peasants from southern and eastern Europe.  Still, evangelical reaction to this "New Immigration" partook only super-
ficially of the kind of nativism, or "intense opposition
to an internal minority on the ground of its foreign (i.e.,
un-American) connections," which John Higham claims for
this period.  Granted that evangelicals displayed fear of
supposed Roman Catholic subversion of democracy, fear of
European radicals and revolutionaries, and eventually a
social Darwinist Anglo-Saxon racism.  Granted even that
clearcut bigotry and racism existed among some.  Yet an
undercurrent of Higham's nativist argument, and that of
Ray Allen Billington's earlier *Protestant Crusade,* implies
that American dislike of the immigrant involved unreasoning fear, at its best, or manipulative opportunism, at its
worst.  By implication, the educated Protestant leadership
ought to have encouraged respect for Catholics, Jews and
immigrants generally, but self-interest led to demogogic
activity instead.  Such a position portrays the immigrant
leaders and followers as meek recipients of American abuse
rather than as active agents, like the Boston Irish, whose
own presuppositions were often hostile to those of their
host culture.  Clearly, late nineteenth century America
still witnessed a multisided culture conflict, whose ac-
tors were less villain than human, which intensified American nationalist emphasis on the Religion of the Republic.[53]

Evangelical ire focused on the Catholics more than
others because of deep-seated theological and ideological
opposition.  Besides, a large portion of the postwar new
immigrants were Catholic.  The Evangelical Alliance nevertheless took little action concerning the spreading influence of Roman Catholicism in America until the early 1880s.
Alliance efforts up until that time were directed: (1) towards continued vigilance in defense of religious liberty
throughout the world; and (2) towards biennial conferences,
held in different cities of the nation, designed to
strengthen American interest in the Alliance and its goals.
The biennial conferences proved particularly important in
that the auxiliary alliances seemed to suffer from a lack
of a program, other than those conferences, adequate to
sustain local evangelical interest.  Even the national

Evangelical Alliance in New York City faltered.   From 1875
to the end of 1882 the New York body held the annual meetings of the Evangelical Alliance for the United States of
America, but its monthly meetings convened only sporadically.[54]

From 1883 on, however, the Alliance became very active.   The reasons for its new activism are not too clear.
One major factor seems to have been a general desire on
the part of the New York evangelical community to plan for
the public celebration of the 400th birthday anniversary
of Martin Luther.   The Executive Committee expected this
celebration to give "thanks to God for the blessings of
the Reformation, especially for the free circulation of
the Word of God, and for religious liberty."   Another reason seems to be the growing sense of malaise among evangelicals concerning the state of the nation and Protestantism
within it.   This general concern received specific stimula-
tion from renewed Roman Catholic attempts to obtain New
York State and City funds for Catholic institutions.[55]

Such efforts occurred sporadically during the late
1860s.   The Executive Committee responded, in 1870, with
the statement that "the Executive Committee views with
great anxiety the encroachments of the Roman Catholics, in
this city and in the United States, upon those principles
of religious liberty, and of equality of all denominations
before the civil law, which have been the glory of our institutions in the past; and which have been illustrated in
the complete independence of 'Church and State.'"   The Alliance further resolved that no government, be it city,
state or national, could appropriate public funds for sectarian institutions.   Therefore, the Alliance appealed to
the New York State Legislature for the repeal of Section
10, Chapter 876, of the laws of 1869 which appropriated 20
percent of the excise taxes of the city of New York to
those private schools educating children gratuitously.
Boss Tweed sponsored this law to win greater Roman Catholic support for his machine, since most private schools
were Catholic.   The Alliance sent its resolutions in memorial form to the governor and legislature of New York
and sponsored large public protest meetings as well.
Leaving no opportunity unused, it even sent Samuel Irenaeus Prime to present the Alliance views to a State Convention on the Public School Question held in Albany
during April 1870.[56]

The bulk of Alliancemen were not ready to accept the
more astute and complicated stance of Methodist editor and
Alliance Councilor Daniel Curry. He believed responsibility

for religious training resided in church and home while
the state should provide and control secular education at
all levels preceding college and seminary.  Bowing to reality, Rev. Curry accepted public funding for religious
schools as an inevitable consequence of contemporary political pressures.  As a result, what separated Curry from
his peers was his public admission that Roman Catholicism
stood condemned for receiving an *unfairly large share* of
public funds, rather than for receipt of funds per se.

>      American ideas of religious liberty re-
> quire that all sects shall be equally tol-
> erated and protected by the laws. If Churches
> are to receive pecuniary favors whether as
> gifts or exemptions, all forms and kinds of
> religious societies must fare alike.  If to
> the ministers or priests of any of the sects,
> as such, shall be granted any rights and
> privileges, the same must be allowed to all
> whether Protestant or Catholic, Christian,
> Jew, or Mormon.  That to certain limited
> and carefully guarded extents such grants
> may be expedient we are not prepared to deny.
> If, however, there is any inequality of dis-
> tribution, then there is injustice—and such
> will be very likely to be the case when it
> is done by special grants instead of by es-
> tablished laws.  Here is one of the great
> vices of our present system of State and
> city grants to Churches and Church schools.[57]

On the other hand, Rev. Curry thought state aid to charitable institutions good but argued that annual inspections
proving their merit and the number of people aided, con-
jointly, ought to determine the amount of funds given to
each institution.  Such aid to religious charities was
meaningful because they dispensed charity more humanely
and effectively than did the state.[58]

     In March of 1875, the Alliance again opposed Catho-
lic attempts to obtain public funds in a memorial to the
Board of Education of New York City prepared by Samuel
Irenaeus Prime, Philip Schaff, William Adams, William E.
Dodge, Sr., Nathan Bishop and S. B. Schieffelin.  Although
the memorial ignored the Catholic critique of evangelicalism in the public school, it avoided arousal of prejudice
or irrationality to sway the public to the Alliance position.  Rather, it utilized a rational and logical argument
based on the evangelical perspective which concluded that
sectarian appropriations endangered the Republic.  This

"Protest and Memorial" judged the public school system of
New York City superior to that of any other city in the
world in its quality, impartiality, and availability to
all.  Such city schools provided those homogeneous and co-
hesive characteristics so essential to democratic society
(and so upsetting to conservative Catholics).  Nothing
could be clearer than "the free education of all the children in the same schools, in the same studies, under the
same teachers tends to the culture of that common sympathy
and union vital to the security of peace and social order
in a Republic, and especially in a great city where the
government is popular and rests upon the intelligence, virtue and unity of the people."  If public funds were divert-
ed to a denominational school system, the memorial predicted other religious and nationality groups would demand
their own systems, "thus frittering away the noble democratic republican system of equal advantages, which has
hitherto been the pride and glory of New York."[59]

Another consequence of public funding for Catholic
parochial schools was the injection of bitter religious
controversy into the educational and political system. The
Alliance memorial thought history proved such controversy
disastrous to the peace of any community or nation.  Implicit in the latter point was the suggestion that good
citizens would avoid arousing such controversy, an argument very favorable to those benefiting from the status
quo.  Hence the law ought to prohibit appropriations to
schools teaching doctrines or using books of a religious
nature or prejudicial toward any religious sect.  Those
who wish religiously oriented schools for their children
must support them at their own expense.  If, by chance, it
were lawful to appropriate funds for sectarian purposes,
the Alliance insisted that they be divided according to
the proportion of taxes paid by each sect so no sect would
be paying for the program of another; but it believed such
impracticable because no division could possibly accord
with the rights of all religious groups. The memorial predicted the public educational system would survive the
current crisis to foster further the good of the whole
people.[60]

This "Protest and Memorial" rested on several assump
tions.  It assumed the nonsectarian religious instruction
still found to some extent in New York's public schools,
and the continued use of the King James Version of the
Bible, did not favor any particular religious group. Rather, those practices fostered the common good by inculcating that morality and virtue thought essential to
stable democratic government.  It further assumed democratic government could only continue to function if the

nation were evangelical in culture, ideals and values.
The peoples of diverse nationalities and cultures which
constituted New York's population had to be educated to
its acceptance.  Such presuppositions were connected always with the other evangelical ideals of freedom of conscience and separation of church and state without any indication of the implicit contradiction between them.  To a
large extent, they would all continue to inform Alliance
arguments against public appropriations for sectarian purposes throughout the remainder of the century.

Many Roman Catholics, to the contrary, believed doctrine required the Church to control the education of its
youth.  Growing alienation from the American public school
led to full conservative and qualified liberal Catholic
endorsement for the creation of a separate national parochial school system (Catholics will build the bulk of the
current system during the late nineteenth century).  The
nonsectarian religion taught in the public schools and the
use of the King James version of the Bible, even if read
without comment, made those schools unacceptable to many
Catholics.  By the 1880s, the Catholic attempts to share
in public funds given to nonsectarian educational and
ameliorative-reform institutions became more numerous and
vigorous.  The evangelicals on their part reacted to this
growing "peril" by increased efforts at molding public and
legislative opinion in defense of the publicly supported
nonsectarian institutions and in opposition to the sectarian system which the Roman Catholics desired.[61]

The Alliance became quite active in this respect in
1883.  In that year, it appointed John Jay, Philip Schaff,
Samuel Irenaeus Prime and James Buckley to a committee
with power to present Alliance views on the use of public
funds for sectarian purposes to the governor and legislature of New York.  Their efforts were published as a public *Protest of the Evangelical Alliance of the United
States Against the Bill Before the Legislature of the
State of New York, Entitled 'An Act to Secure to the Inmates of Institutions for the Care of the Poor Freedom of
Worship.'*  During 1883 the Alliance also selected Episcopalian and strongly anti-Catholic John Jay to succeed de-
ceased William E. Dodge, Sr., as President of the Alliance.  The character of the crisis which evangelicals believed themselves to be facing may be seen in Jay's letter
of acceptance.  In reference to the Alliance *Protest*, he
said: "This resolution exhibits on the part of the Alliance a view in which I entirely concur of the danger
threatened to our religious and civil liberties by the
pending attempts to overthrow the freedom of worship,
which lies at the foundation of the Christian Churches

which the Alliance represents." Hence, Jay believed the
"duty" of "interposing to avert this danger seems to me
instant and imperative." He accepted the presidency from
devotion to the great objects of the Alliance, the promotion of "religious liberty" and "cooperation in Christian
work." Jay pledged to foster these goals, so important to
"the purity and progress of Christianity, and the welfare
and stability of the Republic."[62]

This evangelical concern for the future of American
culture led to Alliance reorganization between 1885 and
1887. The restructured Alliance gained corporate status
under New York State law and thereby became eligible to
receive these large bequests thought necessary for long-
term life and vigor. It created a Board of Managers as
the highest governing body of the corporation but retained
the Executive Committee, now reduced to an efficient size,
to direct the affairs of the Alliance during the year.
Finally, it rounded out its more vital organization by appointing a vigorous personality, Josiah Strong, to the new
post of General Secretary, in December of 1886.[63]

Although its long-term program sponsored social gospel reform of American society, the immediate purpose of
reorganization was conservative. The new and powerful
Committee on Legislative Action, chaired by Methodist
clergyman James King, intended to preserve the status quo
in the realm of freedom of conscience and the separation
of religion and civil authority. It desired to frustrate
the passage of the Freedom of Worship bills which Catholic
interests had persisted in bringing before the New York
Legislature ever since the 1870s. This concerted effort
of Roman Catholics to obtain fulfillment of their needs
precipitated evangelical resistance statewide. Spearhead-
ing reaction, the Alliance organized branches, utilized
pamphlets, statewide circulars, mass meetings, the newspaper, petitions and legislative lobbies to further its
ends. The circulars and documents ranged from five to ten
thousand copies per item and were sent to strategic clergymen, social, business and political leaders whose good
opinion of Alliance goals had maximum impact on the masses
and the government. The first series of Freedom of Worship bills held statewide implications although focused
solely on the "House of Refuge"— the Refuge was run by the
Society for the Reformation of Juvenile Delinquents on
Randall's Island, New York City. The debate revolving
around the bills treated this Refuge as the exemplar of
what Roman Catholics disliked, and Protestants cherished,
about the character of state and state-supported private
ameliorative and reform institutions.[64]

From the evangelical perspective, the nonsectarian
character of the House epitomized the proper relationship
of religion to a civil reform institution. The Alliance
attributed the great success of this Refuge over its past
60 years to "the fact that with jealous care it has been
kept wholly unsectarian. To reform its inmates they are
brought under moral and mental training based on the divine
precepts of the Bible, which form the basis of all Christian morality." Chapel was open ostensibly to clergy of
any denomination to give moral and religious instruction,
while the sick could be attended by the clergy of their desire as long as no attempts were made to proselytize and
no disparaging remarks were made concerning any church or
creed. The Alliance documents concluded that this situation was pleasing to all committed to the constitutional
right of freedom of profession and of worship; it was
therefore unacceptable to some Roman Catholics as well as
to the Catholic hierarchy which, the Alliance alluded, "denies the right of liberty of conscience, and which destroys
where it can religious toleration." In justification of
the belief that Catholicism still adhered to an essentially
antilibertarian position, the Alliance reminded the people
of the *Syllabus of Errors* and other promulgations of doctrine which condemned modern freedoms. Hence the Alliance,
quoting the *London Times,* was certain

> That the Roman Catholic promoters of the
> said Bill hold, with the late Pontiff's
> [sic] Gregory XVI., and Pius IX., that the
> opinion 'that liberty of conscience and
> worship is each man's personal right,' is
> an erroneous opinion, a delirium, a heresy,
> and a crime; that freedom of education and
> worship are contrary to the laws of God;
> and that, as regards religious toleration,
> they hold, with the present Pope, his Holi-
> ness Leo XIII., who recently declared in
> his letter to the Cardinal Vicar, March
> 28th, 1879, that if he possessed the liber-
> ty he claims 'he would employ it to close
> all Protestant schools and places of wor-
> ship in Rome.'[65]

Given this view of Papal dogmatic assertions and pronouncements, it is easy to understand why evangelicals
might suspect any Catholic action appearing to question an
institutional form which had become part of the cultural
fabric: nonsectarian religious training in state and state-
supported institutions. That this nonsectarian training
was establishment of religion never dawned on most evangelicals, even though such training instilled principles and

operated along lines quite in tune with the Alliance doctrinal basis and constitution.  Given hindsight, contemporary evidence now suggests clearly that this supposed nonsectarian training militated against Roman Catholics in
the practice of their faith.  Alliance evangelicals therefore defended, often unconsciously, a kind of established
evangelicalism when they branded attempts to gain religious
rights for Catholics as undermining freedom of conscience
and separation of church and state.  By assuming Papal
teachings dominated the attitudes of many American Catholics, these evangelicals could deem perfidious sometimes
rather innocent Catholic demands.  It must be noted, however, evangelicals were correct that some "innocent" demands laid the legal basis for goals objectionable to the
evangelical perspective, such as transformation of public
education into a denominational system.[66]

     Alliance documents show the Catholic Union, a lay
organization behind the Freedom of Worship bills, wanted
"the appointment of a priest approved by the Archbishop of
New York as (Roman) Catholic chaplain to the said House of
Refuge, with the right to [*sic*] the said chaplain to cele-
brate Mass therein every sunday, to have free access daily
to the hospital, and to be allowed accommodations for hearing confessions of Catholic children in the sacrament of
penance."  The Managers of the House of Refuge refused
these demands as "inconsistent with the interests and discipline of the Institution, and with the Constitutional
rights of the inmates."  The Catholic Union then asked the
state legislature to require that such institutions "'per-
mit at reasonable times the inmates thereof to be visited
by clergymen of the denominations to which they belong,
and the religious services of such denominations to be had
according to its rules and discipline.'"  The net effect
of these bills, the Alliance countered, would be to open
all "public and private institutions of the State receiving
public money to the members of a clerical order which
claims not merely spiritual, but temporal power."[67]

     Roman Catholics and their legislative champions made
their demands on the grounds that: (1) children of Roman
Catholic parents or guardians should be brought up in the
Roman Catholic faith; (2) that children baptized as Roman
Catholics must be trained as such; and (3) that these
rights are particularly relevant to the House of Refuge
because 50-75% of the children therein are Roman Catholic
or of that parentage.  The Alliance captured evangelical
sentiments in its counterproofs.  Argument (1) was invalid
because parents forfeit control over their children when
parents are imprisoned or desert them.  Argument (2) could
not be accepted because the claim that children must be

trained in a faith merely because they were baptized in it
denies the freedom of conscience and worship which is the
right of the child. Evangelicals assumed that institutional training in nonsectarian religious and moral values
still left great freedom of choice as to denominational
affiliation  when the child reached his majority, but that
sectarian teaching, such as Roman Catholic, so indoctri-
nated the child that he could no longer realize such freedom at his majority. The Alliance warned that acceptance
of the baptism argument would set a dangerous precedent in
the light of his Holiness Pius IX's claim that all children baptized as Christians, whatever their denominations,
belonged to the Roman Catholic Church. Under this rule,
all baptized children could be proselytized by Catholics.
Finally, the Alliance "Protests"—plugging into the new
social science stress on collected data—cited statistics
to show most paupers, criminals and illiterates in America
were Roman Catholic. More damning, Catholic parochial
schools produced a comparably higher number of these de-
generates than did the public schools. Hence, the Alliance implied the Catholic demand for redress must be ignored because of the high percentage of Catholics in public institutions. Statistical science seemed to prove
only free institutions outside of Catholic influence allowed freedom of conscience and worship as well as the
full and wholesome development of human potential. The
Alliance concluded its protests with the demand that no
bills be passed which are designed to undermine or alter
that separation of church and state bequeathed by the
founding fathers, a separation condemned by Article 55 of
the *Syllabus of Errors*—this is the "only policy that com-
ports with the harmony and goodwill between citizens of
opposing creeds, so essential to the national peace." It
protested against what it considered to be a Roman Catholic ploy for "the introduction or allowance by the State
of proselytism and propagandism in our penal, charitable,
and educational institutions." It also protested against
the use of state power to deny the constitutional rights
of freedom of conscience and worship to children who are
wards of the state. Finally, it attacked Roman Catholics
for threatening electoral retaliation against any party
which defeated the bills.[68]

These arguments do not mean the Alliance suspected
all Catholics of unconstitutional sentiments and political
opportunism. The debate over the Freedom of Worship bills
often focused on two liberal Catholics belonging to the
House of Refuge Board of Managers, Chief Justice Charles P.
Daly of the New York State Supreme Court and Mr. Nathaniel
Jarvis. Alliance publications very early and quite carefully noted that not all Roman Catholics were un-American.

Although the Catholic Union claimed support for the House
of Refuge by Daly and Jarvis meant these two were unrepresentative of the Catholic clergy and laity, the Alliance
lauded their example as reflecting

> ...the views of several of the more en-
> lightened and liberal bishops and clergy
> of that church, and especially of that
> intelligent and honorable class of Roman
> Catholic laity who, representing the olden
> school from the times of Carroll and La-
> fayette, appreciate their rights and
> duties as American citizens; who desire to
> maintain their loyalty to American insti-
> tutions, who dislike clerical intermeddling
> with their personal and political affairs,
> clerical threats against giving their chil-
> dren the advantages of the public schools,
> clerical dictation to voters at the polls,
> and the introduction in our politics of a
> clerical faction loyal to the Roman Catho-
> lic power;[69]

and oppose the grand conspiracy to overthrow American
freedoms and subject the American state to the "priestly
authority of Rome."[70]

Even though the Alliance facilitated greatly the defeat of these bills, the public uproar to which both sides
contributed was such that one-term President John Jay declined re-election in 1885.  He did this to deny hostile
legislators the opportunity of arousing Catholic animosity
toward the new Civil Service Commission—as political re-
former and president of the Commission, Jay could not sustain the widespread support needed for Commission success
if he remained President of the Alliance.  The furor became so great that James King's legislative committee issued a disclaimer in the preface of its fourth document,
one critical of the Freedom of Worship bills, concerning
the assaults made on Roman Catholicism in the public forum.  In the name of the Alliance and the committee representing the United Charities of New York City, the preface
reasserted that they respected Roman Catholic convictions
and demanded equal rights for them "but when a portion of
them demand what is special and unfair, and what we believe to be *un-American*, we are united in our opposition."
This document pointed out carefully that the United Charities represented Protestant, *Hebrew*, and nonsectarian institutions in order to indicate the wide public and religious opposition to the bills.[71]

Both the United Charities and the Alliance opposed
the newest Freedom of Worship bill (1883). It was "unjust
in its provisions, dangerously vague as to its meaning,
and un-American in its spirit and origin, and as calcu-
lated only to arouse a bitter sectarian controversy."
These charges have some merit. Vagueness of language
opened the possibility that the Senate version of the bill
would apply to all ameliorative and reform, penal, orphan
and charitable institutions even if those institutions received no public funds. This posed a threat to all solely
denominational institutions of a reformatory character and
might have undercut one of their major reasons for being,
the conversion of nonevangelical wards to evangelicalism.
The new Assembly bill provided for: (1) "the free exercise
and enjoyment of religious profession and worship without
discrimination or preference," (2) in any reformatory or
penal institution receiving monetary aid from any munici-
pality; (3) the requirement that such institutions provide
for religious instruction and ministration so as to fulfill the state constitutional guarantee of free exercise
of religious belief and worship, subject to the proper
discipline of the institution; and (4) forbade compelling
inmates to attend religious instruction by clergy from
other than their own denominations.[72]

James King spoke against these provisions before the
Committee on Affairs of Cities of the New York State Assembly. His speech reiterated the arguments of former
documents in far more lucid and logical manner and set
forth further support. A few generalizations concerning
some of the new points might be useful because the evolution of King's thought in the realm of the relation of religion and civil authority is representative of a similar
change in the Alliance position. King repeated the general evangelical suspicions of Catholicism which Papal pronouncements engendered. Although the history of both
Protestantism and Catholicism was blemished by the error
of intolerance, King believed Protestants erred much less
in that direction—the Evangelical Alliance had defended
indiscriminately Protestants, Catholics, or Jews anywhere
in the world from religious persecution. Yet the Alliance
opposed this bill because it embroiled the state in the
sphere of religion where it lacked constitutional authority. This was true particularly because the bill required
classification of children according to denomination at a
time when these wards lacked the maturity to decide the
grave question of their faith. King was certain this
scheme of cataloging was "foreign and Jesuitical, subver-
sive of religious liberty, absolutely un-American, and
utterly unconstitutional." He did not mean to condemn all

Roman Catholics but only the Jesuitism now attempting to
introduce sectarian teachings into the "absolutely unsectarian beneficiary institutions of the State whether they
be the public schools or the penal and reformatory institutions."  Quoting from United States President Ulysses S.
Grant's Des Moines Speech (1876), King demanded the public
schools remain free and unsectarian and that public funds
be denied sectarian use.  He concluded by proposing the
state constitution be amended to prohibit both appropria-
tion of public funds for sectarian institutions and legislative denominational references.  The Alliance decided
only a constitutional provision would protect individual
rights and the principle of separation of church and
state.[73]

     Despite King's efforts to present a fair analysis of
the situation, his commitment to a basic evangelical assumption militated against any real understanding of the
Catholic position: "*Hands off of our unsectarian institutions! is the substance of what we have to say.  And the
unsectarian character of an institution is destroyed when
Roman Catholicism is introduced, because it cannot, from
the very law of its being be unsectarian.*"  This inherent
evangelical inability to conceive of truly nonsectarian
institutions, that is institutions not teaching even a common or evangelical religion, places Alliance arguments in
the contradictory position of defending evangelicalism in
state institutions at the same time it espoused freedom of
conscience, worship and the separation of church and state.
Whatever justification there might have been for evangelical fears of conservative Catholics in America, evangelicals themselves strayed from religious liberty.  By 1886,
James King developed an elaborate historically documented
(although not necessarily correct) critique of conservative Catholicism in America.  Although he distinguished
the dangerous and hated  ultramontane or Jesuit servants
of the papacy from the generally loyal Roman Catholics and
Church in America, King attested to the dominance of the
ultramontane faction over Roman Catholic policies and activities and the danger that they ostensibly posed for
America.  Ultramontane goals and teachings were "at vari-
ance with American principles, hostile to the supremacy of
the State, and to our system of common schools."  The
Catholic Union, an ultramontane organization in King's
eyes, supposedly made false claims of discrimination in
the House of Refuge which both the Catholics on the Board
of Managers and their liberal Catholic supporters repudiated.  Citing such legal authorities as Chancellor Kent,
King assured the public that the practices questioned by
the Catholic Union had existed for over a half-century and

rested on the recognition that the Christian religion was
elemental in the administration of the common law in America.  The lessons from these facts were obvious to King:

> The loyal managers of the House of Refuge
> unanimously recognized the fact which Ultra-
> montanes who profess a primary allegiance
> to a foreign Pontiff are unwilling to accept,
> that loyal Americans of all creeds and par-
> ties who know and appreciate the history
> and progress of the Republic, remember with
> joy and pride, that it was a spirit of re-
> formed Christianity based upon the divine
> truths of the Bible which gave tone to its
> institutions and laws, and nourished the
> morality, the patriotism, the schools and
> the churches of our land.  It is these
> which have secured for Americans...the
> highest civilization in the world....[74]

The net effect of this and similar evangelical sentiments was that the American Alliance could promote sincerely religious liberty and the separation of church and
state around the world at the same time that it defended a
kind of established evangelicalism in basic American institutions.  The evangelicals were merely trying to provide the world with the benefits of the American experiment in religious freedom.  Their view of religious freedom however implied religion in a general sense would have
intimate connections to the culture and to civil authority
in the guise of an evangelical Religion of the Republic.
The evangelicals were certain evangelicalism provided the
only sound basis worldwide for democratic forms and civilization.  It helped mankind internalize that morality and
values essential to a stable and Christian society—one
based on the conjugal family as the bastion of home,
church, school and government—wherein the individual
lived that responsible life characteristic of true freedom.

Robert Lord and his colleagues may be correct that
many evangelicals finally accepted the elimination of religious instruction from public schools and other institutions in order to defeat Catholic demands, but this does
not appear to have been a matter of vindictiveness.  Evangelicals believed the public schools served a homogenizing
and acculturating function thought crucial to the survival
of a democratic society increasingly unsettled by massive
immigration, cultural and religious pluralism, materialism,
infidelity, vice and crime.  Many evangelicals therefore
preferred to accept a secular and national public school

system rather than accede to Catholic demands which lead
potentially to a splintering of that system into diverse
denominational systems as well as to official connections
between church and state which went far beyond those presently acceptable.  The National League for the Protection
of American Institutions, for example was formed at Sara-
toga Springs in August 1889 by Alliancemen and leaders
among the evangelical and Protestant elites in general.
Under the guidance of General Secretary James King, the
League mobilized public support for constitutional amend-
ments on the New York and national levels.  They were designed to separate religion from civil authority in Indian
missions and schools as well as more ordinary American
institutions and public schools, thereby frustrating further excuse for sectarian raids on public funds and eliminating that great divisiveness which religious controversy
created in contemporary politics—they finally understood
why the Founding Fathers of 1789 created such separation.[75]

     The groundswell of League, Evangelical Alliance, and
other powerful bodies demanding amendment, coupled with
internal discord among New York State Catholics over the
merits of the public school, finally led the 1894 New York
State legislature constitutionally to outlaw granting
public funds to private religious schools at the same time
that evangelicalism was withdrawn from public institutions.
Clearly even New York Catholics accepted secularization of
the public schools: the liberals approved while conservatives like Bishop McQuaid of Rochester focused on building
further their parochial school system.  Everyone was tired
of controversy.  Whether in New York or nationally, the
evangelicals in particular found secular public education
palatable given deep confidence that the new nationally
coordinated Sunday School programs, Chautauquas and other
voluntaryist evangelical education institutions could replace successfully the school as a means of inculcating
evangelicalism in American culture.  Besides, they thought
the public schools would still teach the democratic, if
not evangelical, essentials of the Religion of the Republic to the masses.[76]

# CHAPTER SIX

# ECUMENISM, NATIONALISM AND AN EVANGELICAL

# SOCIAL GOSPEL, 1883-1900

At the same time the Alliance endeavored to protect religious liberty at home and abroad, it continued to participate in international expressions of evangelical unity. It sent delegates to every major World Alliance conference of the period: Basle (1879), Copenhagen (1884), Florence (1891), Chicago (1893), London (1896) and London (1907). This activity is significant in that the U.S. Alliance reflected internal tensions within the larger American ecumenical community. By 1886 evangelicals tended to express their identity by supporting either international ecumenism or pragmatic denominational cooperation in the home culture. Quite obviously nationalism and internationalism imbued the Alliance from its beginnings, one or the other often receiving temporary emphasis during specific periods. Both ways, after the Civil War, merged Christian union with those ideals inherent in the Religion of the Republic while simultaneously stressing Christian cooperation as the pragmatic method suitable to incarnating Protestant unity and democratic republicanism in human reality. At issue was whether this evangelical and republican mission to mankind would be incarnated faster through a national or international focus. Attempts to balance the two directions, so often successful in the past, now failed due to the rise to power of new leadership and to contemporary urban and labor crises which no longer could be explained away as the fault solely of immigrants and Catholics.

During the 1880s men like William E. Dodge, Jr., John Jay, James King, and Josiah Strong came to power in time to shift U.S. Alliance focus away from World Alliance attempts at greater cohesion and towards solutions of national problems thought to threaten the existence of the evangelical Republic itself. Initiating the social gospel and religious reform movements earlier than William G. McLoughlin believes (by the mid-1880s rather than 1890), I maintain these men were among his "prophets of the Third Great Awakening" (1890-1920) who "had to undertake an enormous rescue operation to sustain the culture. They

had to redefine and relocate God, provide means of access
to him, and sacralize a new world view" which came to
grips with the emerging process oriented sciences, social
sciences, biblical criticism, modernity, the urban and industrial world.  "The new answers were formulated as the-
istic evolution, Progressive Orthodoxy, and Christian sociology."[1]

     Much of the best literature, such as that by C.
Howard Hopkins, Henry F. May, and Aaron I. Abell, portrays
this social gospel as liberal in character.  Obviously
Congregationalists Washington Gladden and Josiah Strong
tried to adjust Christian thought and practice to meet
modern needs, Baptist Walter Rauschenbusch later created
a theology for the movement, and other clergymen like Congregationalist George D. Herron and Methodist Harry F.
Ward toyed with various forms of Christian socialism.  The
reform efforts of these turn-of-the-century Protestants
aroused fundamentalist and subsequent neo-orthodox counter-
attacks which, in turn, solidified the liberal image of
the social gospel.  Recently, Ronald C. White, Jr. and C.
Howard Hopkins published *The Social Gospel: Religion and
Reform in Changing America* (1976) to remind us of the
many-sided nature of the movement.  My short selection on
the Evangelical Alliance in that volume hinted at some of
the conservative facets of the movement, attuned to Mc-
Loughlin's "rescue operation," which this chapter treats
more fully.[2]

     Although Alliancemen helped to lead the way in these
matters, I must stress  they and their middle road evangelical following pursued that conservative agenda inherent in the social gospel: change economic conditions, reform society, aid the poor, but save the souls of men and
christianize the society to sustain the evangelical Religion of the Republic and attain the Kingdom of God on
earth.  Such conservation is elemental to the nature of
apparently liberal reform.  Hence this very era of ascen-
dent liberalism and modernity, this period of the Third
Great Awakening, spawned the Progressive politics of Theodore Roosevelt and Woodrow Wilson, regulated big business,
attacked the urban boss system, and did all manner of
things thought liberal but actually intended to retain
that free enterprise capitalism and democratic government
responsive to the people.  Such retention can be applauded
yet these same leaders and middle class reformers capped
nineteenth century anti-immigrant and anti-black trends by
closing the door to immigrants with the Quota System (1921
while squelching further black aspirations by nationalizing the segregation system.  Obviously Anglo-Saxon racism,

Social Darwinist reinforcement for the notion that colored peoples are inferior, and all sorts of invidious factors influenced these trends.  Still, as the history of late nineteenth and early twentieth century Methodism shows, many evangelicals were won over to the liberal cause of labor unions (based on demands for a living wage supportive of those evangelical ideals of house, home, family, church, school) at the expense of another quite old liberal commitment, an open door to immigrants.  Using an argument relevant to American culture ever since, labor unions helped to convince the faithful that labor's just cause was impossible unless the source of cheap labor which forced wages down to impoverishment, the immigrant, be kept out.[3]

Yet this paradox of contradictory goals inherent in the liberal agenda was not apparent to Americans during the late nineteenth century.  Rather, adherents of international ecumenism or national interdenominational cooperation assumed feasible the worldwide incarnation of their evangelical republicanism because evangelicals abroad and at home appeared to recognize and accept the existence of that core evangelical identity articulated by the Alliance and so elemental to increased ecumenism and cooperation. The issue therefore was not one of identity, but of program:  Would international cooperation or social gospel reform at home best build Christian union and expand democratic freedom?  De-emphasis but survival of internationalism among Americans meant the U.S. Alliance sponsored simultaneously two potentially contradictory programs.  By the mid-1890s, the more international as well as conservative evangelical elements of the Alliance reasserted themselves to the point where they hindered and then rejected General Secretary Josiah Strong's nationalist and increasingly modernist programs.

In 1886, then, U.S. Alliance internationalists and nationalists began to diverge as to program as well as conception of the true nature of Christian unity.  The international element intended to strengthen evangelical unity and express evangelical identity through creation of a more powerful world Alliance.  Taking liberal ground against denominational provincialism, it hoped ultimately to attain Protestant and possibly Christian federation worldwide, a semi-organic form of union, because the Church of Christ could recognize neither national boundaries nor nationalist limitations.  In contrast, the national element thought expression of evangelical identity and achievement of unity possible only through solution of those problems plaguing the nation.  No world church could be possible until grassroots Christian unity existed on the national levels. In this context, pragmatic

cooperation among local churches and, eventually, national
denominations augured more immediate probability of success for Christian union than efforts on the international
level.  Both liberal approaches, especially the nationalist, therefore verged away from the traditional evangelical view of Christian union as fellowship among individuals, part of the invisible and universal Church, and espoused implicitly denominational federation as not only
possible but necessary.  Their vision and effort contributed respectively to the backgrounds of the World and
actual creation of the Federal Councils (later, National
Council) of the Churches of Christ.

        Philip Schaff continued to inspire the internation-
alists while William E. Dodge, Jr. and Josiah Strong led
the nationalists.  Schaff's position must now be clarified
if the "new departure" begun in 1883 and made official
policy by 1886, with the hiring of Josiah Strong as general secretary, was to make sense—the Dodge-Strong nationalist social gospel program will be explained later.
Schaff took ecumenical ground of such irenic breadth that
he went beyond most internationalist and nationalist contemporaries and is now cited by scholars as significant to
modern ecumenism.  His peers in the American executive
structure sent him as their official representative, or
leading delegate if there were others, to most of the late
nineteenth century World Alliance meetings and usually
paid his expenses even if vacationing in Europe.[4]

        The breadth of Schaff's position may be seen in his
paper before the Copenhagen Conference (1884) on "The Discord and Concord of Christendom; or, Denominational Variety and Christian Unity."  In a startling affirmation for
an evangelical of his day, Dr. Schaff reminded his audience that the Greek, Roman Catholic, and Protestant divisions of Christendom were *all* valid elements of the Church.
Protestantism, nevertheless, represented a signal advance
over the other two in its achievement of evangelical freedom, direct access to scripture and God's grace, direct
union and communion with Christ, and general priesthood of
believers—hence the most powerful and progressive nations
of the world adhered to Protestantism and to civil and
religious liberty.  Such division, however, should not
justify that spirit of intolerance and exclusiveness which
enabled each body to believe it alone the true church of
Christ.  Schaff assured the Conference that denominationalism and confessionalism posed no danger to reunion as
long as they did not become sectarian.  "Denominationalism
or confessionalism grows out of the diversity of divine
gifts, and may co-exist with true catholicity and large-

hearted charity. But sectarianism is an abuse and excess
of denominationalism, and is nothing but extended selfishness," a selfishness destructive of the spirit of unity.
Schaff testified happily that tendencies towards reunion
were triumphing over sectarian exclusiveness.[5]

The compatibility of denominationalism and church
unity rooted in the divine law of unity in diversity.

> The one universal Church, founded by
> Christ for all ages and nations, is
> adapted to every grade of society and
> culture, from the lowest to the high-
> est....Every Christian church or denom-
> ination has its special charisma and
> mission, and there is abundant room and
> abundant labor for all in this great and
> wicked world. The Roman Church can not
> do the work of the Greek, nor the Protes-
> tant that of the Roman, nor the Lutheran
> that of the Reformed....The cause of
> Christ would be marred and weakened if
> any one of the historic churches should
> be extinguished, or be absorbed into an-
> other. Every denomination ought to be
> loyal to its own standards, and walk in
> the paths of its ancestry, provided only
> its *esprit de corps* do not degenerate
> into spiritual pride and sectarian
> bigotry.[6]

Convinced of the timelessness of historical truth, Dr.
Schaff noted the Christian Church lacked visible organic
unity despite apostolic adherence to one faith motivated
by one love. Consequently, history indicated unity of
spirit rather than unity of form essential for the Church.
God would retain the best of the historic church and eliminate human imperfection from it in His own good time. He
"would bring cosmos out of chaos, and overrule the discord
of Christendom for the deepest concord."[7]

Schaff believed firmly that duty required each man
sustain the finest of his particular religious tradition
while recognizing and cherishing the great agreement of
the churches in canonical scripture, creed, doctrine, tradition and morality. Fraternal fellowship ought to be
cultivated in such fashion that the constant search for
divine truth will be carried on in the spirit of love and
charity towards erring brethren; only spiritual weapons
may be used against sin and error. Moreover, history shows

all tendencies toward union must rise out of Christian
freedom, rather than coercion, and must preserve unity in
diversity.  One can look forward to the ultimate union of
evangelical Protestantism and evangelical Catholicism when
universal humiliation and repentance and the elimination
of error from the visible Church has been achieved.  "Then,
but not till then, may be realized the dream of a Johan-
nean Church of love that shall exclude all defects of the
Petrine Church of authority and the Pauline Church of
freedom, and melt the excellences of both into a higher
unity."[8]

This vision of the future church made it impossible
for Schaff to accept the Roman conception of unity, absorption of all other churches.  It also proscribed a negative fundamentalist union based on rejection of all distinctive creeds in favor of the Bible.  Such an approach
reduced the holy Catholic Church to a Bible society and
really could not undo history because any discussion of
the Bible would lead to a revival of theological schools
and churches.  Nor would it allow unity based upon an eclectic creed because religious parties found syncretistic
compounds unacceptable.  A creed must be an organic growth
whose living unity resulted from inspiration by the spirit
and truth.  Therefore the only possible basis for unity
was "a *conservative* union, which recognizes, from a broad
and comprehensive evangelical catholic platform, all the
creeds in their relative rights as far as they represent
different aspects of divine truth, without attempting an
amalgamation or organic union of denominations.  This
seems to us the only view which consists with a proper respect for God's work in the history of the past."  This
developing train of thought, so broad in its ecumenical
vision, reached full fruition in the paper which Dr. Schaff
presented to the World Parliament of Religions at Chicago
in 1893.[9]

Unhappily for world ecumenism, the American Alliance
turned its focus inward just when the international movement attempted to finish the work of the 1846 London Conference.  The Eighth General Conference of the World Alliance, held in Copenhagen in 1884, authorized creation of
an International Committee as a central executive.  Meeting during August 25-26, 1886, the Committee heeded Philip
Schaff's advice by submitting its organizational rules to
the national branches for their approval.  Dr. Schaff
hoped the American branch would endorse the rules subject
to the understanding that Committee decisions of a legislative character became effective only if ratified by
either the national bodies or General Conferences.  On the

other hand, both William E. Dodge, Jr. and John Jay, fellow members of the special American committee formed to
deal with this issue, disliked the International Committee
because it over-represented the insignificant branch Alliances, thereby threatening to bind the whole movement with
decisions passed by a bare and unrepresentative majority.
Their nationalist "Majority Report," paralleling contemporary American isolationism and abhorrence of entangling
military alliances, suggested Americans ought to remain
outside of, but sympathetic with, the International Committee: "It seems that the perfect freedom of action,
which in our own case is essential to command the confidence of the American people, and accomplish our weighty
work, whether national, state, or municipal, might be
gravely interfered with by being subjected to the powers
assumed by this Committee."[10]

The American Board of Managers endorsed the "Majority Report" with the understanding that its action did not
preclude cordial cooperation with the European brethren
and International Committee. Eventual reduction of the
Committee to an advisory status, a change which eliminated
what Josiah Strong considered the real bone of contention,
won ultimate American approval of the Committee at the
cost of precluding any possibility for development of cen-
tralized Protestant authority on the world level during
the nineteenth century. The Board decision reflected fear
of such authority as well as realization that American
evangelicals were far too concerned with national problems,
and possibly far too nationalistic, to affiliate with such
a foreign movement. As a former critic of the Alliance,
Episcopal clergyman J. H. Ward suggests,

> Before this organization became thoroughly
> American in spirit and purpose it was
> identified so closely with the English
> section of the Alliance that it failed to
> satisfy Churchmen as to the wisdom of its
> aims. It seemed to be in the hands of men
> whose religious sanity could be questioned.
> in its resuscitated form it has reached
> under their management a point of develop-
> ment where it represents very largely the
> methods by which the religious and social
> reforms of the community may be conducted
> with more satisfactory results than have
> heretofore been possible.[11]

This concern over American problems explains only
partially the American Alliance shift away from vigorous

international ecumenism towards a social gospel focus at
home.  The proliferation of denominational alliances and
congresses also induced American religious figures to re-
assess the proper relation of religious unity to cultural
problems.  The Presbyterian Alliance, an international organization of Presbyterian and Reformed denominations, was
the first such alliance.  James McCosh, Philip Schaff, and
William Blaikie prepared the way so well that plans for a
Presbyterian world body crystallized during the Evangelical Alliance Conference of New York (1873).  If Presbyterian efforts of 1873 jelled as an Alliance of Presbyterian
and Reformed at Edinburgh in 1877, Methodist discussions
of the mid-1870s bore fruit in the London Conference of
1881.  As was true of the Presbyterians, Methodist Bishop
E. O. Haven claimed the rising ecumenical spirit in his
world church family arose from Alliance activity: "much of
the improvement in the spirit of Christians toward each
other is due to meetings...of the Evangelical Alliance.
It is not true, as some superficial observers may think
that these meetings affect but little, because their results do not take immediate form.  They contribute to silent spiritual potencies, that work through all appropriate agencies, and renew the face of the earth."  Haven
concluded that "an Evangelical Alliance of our own, of
course subordinate to the great and general one, would
surely be followed by gracious results."  The difference
between trends toward denominational alliances and prewar
churchly efforts to eclipse evangelical ecumenism, by
stressing loyalty to the denomination above all else, is
that most leaders of late nineteenth century denominational ecumenism were major figures in the U.S. Alliance and
known for their breadth of ecumenism.[12]

     Nevertheless, birth of the first denominational al-
liances due to influences of the World and American Evangelical Alliances testify to the latter being almost too
successful in sponsoring Christian union.  As an untitled
article from the columns of the *New York Evangelist* pointed out in 1884, worldwide Presbyterian, Methodist, and
Anglican "organizations have sprung forth from the Evangelical Alliance, and they are largely doing the work which
it formerly accomplished," but with greater success due to
superior organization.  Furthermore, displacement of the
Evangelical Alliance occurred because "a higher conception
of Christian unity has arisen since the organization of
the Evangelical Alliance—a unity which consists not in
ignoring of all differences in order to unite on essentials
but a unity which consists in the mutual recognition and
toleration and free and manly discussion of differences
within the same organization."  Such an observation

obviously ignored the fact that members of the same church
group could discuss doctrine more fully than an Alliance
involving members of diverse church groups, yet it will be
repeated often during the 1880s by men like Episcopal
Bishop A. Cleveland Coxe. American Alliance leaders understood the implications of the article recommendation that
the world body foster interdenominational cooperation, concerning the common interests of Protestantism, either by
an executive commission embracing all denominations or
through denominational alliance representation on the Evangelical Alliance executive board. They heeded the article
warning that the World Alliance verged on a colorless evangelicalism pleasing to no one which would force out the
better elements unless it adjusted to the times.[13]

In February of the same year, Bishop Coxe criticized
the American branch per se. Coxe thought Christian disunity, compounded by Christian individualism, scattered
that moral and social strength needed by Christianity to
checkmate the monstrous social evils which threatened the
work of America's forefathers. He hoped a great Christian
Alliance might be created in America out of the fusion of
the National Reform Association——a body desiring to amend
the Constitution to make Christianity the official national religion——and the Evangelical Alliance, subject to the
liberalization of their membership and goal requirements.
As far as the Alliance was concerned, Coxe applauded recent
activities to defeat the Freedom of Worship bills and other
Roman Catholic assaults on the nation, but charged its
Basis divided Protestants at a time when preservation of
Christian civilization required unity. Applauding Horace
Bushnell's criticisms towards the Alliance of a generation
ago, Coxe believed the Basis kept thousands outsides its
ranks, particularly in Europe where the term evangelical
means Calvinistic and alienated Methodists and Lutherans
devoted to the cause of unity. He also criticized the Alliance method of union as an agreement to avoid discussion
of religious differences. In his mind, the properly formulated movement allowed men of divergent convictions to
cooperate "for practical efforts in the nation, or for social ends limited, *in spite of* real differences...openly
avowed and understood." American Protestants had to cooperate "to develop and maintain Christianity as the social base of our people."[14]

As the American actions concerning the International
Committee suggest, the type of criticism in the *New York
Evangelical* proved less germane than that set forth by
Coxe. The Alliance would continue to foster Christian
union and religious liberty but the cumulative impact of

cultural and religious pluralism and urban-industrial dis-
locations during the 1870s and 1880s inspired the U.S.
body to reformulate its program towards one of social mission.  The process of reformulation occupied the period
from 1883-1886.  It began under the auspices of such elder
statesmen as William E. Dodge, Sr. and Samuel Irenaeus
Prime only to be carried out by a younger generation of
men like William E. Dodge, Jr., R. R. McBurney, Henry B.
Chapin, George Wenner, James King, Josiah Strong, R. Fulton Cutting, and Charles Stoddard.  Many of the latter belonged to the movement during the 1870s and rose to power
with the death and retirement of their predecessors.  This
three-year reassessment of goals revolved around the need
for reviving the national conference, appointing a general
agent and delineating his duties, and promoting Christian
unity, religious liberty and practical Christian cooperation.  The Alliance desired a salaried and permanent general secretary as early as April of 1883 but financial
difficulty required a voluntary general secretary relying
on borrowed quarters.  This personage acted as librarian
and correspondent.[15]

     As pointed out in Chapter Five, refinement of goals
and program led to streamlining of the Alliance structure.
This constitutional reorganization is noteworthy in two
ways.  First, reorganization of the Executive Committee
obliged the newly-elected President and social gospel advocate, William E. Dodge, Jr., to appoint a new slate of
men; a businessman and layperson was really making major
decisions for an important evangelical body.  His selection placed a coterie of younger men in power:  Chairman,
Rev. James King; R. R. McBurney; Rev. Charles Stoddard;
Rev. Merritt Hulburd; Rev. R. S. MacArthur; John Jay and
John Paton.  They were chosen to carry the heavy burdens
of an expanded program which the elder statesmen were too
old to sustain.  Careful perusal of the "Minutes," however
shows these past executive officers participated actively
in Executive Committee meetings as constitutionally desig-
nated *ex officio* members and also influenced the decisions
of the Board of Managers, the governing body of the Alliance.  Second, the constitution required that the Executiv
Committee fill the newly-created position of "General
Agent" or Secretary.  Difficulty still arose concerning
definition of that office because Alliance long-term goals
had not solidified.  For a time, it appeared the general
secretary might mobilize evangelical forces in New York
State for defense of religious freedom and separation of
church and state, but Executive Committee refusal to cooperate with the overly-narrow "Central Committee for Protecting and Perpetuating the Separation of Church and Stat

in fund-raising and propaganda efforts kept Alliance ave-
nues of change open.  The secretary's role became clearer
by November 1885, when the Executive Committee revived the
biennial and national conference technique of the 1870s
and planned a national conference, to be held in Washington, D.C., for December of 1886.  In April 1886, it decided to "enter upon an enlarged and aggressive work" with
the help of a permanent general secretary which it hoped
to choose as soon as the financial means became available.[16]

        In an attempt to win wide support for the projected
conference, President William E. Dodge, Jr. used his extensive social and religious influence to gather approxi-
mately 150 important Protestants at a reception in his
home.  Such major figures as John Jay, Arthur Brooks,
James M. King, William R. Huntington, Lyman Abbott, Robert
S. MacArthur, James McCosh, Bishop John F. Hurst and Russell Sturgis, Jr. gave short but spirited addresses favoring an expanded program for the Alliance.  As minister to
Brooklyn's Plymouth Church Lyman Abbott recorded, "in a
few terse words," President Dodge "outlined the great problems presented for solution before the American people—
the relation of religion to education, Mormonism, the temperance question, evangelistic work in the cities, the
labor problem, etc." —and called for Christian cooperation
in their solution.  Although the content of others' statements is not known, President Dodge captured their intent
in a June address to the Executive Committee.  He persuaded
the Executive body to return to committee the preliminary
plan for the Washington Conference with the instruction
that speakers be selected to represent all denominations
and regions of the nation.  Thematically, the Committee
must stress the "possibility and necessity of cordial cooperation of the various denominations in studying the
great and pressing questions of the times, and in working
together to prove the certain adaptation of the simple
teachings of Christ to solve all such questions.  Secondly,
to give full time for the discussion by the Conference of
the practical methods of such united action."[17]

        Rev. George B. Safford, secretary for the Committee
on Conferences, expanded on this theme in his official capacity.  The Washington Conference was part of a larger
Alliance plan to "manifest and strengthen Christian unity,
and to promote cooperation in Christian work" so obviously
lacking among denominational agencies.  Such cooperation
was absolutely necessary if the individually weak denominations were to coalesce sufficient power for the gospel to
triumph over the perils facing Christianity in America.[18]

     The Committee on National Conferences—William E.
Dodge, Jr., Rev. L. T. Chamberlain, Rev. Charles Stoddard
and R. R. McBurney—had the duty of initiating the expanded Alliance program by laying the groundwork for the Washington Conference.  After several months of effort, the
four men discovered the program still suffered "a certain
fundamental lack in conception."  By October 22, the Committee gave the Executive Committee a different program
based upon conclusions "neither wholly new nor largely
novel" to Alliance tradition, yet suited to the varied
challenges of the time.  Its catalog of perils reflected
evangelical experience concerning increasing cultural complexity, pluralism and moral corruption in the United
States.  The crisis appeared immense:

          There is something in the sheer vastness
          of modern movements—social, intellectual,
          moral—something in their very rise and
          rush and range, which distinguishes this
          period from all that have preceded.

               'The wicked now
          'Are winged like angels.  Every knife
            that strikes
          'Is edged from elemental fire, to assail
          'A spiritual life.'[19]

Immigration swelled the population and contributed a dangerous heterogeneity to culture and religion (especially
as it appeared the mainstay of the new labor union movement which seemed to threaten capitalism).  Population
shifted to the cities and overflowed the western frontier,
thereby changing the context and locus of power for American culture.  The geometric growth of Roman Catholics and
the expansion of Mormonism into states neighboring Utah
threatened the political fabric of the Republic.  (Evangelicals assumed both religions so controlled their members that they voted according to Church dictates, thereby threatening that independence of mind requisite to democracy.  Evangelicals also held Mormonism repugnant for
its polygamy and assumed crimes of violence.)  To cap it
all, a high level of illiteracy and intemperance provided
the means for socialism and secularism to attack the moral
base of America at the very time when a "tendency to class
distinctions within" "and without the Church" (evangelical
denominations now appealed primarily to the middle class)
hindered the one agency capable of defending the nation.
These developments were "evil" because they threatened the
reality upon which American evangelical identity rested.
Introduction of conflicting moralities, cultural attach-

ments and religious allegiances augured ill for the evangelical Religion of the Republic and its national mission.
How could evangelical America transmit its high culture,
morality, and proper religious perspective to the world if
America ceased to be evangelical?  The dangers appeared to
be real.  The American mission was at stake.[20]

     Despite this gloomy picture, the report offered much
hope.  The American heritage and resources—a nation resting upon "Christian principles, customs, institutions,"
and general public adherence to the "inspirations of Biblical truths"—provided sufficient basis for Christian
forces to unite according to "loyal cooperation" and to
meet successfully the emergency.  Although the record of
evangelical comity is flawed, tradition and present position providentially designed the Alliance to guide the
faithful to victory.  "It stands, in doctrine, upon the
Catholic basis of Evangelical Christendom.  It possesses
the confidence of the churches of every name.  It has a
clear possibility, and to some extent a reality of organization adapted to the required service.  In its genesis
and genius it is an alliance.  By its very terms therefore,
it honors each ally.  There is nothing to forbid its re-
joicing in the distinctive success of each and every member of its great federation."  The new mission therefore
would be true to Alliance tradition.  General Conferences
would be councils of war preparing for future campaigns
through analysis of past ones.  Alliance publications
would broadcast their findings across the nation.  Careful
proliferation of branch Alliances would provide local
agents to mobilize assaults upon the "common perils of the
land."  The report, in effect, called for the application
of past cooperative methods to the total spectrum of national problems, not simply to Christian union and religious liberty.  This new departure replaced implicitly the
old conferences method of cooperation-in-discussion, concerning religious problems, with one of cooperation-to-
wards-action involving problems of society as well as religion.  The only thing hindering fulfillment of such a program, the report suggested, was the absence of a suitable
secretary to coordinate activity.  Although Congregationalist minister Josiah Strong's name was not mentioned,
committee interviews indicated he might be contracted if
the Alliance adopted this strategy.  William E. Dodge, Jr.
and his three colleagues were struck with the notion that
God reared Strong for Alliance service and the Alliance
for divine mission: "There exist, then, the crisis of
peril, the sufficient resources, the providential organization, the seemingly appointed man."[21]

Sydney Ahlstrom asserts correctly that Josiah Strong
"was the dynamo, the revivalist, the organizer, and alto-
gether the most irresponsible spirit of the Social Gospel
movement" whose contributions were such that there might
not have been a movement without him. Using Ahlstrom's
language but changing its focus, a boundless "confidence
in applied science and guided evolution" characterized
Strong's approach to organization and made his overall
perspective so modern, telling and appealing to many contemporaries. He participated in what historian Robert
Wiebe characterized as America's turn-of-the-century
"search for order" underneath seeming urban chaos.[22]

Proud heir to a New England cultural heritage and
graduate of Lyman Beecher's Lane Theological Seminary
(1871), Josiah Strong held various home mission and regular Congregationalist pastorates from Cheyenne, Wyoming to
Cincinnati, Ohio. His first book, *Our Country: Its Possible Future and Its Present Crisis* (1885), catapulted
Strong to evangelical leadership and helped to precipitate
the social gospel movement. Its almost electric message
combined the traditional home mission argument that the
barbaric American West must be won to evangelical republicanism for the health of the nation, with a new perception
that an equally barbaric city had emerged as the "nerve
center" of modern American society. His lifelong message
juxtaposed an evangelical jeremiad of American declension
with the hope of so saving American souls, and advancing
what was, in effect, the evangelical Religion of the Republic, that the Kingdom of God would be established on
all earth. In Lyman Abbott's words, Strong wished to create the "Republic of God" on earth. The first step, to
sustain the evangelical republic itself, called for restoration of good citizenship and government while prescrib-
ing denominational cooperative support for a radically
Christian stewardship, towards westerners and urbanites,
as the only remedy for the crisis.[23]

Given the crisis, organization and prophetic leader,
both the Alliance Executive Committee and subsequent October 29 session of the Board of Managers responded enthusiastically to this momentous Committee on National Conferences' report. The Board was convinced, "as representative of the evangelical sentiment of the Christian churches, and [given] the great needs of the times," the Alliance must "study carefully and wisely, the various perils
and conditions which at present menace the Christian
Church." It ordered the Executive Committee to gather
"information and statistics" which would educate the Christian public concerning its peril and convince the

denominations of the necessity for cooperation in their
extremity. The Christian leadership should be prepared to
transform the Alliance conferences into national tools for
cooperative effort and to create branch Alliances as local
vehicles of cooperation. The Executive Committee must
elaborate further such plans for practical cooperation—at
all levels of rural, town and city life—"as shall give
directness and force to the deliberations of the conferences and gatherings which may be held."[24]

The final action of the Board during this extraordi-
nary October 29 session was to approve Josiah Strong,
sight unseen, as General Secretary. In addition to the
official letter asking Strong to be General Secretary,
William E. Dodge, Jr. wrote under his own hand to explain
the full context and meaning of the invitation. Noting
that congenial unanimity ruled this momentous Board meeting, Dodge emphasized to Strong that Rev. Robert S. Mac-
Arthur, the leading New York Baptist clergyman, appeared
unwilling to cooperate with the new program during the
summer, but now "not only heartily endorsed all that was
done & promised money and aid; but in addition proposed
that his newly renovated and enlarged church, which is one
of the finest in the country, should be the place where a
reception should be given you by the Alliance as a house-
warming for the building." Dodge assured Strong, "this
for his denomination means very much," implying that even
"conservative" elements of the Baptist fold might support
the new program far more than the old. After describing
the proposed plans in detail (a program which arose from
Alliance imperatives, but appears to have been formulated
in terms congenial to Strong after previous consultation
with him), and noting those specific areas of Board discussion, Dodge emphasized the Board thought the nation
"ripe for a larger work—that American needs, common sympathies & American dangers had prepared the hearts of
Christian people of all names to co-operate heartily under
new leadership—And, all felt the Alliance was called to
the work & had before it the possibility of a work for the
Master & the Country greater than anything this century
had seen." President Dodge assured Strong,[25]

> ...nothing could be more delightful than
> the perfect unanimity and cordiality with
> which your nomination and election were
> made. The whole thing from the beginning
> has been so strangely led & marked by Pro-
> vidence—Our plans taken out of our own
> hands—as to the Conference at Washington—
> and as we have studied & prayed—a strong,

positive light has seemed to open a great
work & a great need.

Your name has come to us with the same
leading from above. Your own study & preparation & experiences all lead in the same
way & as stated in the Resolution sent to
you, I believe the office tendered you, so
cordially, can easily be made, with proper
study, organization & work on the part of
all of us, equal to any in the land for
effective influence & usefulness.[26]

Dodge concluded with promise of full support and creation
of valuable friends all over the land if Strong joined in
the proposed work.[27]

Josiah Strong accepted and was invested with office
at a special session of the Board on December 27, 1886. At
this meeting, the Board approved Dr. Strong's revision of
the October Report, a revision authorized by the powerful
Committee on National Conferences. The support of this
enlarged body—Rev. C. A. Stoddard, Rev. L. T. Chamberlain,
John Jay, C. T. Rowe, R. R. McBurney, Rev. Henry B. Chapin,
and William E. Dodge, Jr.—assured a speedy and successful
hearing for Strong's revision.[28]

The Alliance and Josiah Strong were ready for a social gospel program because both, during the late 1870s
and early 1880s, underwent a parallel evolution in their
understanding of the demands which the changing character
of American religion and civilization required of evangelicals. Both the man and the ecumenical body desired to convert the multinational, heavily Roman Catholic and Jewish
urbanites to the evangelical Religion of the Republic, to
"Americanize" them. On the other hand, both tended toward
activist assessment and then adjustment of those elements
of American culture which proved harmful to protesting mi-
norities and could be changed so as to enhance the evangelical base. Each evolved logically from anti-Catholic
stance to energetic social gospelism (which still included
anti-Catholicism), premised upon basic evangelical belief.
Both aspired to creation of an *evangelical* kingdom of God
on earth but realized cooperation of Protestants of all
hues essential to success. The Alliance however lacked a
full-time dynamic leader and the man aspired to a national
base for his operation. Both responded enthusiastically
to their mutual discovery. Consequently, the October Report declared providence hid Strong until the Alliance was
ready to use his services. The Alliance found Strong

really attractive because of similarities of conception,
and Strong found the Alliance appealing because its developing program and potential for great national activity
could help him redirect and strengthen evangelical Protestantism in its purpose and programs.  This mutual compatibility of the movement and the man proved for harmonious
relations from 1886 until 1898 when the man veered too far
away from the evangelical center, at which time the movement and the man gladly parted company.[29]

        Josiah Strong restated the themes of the October Re-
port with rhetorical insight clearly his own.  Issued as
Alliance *Document* XXII and later as part of *Document* XXV,
it sounded the clarion call for evangelical America to
mobilize against the perils of the time.  True to Strong's
*Our Country* and the Committee on National Conferences'
October Report, the December Report assessed the manifold
perils facing the nation and prescribed a remedy which
evangelicals could understand: "The gospel is the great
remedy for the evils which afflict us.  Wise legislation
and education can do much to mitigate them, but cannot
eradicate them.  Sin is the root evil of society.  God's
remedy for sin, therefore, is the radical remedy for these
evils."  But, the gospel cannot be carried effectively to
the nation without organization and cooperation.  Strong
knew organization was the key to success "whether in commercial, business, political, or religious enterprise" in
the nineteenth century.  Because careful cooperation would
reinforce every denomination, he thought the Alliance impelled by providence to guide the cooperative organization
of churches.  The term cooperation, however, did not imply
any intention to sponsor organic unity.  Strong did not
want any such misunderstanding to alienate the denominations from the movement.  "We recognize both the existing
necessity and value of sanctified denominationalism, which
has its roots in historic values, and in difference of
taste, temperament, adaptation, and methods.  We seek not
a union of denominations, but the organization of individuals for the cooperation of denominations."[30]

        And, in tune with the more pragmatic nature of the
new Alliance program, cooperation would contribute to another practical goal, the Christianization of American
civilization.  Evangelicals now realized their euphoria
over attaining this state by 1870 proved premature in the
light of subsequent urban and industrial crises, particularly the railroad strikes of 1877 and the very upsetting
Haymarket anarchist bombing and riot of May 1886.  Since
its beginnings, the Alliance knew achievement of its goals
required education of the public.  Recognizing the great

power public opinion exercised over the affairs of men, it
seemed obvious that mobilization of the churches would redirect public opinion and thereby eliminate the perils
blocking attainment of a Christian America.  Implementation of such a goal obviously implied practical action.
The Report suggested a modified plan for using traditional
methods: completion of a grass roots branch system and mobilization of national conferences and a central headquar-
ters to distribute information and educate the public.  It
assumed the basic problem at hand to be ignorance concerning the causes and nature of American problems.  This information gap would be remedied in part by proliferation
of local and state Alliances.  They would channel information to the national body and transmit Alliance know-how
to the local churches.  Acquisition of information on the
local level would be facilitated by a radically new method
of information discovery, borrowed by Strong from Rev.
Frank Russell, called house-to-house visitation.  Believing "the very first step toward a *better* condition of
things is an accurate knowledge of the existing condition
of things," the report insisted that interviewing personally the populations of whole regions and cities essential
to success.[31]

The national conferences would educate the public
further by providing information derived from practical
experience concerning the solution of the various problems
facing the nation.  Each successful conference would increase the popular audience for the next so that the publication of conference proceedings would eventually take
evangelical solutions to the bulk of the nation.  In order
to assure the proper mushrooming effect of the conferences,
the Report called for a year's delay in the projected
Washington Conference in order to expand the branch Alliance system.  This conference process and resultant published record would complement the visitation system by
providing the informational resources to enable the Alliance to function properly as a bureau of information for
the evangelical world.[32]

The Report emitted a spirit of enthusiasm, despite
the magnitude of the undertaking, because its authors were
imbued with that sense of staggering world mission inherent in the evangelical identity——"the Alliance is called
of God to a sublime opportunity.  To save our American
civilization and thoroughly season it with the salt of
Christianity is to give a Christian civilization to the
world."  Of course, the published version of this statement claimed this a mission of the churches, rather than
the Alliance——one must avoid arousing denominational fear

that the Alliance aspired to become a superchurch. The
Board of Managers endorsed the suggested campaign in toto
and instructed the Executive Committee to begin immediate
implementation. Achievement of consensus as to direction
and methodology freed such an enormous pool of energy that
the Alliance launched into twelve of the most vigorous
years of its existence. It sponsored three major national
conferences, published numerous documents, carried out
grass root campaigns to develop local and state Evangelical Alliances, and injected into the church scene a socio-
logical technique—the information canvass—which provided
the first concrete factual information concerning church
constituencies and their problems. Although this program
never succeeded fully, it did inform Americans about those
problems of modern civilization which hindered winning
completely the people to evangelical Christianity.[33]

By 1889, the change in public image was such that a
once hostile Episcopal critic Rev. J. H. Ward considered
the American Alliance responsible for setting that properly board tone of spirit needed to guide the denominations
to a common purpose. The American body now realized self-
congratulations, made by the evangelicals of the 1870s
concerning the successful Christianization of the nation,
smacked of irrelevance when America appeared to be undergoing a general moral and spiritual degeneration affecting
all aspects of its culture. The masses no longer seemed
to attend church. The sanctity of the family and home appeared to be in question. And, the clergy was declining
in stature. Even preaching the gospel no longer answered
fully those problems. For instance, lawyer, professor, and
former U.S. minister to Britain Anson D. Phelps praised
Alliance work and its Washington Conference to William E.
Dodge, Jr. He informed Dodge that "free government means
to us a government in the hands of the lowest and worst
class of foreigners, organized and stimulated by dema-
gogues of our own race and theirs" (sentiments expressed
already in somewhat more low key fashion by Josiah Strong
in *Our Country*). Phelps asserted categorically,[34]

> Unless we can take up arms against this
> influx of foreigners, and the suicidal
> policy that makes them all voters as soon
> as they arrive (virtually, for the natural-
> ization laws are a farce), we shall see a
> condition of things before long to which
> the Southern Rebellion was child's play.
> The dying out of religious faith to so
> large an extent among the masses of so-
> called 'Protestants' seems to me another

> dangerous feature in our modern life.  And
> politics, certainly, descends to a lower
> depth at each turn of the wheel.  I cannot
> assume to propose a remedy.  It is well for
> such men as compose the Alliance to take
> counsel together.
>
> My own view is that free government can-
> not be made to stand except by a thorough
> purification of the electorate, which in
> this country should include the exclusion
> of all foreigners.  Through what revolution
> this is to be accomplished no one can now
> predict.  Probably through an intermediate
> military despotism.[35]

The Alliance, of course, never endorsed such extreme views,
although it did partake of the middle and upper class
Anglo-Saxon racism and crisis mentality implicit in Phelps'
statement.  The evangelical Republic was in grave danger!

The source of difficulty was that much of evangelical Protestantism broke away from the common man when its
constituency became middle class at midcentury.  Many of
those churches which were evangelical from their inception,
such as the Methodist and large portions of the Baptist
folds, appealed originally to the simple rural and mill
town folk of America.  Yet their emphasis on the work ethic and insistence that members avoid such corrupting (and
expensive) habits as liquor, tobacco, and theatre meant
evangelicals accumulated property and rose in social
standing to a middle class status.  Their situation im-
proved further, as was true of most native Americans, when
rapid post-Civil War industrialization drew so many foreign immigrants into the labor pool that a concomitant
growth in the managerial and white collar force was essential.  The latter opportunities fell primarily to those
having mastery over the American language and cultural
values.  Evangelicals, particularly those in the urban
areas, benefited enormously from these new positions but
tended to look askance at the increasingly heterogeneous
labor force at their disposal.  One reason Protestantism
lost track of the common man was not just that he was increasingly an immigrant, for many important evangelicals
such as German Reformed become Presbyterian Philip Schaff
(Swiss) and Methodist William Nast (German) were of European origin, but that many of the immigrants after 1880
derived from southern and eastern Europe.  For example,
roughly one million persons came from that area compared
to four million from northern Europe during the decade

from 1880 to 1890. Although this "new immigration" did not
exceed annually that from northern Europe until after 1896,
it changed significantly the cultural context of American
labor. The new immigration displaced that of Germanic origin as the source of *unskilled* laborers in American indus-
try and mining. Nearly all Americans (and this may even
be true of the Indians) originated from immigrant ancestors
but, until the 1880s, most came from Germanic and Celtic
sources. If pre-Civil War evangelicals had religious and
cultural difficulties with the English-speaking Irish, they
now found an almost incomprehensible gap between themselves
and the Latin Catholics, Greek Orthodox, and eastern Jews,
given the strange languages and peasant customs of the
latter.

In the beginning, few evangelicals thought this separation from the common man important and even fewer, some
liberals, realized that reforms and social service as well
as heartfelt preaching of the gospel were in order if the
masses and the nation were not to be lost permanently.
Josiah Strong was one such liberal, and his recruitment by
the Alliance shows its commitment to the investigation and
repair of the health of Protestantism and the nation. As
John Hutchison points out, the steadily growing Alliance
made Josiah Strong General Secretary to foster the social
gospel. "Strong, who had just come into national prominence for his book *Our Country,* was one of the first religious leaders to concern himself with social reform and
social service. Preaching a new gospel which 'changes environment' as well as individuals, which was directed not
only to the soul or spirit but to the whole man, which
spoke of applying the teachings of Jesus to human society
and of building the kingdom of God on earth, Strong was a
pioneer in the social gospel and social service."[36]

Born in Napierville, Illinois, on January 19, 1847,
Josiah Strong grew up in an evangelical Congregationalist
family committed to social causes and proud that the famous abolitionist actor in "bloody Kansas" (1855-1858) and
the later raid on Harpers Ferry (1859), John Brown, stayed
in the Strong home and regaled boy and family with stories
concerning his just cause. Graduating from seminary in
1871, Josiah became a Congregationalist missionary on the
western frontier in Cheyenne, Wyoming, and thereafter held
successive positions as: chaplain and instructor at Western
Reserve College; pastor in Sandusky, Ohio; Superintendent
of the Home Missionary Society of Ohio, Kentucky, West Virginia, and Western Pennsylvania; and pastor of the Vine
Street Congregational Church of Cincinnati, Ohio. These
experiences gave Strong such breadth of insight that his

revision of the Home Missionary Society pamphlet, *Our Country,* restated old themes, inherent in home mission literature from the time of Lyman Beecher and Horace Bushnell,
with such timely and persuasive stress on the challenge of
both urban and disappearing rural frontiers that he catapulted to national prominence—Josiah Strong propounded
the frontier thesis of American democracy well before historian Frederick Jackson Turner but was far more sanguine
about the survival of democracy in the urban world than
the latter.  His connection with the 1885 Cincinnati Interdenominational Congress contributed further to his preparation for the Alliance by familiarizing him with Rev. Frank
Russell's visitation system and other social gospel techniques.  Russell later summarized his efforts in an Alliance pamphlet, at Strong's behest, and then joined the Alliance as field secretary in 1888.[37]

       Merging with developing social Christianity, however,
did not imply Alliance repudiation of the evangelical tradition.  In fact, most of the leaders and supporters of
the social gospel were evangelical!  Soon after Josiah
Strong entered office, the Executive Committee and Board of
Managers stressed the evangelical nature of their movement
by reaffirming the Alliance Basis in its entirety.  Philip
Schaff managed to liberalize the conditions of membership
to allow a person to sympathize with, rather than endorse,
the principles of the Alliance, but the Board insisted the
sympathizer be evangelical.  Only cooperation among those
of similar identity seemed possible.  Still, it became
easier to work with the Alliance after revision of Article
II in the constitution: "The object of this Association
shall be the furtherance of religious opinion with the intent to manifest and strengthen Christian unity, and to
promote religious liberty and cooperation in Christian work
without interfering with the internal affairs of different
denominations."  As President Dodge later suggested to
Episcopal Bishop Alonzo Potter, the new Alliance policy
freed branch Alliances and affiliated societies from manda-
tory adherence to the Basis, thereby removing a source of
irritation to the Bishop and other contemporaries.  Such
changes won the Alliance greater breadth of membership but
still proved restrictive enough to embroil it in controversy from time to time.[38]

       The Alliance also continued its policy of avoiding
theological debate.  Even as late as 1895, Josiah Strong
resigned an editorial position with Rev. George Herron's
the *Kingdom* because the Executive Committee feared his association with this periodical might compromise Alliance
programs by dragging the social mission of the church,

applied Christianity, into the theological arena.  Realizing the wisdom inherent in this policy, Strong, in turn,
warned the *Kingdom* that men of all theological stamp could
be convinced of the necessity and utility of applied Christianity only if theological issues were ignored: "I believe
it to be true that we have no theology in harmony with the
established results of science and of scientific criticism,
and we are bound to have a new theology, *but let that come
later.  If the movement in behalf of applied Christianity
becomes identified with a strange theology (Whether true
or false) it will postpone the acceptance of her social
mission, by the church, for an entire generation.*"[39]

By May of 1887, this rapid chain of policy decisions
enabled the Alliance to turn much of its attention toward
preparation for the Washington Conference.  Although the
bulk of the details fell upon Josiah Strong's shoulders,
he was ably supported by others.  President Dodge, for example, used his extensive influence through personal correspondence to obtain public endorsement of men like Bishop A. Cleveland Coxe, despite their earlier criticism, for
the Alliance program and projected conference.  The new
Alliance image coupled with the able leadership of men like
Dodge and Strong bore great fruit.  The elite of American
Protestantism signed the "Call for the Washington Conference."  Forty-six of those eighty-six figures—men like
Methodist Bishop John F. Hurst, Moravian Bishop Edmund de
Schweinitz, Baptist and University of Rochester President
Martin B. Anderson, and President of Princeton, James Mc-
Cosh—were members of the Alliance as of June 1886, and
many had belonged since the 1870s.  Of those identifiable
according to religious persuasion, there were ten Methodist bishops, four Episcopalian bishops, two Presybyterian
Moderators, two Moravian bishops, one Congregationalist
Moderator  as well as three Congregationalist, one Presbyterian, one Methodist, and one Dutch Reformed college
presidents.  Obviously, the Alliance now appealed to the
denominational power structure more than ever before.  Of
the remaining 42 identified, 34 were prominent clergymen—
several holding powerful editorial positions.  In aggregate,
there were 18 Presbyterians, 17 Methodists, 12 Congregationalists, 8 Episcopalians, 4 Baptists, 3 Dutch Reformed,
2 Lutherans, 2 Moravians, 2 Quakers, and 1 Disciple of
Christ.  Although the Presbyterian and Reformed were still
represented in strength, the attachment of ten Methodist
bishops (both north and south) represented a heavy influx
from the largest *organized* evangelical denominations to
the Alliance cause.  The addition of some Baptists, Quakers
and even a Disciple editor indicates the exclusivist
Arminian groups found the Alliance appealing

in this age of crisis.    Finally, it   should be
noted that many of these religious leaders were southern.
The net effect of the new departure therefore was to make
the Alliance more denominationally acceptable, nationally
representative (although still urban in orientation), and
socially concerned.  It had always been evangelically liberal theologically and to some extent politically, but now
appealed as well to leading social and economic theorists
and activists.[40]

        That the Washington Conference was intended to mobi-
lize evangelical social activism may be seen in the crisis
mentality and careful rhetoric of the general secretary.

> Thoughtful men are convinced that the
> closing years of the nineteenth century
> constitute a momentous crisis in the his-
> tory of the nation.  There is a march of
> events which will not tarry.  The neces-
> sity of planting Christian institutions
> in the formative West, and of strengthening
> them in the older states, the duty of
> overtaking the rapid growth of our cities
> with adequate church provision, the impor-
> tance of closing the widening chasm between
> the church and the multitude, and of bring-
> ing the regenerative power of the gospel to
> bear upon every character and life, demand
> the instant recognition of the Christian
> church and the full exercise of all its
> energies.[41]

The only remedy for these faults in American civilization,
declared Strong, was application of the gospel through intelligent, comprehensive cooperation.[42]

        Convened from December 7-9, 1887, the Washington Con-
ference informed its vast audience, and nation as well, of
the perils confronting American civilization and the interdenominational application of the social teachings of Jesus
to their solution.  As John Hutchinson suggests, the "tenor
of this conference was set by the opening address of the
president."  Dodge made clear the Conference resulted from
careful study by the Board of Managers of the vast social
and economic changes affecting the nation.  That study revealed the need for a permanent general secretary to educate Christians concerning the nature and solution of national problems, as well as the power requisite to their
solution.  Interdenominational competition heretofore
undercut the potential power of American Christianity, "a

power which, if wisely directed, could bring to bear upon
all social questions and all disturbing elements the influence of the simple teachings of Christ, which we believe
contain the solvent for all perils and dangers, and which
can alone bring about a real brotherhood and mutual confidence between all classes and conditions of people." Such
"*applied Christianity*" can meet all the needs and relations
of man to man and make the brotherhood of man under the
fatherhood of God, "in one household," the watchword of the
church. President Dodge advised his auditors that these
various ends required local Christian resolution. He assured the audience such cooperation would not endanger denominational integrity and would increase the spiritual
health, vigor and unity of the church.[43]

In a similar vein, Methodist Bishop Edward G. Andrews,
Vice-President of the Washington, D.C., Alliance, thought the
words *peril, opportunity, cooperation,* central to the meaning of the conference. As was true of the chorus of speakers that followed he paralleled President Dodge's analysis
of the perils facing the nation and pinpointed their roots
in "the persistent evil of human nature itself." Citing
the experience of Lyman Beecher with the 1818 disestablish-
ment of Congregationalism in Connecticut, the Bishop warned
that apparent threats to the church might prove beneficial
ultimately: "It is possible thus that some of the things
which we fear, things not sinful in themselves, may turn in
ways which we do not now know to the furtherance of the
Gospel. I speak of urban growths, of immigration, of Romanism in America, and of some forms of socialistic tendency." Providential reservation of America for Christian
people consequently offered further help and, if the nation
does its duty, it will hasten the coming of the "kingdom of
God" to earth. "It marks an advance in the Kingdom of God
among men, that the great evangelical bodies, having at
length reached a *consensus* of essential doctrine (a *consensus* set forth with rare wisdom by the First Evangelical
Alliance held in London in 1846), are now disposed to busy
themselves less with controversy concerning creeds and
governments and ceremonies, and more with the practical
application of Christianity to the salvation of individuals
and of society. They tend to concord and co-operation."
Bishop Andrews reminded his audience the Alliance and its
Conference did not presume to define the true character of
the Church or to interfere with the role of the denominations as the Christianizing force in the United States.
Rather, the Alliance and Conference proposed to clarify
that unity underlying religious diversity. Inherent unity
could be made apparent "not by impracticable efforts at
uniformity, not by direct efforts to belittle the signifi-

cance of our characteristic differences, but by a new vision in each church, of the supreme importance of the end
for which all churches stand, namely, righteousness."[44]

        The papers which followed that of Andrews, on Decem-
ber 7th and 8th, dealt with particular topics of peril
such as "The City as Peril," "Immigration," "The Misuse of
Wealth," "Estrangement from the Church," "Ultramontanism"
and "The Saloon."  These detailed elaborations of themes
mentioned by Dodge and Andrews heightened the sense of
danger facing evangelical Americans, thereby preparing the
audience for the last, and in many ways most important,
day of the conference.  Friday's presentation capped the
earlier ones by stressing cooperation among evangelicals
as the means to solving American problems.  The arguments
in favor of cooperation are varied and will take some explanation before the understood character of the term is
clear.  Rev. Richard Storrs, for example, cited evangelical disunity and rivalry as breaking that "law" of cooperation inherent in the nineteenth century, thereby enabling
destructive forces to well up unopposed on the American
scene.  Business, government, reform and labor movements
all used this law so successfully that Storrs knew evangelicals mistakenly feared that cooperation led to organic
union.  To the contrary, he affirmed cooperation short of
organic union as quite sufficient to make "our Christian
civilization secure and permanent."[45]

        This tendency to see preservation of evangelical
civilization as the ultimate goal of cooperation appears
again and again in subsequent speeches.  Like Storrs,
Methodist Bishop Samuel S. Harris argued only cooperative
Christian effort could assure the survival of that Protestant character of American civilization which rested on
the principles of the fatherhood of God and the brotherhood of man laid down by Jesus of Nazareth.  Providence
indicated America may be the site for completion of the
divine plan,but this wondrous development will not occur
unless Christians band together against the organized
forces of evil.  Although such evil rooted in human sin,
the gospel remedy could not be implemented until cooperation replaced Protestant division.  Only when cooperation
reveals those key Christian truths heretofore obscured, by
lesser verities and mere opinion, will evangelicals manage
to "fulfill the mind of Christ and to convert the world."[46]

        In reference to the problem of Protestant division,
Congregationalist and social gospel leader Washington
Gladden denied any desire for uniformity of belief, polity
or ritual.  Divine power expressed itself in so many ways

that diversity of operation could not be avoided but must
not be used to justify denominational jealousies and rivalries.  Most Christians admitted such discord resulted from
human perversity, argued Gladden, and many hoped to go beyond discord to some form of unity.  Since Gladden was convinced that "sentimental unity is nugatory" and "liturgical
uniformity and consolidated government are impracticable,"
the only remedy left for the curse of schism was cooperation.  Denominational recognition of a "parity of churches"
—that is, an agreement not to proselytize communities
well-churched by other denominations—would be the first
practical step toward the kingdom of God.  Gladden's next
step anticipated Frank Russell's and Josiah Strong's discussion of the visitation system.  He called for creation
of regional lay-ministerial associations designed to discover community problems and their possible solution without reference to doctrinal and ecclesiastical issues.  In
effect, Gladden believed the laboring masses could be won
back only when the churches divided up their community into
spheres of operation and then initiated permanent "institutional work" which met the spiritual, educational and physical needs of the people—he was calling for the institutional church with its classrooms, gymnasiums, baths,
kitchens, day care centers, and clinics.[47]

Philip Schaff, during the general discussion period,
also stressed the vital need of the churches to cooperate.
Only then would the nation assimilate the immigrant and
the churches precipitate the kingdom of Christ through conversion of the world.  Convinced church separation was ending, Schaff reminded the audience that the Alliance may encourage Christian cooperation, but the coming kingdom relied on action by the churches alone.[48]

These speeches in turn set the stage for practical
suggestions as to the best channels for cooperation.  In
his speech on the "Methods of Co-operation in Christian
Work," Josiah Strong indicated the complexity of modern
civilization and its cooperative foundation through bio-
logic analogy: "The higher the form of life, the more complex is its organization, and the more perfect is the cooperation among its several organs.  The same is true of
civilization."  Unhappily, Strong thought Protestantism
lagged one hundred years behind in this realm, consequently
endangering the nation's civilization—"there must be pre-
served a certain parity of growth between the material on
the one hand, and the moral and spiritual on the other.  So
far as the former outstrips the latter, our civilization
becomes materialistic, our prosperity becomes our peril."
The Alliance, said Strong, responded to the providential

call for remedying this great defect by inauguration of a
cooperative program for the churches.  It invited the clergy and laity of each community to band together into local
alliances.  Such interaction of evangelicals from all denominations would facilitate cooperation in the following
realms.[49]

> I.  Co-operation in the study of sociologi-
> cal and industrial problems and the application
> of Christian principles to their solution.

> II. Co-operation in reaching our entire
> population with the gospel, and

> III.The co-operation of the Christian mil-
> lions of the land for the accomplishment of
> needed reforms, and for the defense of cherished
> American institutions.[50]

These goals were to be attained through the methods detailed in the Report of December 1886, methods which
Strong again explained.  The key tool of the local Alliance would be house-to-house visitation.  This system divided the households of a city or region so that each
could be canvassed by a layman, preferably a female—
ladies gained easier admittance than men to strange homes
because they appeared less threatening and potentially
more sympathetic, from the perspective of the householder.
(Here is another example, albeit an approved one, of the
increasing role played away from home by middle class
women.)  The continued monthly personal attentions of the
visitor would reveal the basic human problems, thereby enabling the evangelical churches to transform the social
environment through material aid to the needy and win back
the masses.[51]

Secretary Strong was most upset that the churches
continued to ignore the social teachings of Jesus: "as
Christ's teaching contain the live doctrine of God, the
true doctrine of man and of salvation, so also they contain the true doctrine of brotherhood, of social relations."
The local alliance and visitation system would teach the
churches their duty in this realm, with the further advantage of increasing the spirituality and effectiveness of
the church as a whole.  To be effective, however, local
cooperation must engender state alliances which can mobilize Christian power in areas where the enormity of the
work overwhelms the local churches.  Although cooperation
aims ultimately at the salvation of man, immediate social
transformation should result from mobilization of ten or

twelve million Christians.  They will obtain moral legislation as well as defend the Christian sabbath and public
school.  Strong thought even the latter achievements justified such organization.[52]

    Following Strong, Dr. Frank Russell explained the
origins of the visitation system and his use of it in Oswego, N.Y.  The visitation system began among a small
group of clergymen led by the president of Gambier College
(Ohio), Rev. S. A. Bronson.  This little group devised a
means to reach that vast unworked spiritual field of America which evangelical disunity caused to be neglected.
Premised upon dearth of knowledge concerning the urban and
rural poor, their visitation system assumed lay interaction with the masses would end the information vacuum,
break down suspicions between churched and unchurched,
thus opening the latter to gospel influence, and enable
religious charity to benefit directly needy persons and
families.  Russell perfected their method through actual
use.  His experience with the visitation system corrobo-
rated Strong's claim that it provided the churches with a
great deal of information concerning their communities,
while increasing spirituality by involving the laity in
Christian service.  Russell concluded visitation reduced
the prejudices which estranged faithful and nonchurched
from each other and helped ostensibly to heal most community disorders.[53]

    Such arguments proved so persuasive that a correspon-
dent to the Methodist *Christian Advocate* concluded the
Washington Conference "cannot fail to be of great influence in promoting the co-operation of Protestant Christians throughout the country in seeking to save the masses,
and to guide the Nation safely through the perils of our
time."  Subsequent Alliance assessment suggests the widely
publicized conference did convince many to apply the teachings of Christ to social problems by means of cooperative
effort.  Inspired by the conference, the Alliance expansion program went forward so rapidly that in November 1888,
a Syracuse convention of New York State branches organized
a permanent state level executive committee.  This committee relieved the Evangelical Alliance for the United
States of America of the burdens local to New York so it
could organize other states.[54]

    Then, in December of 1888, Josiah Strong, William E.
Dodge, Jr., George U. Wenner, John Jay, and several other
Alliance figures participated in a conference of various
denominations and mission societies located in New York
City.  It created the Chickering Hall Committee on Evangel-

ization to carry out cooperative house-to-house visitation
with the hope of discovering the religious condition of
the city and furthering the evangelization of the people.
The Chickering Hall Committee apparently had nonevangelical
members, a fact which led the Alliance Executive Committee
both to deny publicly that it was an arm of the Alliance
and to re-emphasize its own visitation programs.  The Alliance was too evangelical to allow even the appearance of
compromising its position.[55]

     The peril psychology involved in the Washington Con-
ference (1887) underwent a subtle shift during the period
leading up to the Boston Conference (1889).  The alteration of emphasis between the first Conference title, *National Perils and Opportunities,* and that of Boston, *National Needs and Remedies,* reflects growing confidence in
the ability of evangelical Protestantism to solve contemporary problems.  Protestant leaders now believed applied
Christianity provided the solution for most social and religious problems.  As one outside and formerly hostile
commentator noted, the Boston Conference responded to two
great issues.  "One was that the application of Christianity should be as comprehensive as the life of humanity,
and that nothing in our social life is beyond its reach.
The other was that it is possible to introduce a method of
Christian co-operation by which the scattered people and
the unreached elements in our social life may be brought
into immediate and helpful comment with the existing Churches."  Belief in the efficacy of the social gospel engendered the confidence which imbued the great Alliance Conferences at Boston (1889) and Chicago (1893) and won them
such widespread public attention.[56]

     Over 500 delegates and a multitude of Bostonians con-
verged on the Conference in Boston during December 4-6,
1889.  Its proceedings, keyed to social gospel reform, provided detailed information about immigration, the city and
rural areas, Christian legislation, the relation of church
to state and Roman Catholicism.  It stressed above all the
continued need for interdenominational effort to apply
Christianity to American culture, testimony to the intran-
sigent conservatism of the majority of evangelicals and
their churches.  (Liberal evangelicals will gain control
ultimately of the power structure of churches like the
Methodist Episcopal and Baptist and carry them into the
social gospel, by the early 1900s, despite their more conservative constituency.)[57]

     President Dodge opened the Conference with the re-
minder that much had been achieved since Washington but

great problems remained to disturb the nation. He also
reminded evangelicals that the responsibility for applied
Christianity rested with the denominations rather than
with the Evangelical Alliance. The Alliance only attempted to "promote unity of feeling, sympathy and cooperation"
and to relay information needed by the denominations for
successful fulfillment of these goals. That denominational distinctions arose from accidents of history, time, and
place, induced Dodge to warn against allowing them to
stand in the way of hearty Christian cooperative work and
social reform. Evangelicals would never win the confidence and support of the godless until they learned to cooperate on the basis of their similarities, a state neither endangering faith nor compromising denominational affiliation. Now is the time, said Dodge, to apply Christ's
life and words to solution of all human problems and
sins.[58]

Secretary Strong cited the Washington Conference as
representing a "new era" of church relations because it
went beyond the fraternal position of the great 1846 London Conference to one which called for actual cooperative
efforts by evangelicals. Experience with the cooperative
method, however, revealed that an inadequate supply of
trained leaders diminished the ability of the proliferat-
ing Alliances to survive as viable working units. As
Strong pointed out, Field Secretary Dr. Frank Russell attempted to correct this flaw. He organized one state at a
time until enough urban Alliances existed to create a viable, permanently staffed, state level body capable of
functioning without him. Russell created such an Alliance
on the New York State level, but the national Alliance delayed announcement of its success until now in order to
prevent hasty imitation elsewhere. Although the national
body aided as well those communities within reach which
desired to organize, Alliance silence allowed realistic
assessment of its statewide pyramid.[59]

Such assessment revealed local Alliance survival required inspired leadership. The United States Alliance
also discovered that cooperative efforts were hampered by
rather widespread popular indifference and sectarianism,
and by the inexperience of those church members who participated in the visitation system. On the other hand, the
visitation system aroused such enthusiasm that potential
church members and supplicants occasionally numbered more
than clergymen could handle. Josiah Strong hoped continued use of the visitation system would provide enough experienced laity to relieve the clergy of the latter problem. In any case, its successful utilization in

Binghamton, Rome, Kingston, New York City, and Brooklyn,
New York, as well as in Baltimore and Philadelphia, convinced Strong the inherent principles of personal contact
and cooperation offered solution to the great problems of
rural and urban evangelization.  Those principles were "so
scriptural, so natural, so reasonable, so necessary to the
coming of the Kingdom that their final triumph is to me as
certain as the sure triumph of the Kingdom itself."[60]

     Even though the Alliance developed a methodology use-
ful to both rural and urban areas. it focused primarily on
the urban world.  Hence, the Boston Conference amplified
the needs of the city.  The perils which faced America
were concentrated in the city and it was the city for
which Strong thought Alliance methods most appropriate.
Christ proved self-sacrifice, personal contact, and cooperation essential to  reaching the entire world, but Strong
noted the churches relied instead on the indirect and non-
personal methods of denominational agencies funded by
Christian pocketbooks.  The only remedy for this selfishness was self-giving love for one's neighbor.  The only
remedy for disorders of the city, consequently, was constant and friendly intermingling of the urban church members with the rest of the city populations through continuous visitation.  Only then will the Christian community
perceive and eliminate the multitude of evils which separate the classes.  On the other hand, Secretary Strong
knew even massive individual Christian effort would not
save the city, and thereby save American civilization, unless the churches followed St. Paul's dictum of acting as
the coordinate parts of the body of Christ.  Quoting similar passages from scripture, Secretary Russell applauded
the recent denominational tendency to go beyond mere discussion of differences towards cooperation in the use of
the visitation system and in other Christian activity.[61]

     Both the Washington and subsequent Boston Conferences
catapulted the Evangelical Alliance once again to a position of national leadership among evangelicals.  Both were
quoted widely in religious and secular papers.  Both were
attended by evangelicals from every corner of the Union.
Both were staffed by leading thinkers and religious and
social reformers of the day.  As Lyman Abbott said after
the Boston Conference, "the Evangelical Alliance leads in
the direction in which the church must move, if it is to
move at all.  There must be unity of action, born of the
sense of the divineness of the task and its urgent necessity, which shall make denominational differences look as
insignificant as they really are when one sees them against
the background of eternal truth or the foreground of human

need.  With unity there must come immense impulsion outward
and forward."  The Alliance had become a chief agency in
the national mobilization against monstrous perils, subsequent to a reorientation of direction, and its new approach
was symbolized by that innovation of conference topic which
allowed intelligent discussion of socialism by evangelical
laymen like economist Richard Ely (and appreciative applause from his audience).  Abbott concluded the Alliance
carried out admirably its new social gospel departure to
Christianize American society.[62]

It was this developing social gospel message which
Alliance stalwart and Episcopalian Rev. C. C. Tiffany carried to Italy's Florence Conference of 1891.  He told his
auditors that the object of Christianity was not merely to
get men safely out of the world but to make them useful
factors in it.  Unhappily, he noted the "social conditions
physical, legal, and influential often crush the possibility of many men and women to receive the Gospel truths."
How can men and women live decent Christian lives or bring
their children up in Christian fashion when all share the
poverty, squalor, and lack of privacy of tenement living?
"In view of such festering dens of vice, is not tenement
house reform a Christian task?"  Tiffany obviously thought
the church had to change social conditions as well as to
convert the individual soul, "for the kingdom of God is
meant to be a kingdom of righteousness here, as well as a
kingdom of glory yonder....and that kingdom is to control
the environment of life which shapes its nature, as well
as to touch the inner springs of action."[63]

Subsequent to the Boston Conference, the Alliance attempted even more vigorously to expand its branch system
and teach the churches their social mission.  Further experience with the actual functioning of local Alliances induced the national body to suggest cooperative structures
which varied to meet the different needs of towns, counties
and cities as well as the different levels of preparation
for such work on the part of the communities desiring to
organize.  Successful organization of New York State freed
Dr. Russell to tour several of the major seminaries and
cities of the North and Midwest, as well as the New York
Chautauqua, in an attempt to transmit Alliance principles
to a wider audience.  His tours bore fruit in the form of
community and seminary sponsored visitation systems and the
creation of a series of local Alliances capped by a State
Committee in Michigan.  Despite this fact, the work entered
upon so enthusiastically in 1889 proved disappointing by
1892.  As Secretary Strong noted, many churches refused to
cooperate.  Others thought visitation a means of expanding

church attendance rather than of discovering and meeting
the life needs of the people.  Only when the church actively shows personal interest in the problems of the masses,
will those problems be met successfully.  For this reason,
Strong and Russell attempted to develop a new program designed to educate the churches, and especially clergymen,
in the need for personal contact and cooperation in Christian work.[64]

Josiah Strong spent much of 1893 preparing *The New
Era or the Coming Kingdom* as a vehicle for that education.
His naturalistic tendencies become apparent in this attempt
to show cooperative social gospel activity agreed with the
"fundamental laws and principles" inherent in human society,
prescribed by God, and revealed by revelation, history, and
nature.  It was Strong's conviction that the new era in human progress was dawning consequent of modern science and
social science.  In fact, he raised scientific discovery to
the level of scriptural revelation when he asserted the
"truths of science are God's truths, that its laws are
God's laws," that British social philosopher Herbert
Spencer's "unity in diversity seems to be the fundamental
law of the universe."[65]

God, or to use Strong's enlightened term, "Infinite
Intelligence" created a physical universe harmoniously
rooted in natural laws but man failed to use his endowed
reason and freedom to go beyond discovery of those laws towards fulfillment of their moral implications.  Given human
frailty, God sent Christ to teach that attracting law of
the moral universe, akin to the law of gravity in the physical, love.  Christ taught man a love which allows for human diversity, individualism, while sustaining unity among
men and between man and God: "'*Thou shalt love the Lord thy
God with all thy heart, and with all thy soul, and with all
thy mind,*' and '*Thou shalt love thy neighbor as thyself.*'"
Hence, the pendulum swing between individuality and social
organization now favored further social organization.
Obedience to such divine laws, in the social realm, meant
the individual should be attuned to the divine will and
therefore to other men, to society as a whole.  Modern
science contributed to the forces of steam and electrici-
ty and they in turn unleashed the centripetal force needed for more advanced social organization, through improvement of transportation and communication.  On the other
hand, the same forces balanced the process by insuring
that worldwide clash of ideas which strengthens the tendencies of the individual to perfection.[66]

The one roadblock to this march of human progress,
in Strong's eyes, was the inability of the church (or

"social conscience") to "control the entire life of the
social organism" because "there is no organization through
which it can express itself." Indeed, failure of the
church to obey the teachings of Christ set limits to conscience which hindered rather than advanced the coming
kingdom:[67]

> The church largely lost sight of Christ's
> humanity, and Unitarianism was the result.
> The church has not sufficiently insisted
> that salvation means salvation from sin,
> hence the caricature of sanctification
> taught and illustrated by the modern per-
> fectionists. In like manner the church
> has neglected Christ's teaching concerning
> human brotherhood, which is based on the
> divine Fatherhood, and there results the
> fatherless brotherhood taught by atheistic
> socialism, which is a caricature of Christ's
> teaching.[68]

Strong knew individual and societal perfection, prerequi-
sites to the coming kingdom, would occur only when the
churches obeyed Christ and attuned themselves to this so-
ciological age through use of methods resting upon the
principles of "personality" and "organization," house-to-
house visitation and interdenominational cooperation. Accordingly, Strong endorsed federation-at-the-bottom, or
cooperation of local churches and communities. Federation-
at-the-top, or denominational federation, suffered because
it could reform only as fast as its most conservative and
slowest member. Even federation-at-the-bottom, Strong
warned, would not win the masses to the gospel and prepare
the way for the kingdom until churches and faithful truly
sacrificed for the rest of the people and accepted the responsibility of reforming government and society as well.[69]

This increased Alliance demand, that churches accept
their social obligations, dominated the proceedings of the
World Evangelical Alliance Conference held in Chicago
during October of 1893. The Americans hoped originally to
sponsor this conference in 1891 but the proposed Florence,
Italy Conference pre-empted the date. As was true of the
1873 New York Conference, such delay proved pleasing when
plans for a Columbian Exposition at Chicago seemed to "afford an exceptional opportunity to present to the world
the ideas and institutions which lie at the foundation of
our civilization and are the chief source of our material
prosperity." Unlike the 1873 Conference, however, the
late nineteenth century Alliance decided to focus on the

social mission of the church rather than American self-
congratulation.  This was especially true since the 1893
Alliance Conference would occur last in a series of religious congresses convened during the exposition as part of
the World's Congress Auxiliary.  The earlier convocations
in the series proposed to discuss the more traditional
themes of Alliance conferences (the religious condition of
Protestantism, Christian liberty, Christian union and cooperation), thus freeing the World Alliance Conference to
stress applied Christianity.[70]

    As John Hutchinson suggests, the Alliance congress
at Chicago marked the high-water mark of the movement and
indicated quite clearly the "increasing convergence of the
two interests in church union and in social problems."  It
commenced with a speech presented by Charles C. Bonney,
President of the World's Congress Auxiliary.  He portrayed
the Alliance as an agency for uniting heretofore divided
religious forces into an evangelical demonstration of applied Christianity.  President William E. Dodge, Jr. carried this theme further.  Believing in the unity of the
faithful, this conference was designed by its sponsors to
be "a school of instruction in practical and successful
Christian work" achieved through cooperative effort.[71]

    This discussion of practical work exceeded in scope
and experience that presented by former Alliance congresses.  It called for transformation of society as well
as the saving of individual souls, if American civilization were to flower into that Christian form so essential
to the establishment of the kingdom of God on earth.  This
focus on practical activity sprang from the roots of Alliance purposes during these years and yet definitely related to the deepest spiritual root of all, the desire to
attain that Christian unity for which Christ had prayed.
The Chicago Conference witnessed the flowering of that conception of unity in cooperation and action which inspired
the American Alliance since the early 1880s and foreshadowed its culmination two decades later in the Federal Council of Churches of Christ in America.  As Rev. Simon J.
McPherson of the Second Presbyterian Church of Chicago
stated, in his "Address of Welcome," church union might be
impossible presently but "co-operation, or federation, of
evangelical churches in practical work is already emerging
in the yearnings of consecrated hearts and in the workings
of such bodies as the Evangelical Alliance."  The Alliance
teaches the churches they can cultivate loving fellowship
and pragmatic cooperation without endangering their differences.  In fact, the greatest insight contributed by the
Alliance is that Christ alone must be exalted by the

churches, rather than Luther, or Calvin, or Wesley, as the
source and content of their Christian being and unity.[72]

In a similar vein, Bishop A. Cleveland Coxe deplored
destruction of the visible union which once characterized
the church of the Caesars.  The church must be restored as
the unified body of Christ.  The only possible basis for
comity with Roman Catholicism and Greek Orthodoxy however
would be scriptural.  But unity may not be achieved until
Protestant and Latin churches heal internal divisions and,
then, Protestant, Catholic, and Orthodox police their religious principles and forms according to the scriptural
understanding of the Continental Reformers.  In accord
with contemporary Episcopalian position, Bishop Coxe considered the Anglican Lambeth Proposals (1888) as expressive of the essence of Christian comity when understood in
their worldwide intent.  He warned Americans must avoid
the conception of church unity as the unification of American denominations.  Failure to listen may lead to the
creation of an American sect, when compared to the world
scene, which will reopen the warfare of the church and
contribute further to schism.  The only way to prevent
this, Coxe concluded, is to accept the New Testament remedy "of one common and primitive rule for the perpetuation
of the sacred ministry," the episcopacy.  Quite obviously,
many thought scripture denied this church form, especially
when the Lambeth principles made sectarian claim that true
unity could be attained only through absorption into the
Episcopal Church.[73]

Like Rev. McPherson, President James McCosh thought
federation of the denominations the most feasible format
for unity at the time.  As was true of many Alliance
spokesmen, he believed such federation possible only after
the churches learned to cooperate in ministration to the
nation and its people.  In particular, Josiah Strong repeated *The New Era* espousal of federation-at-the-bottom.
The need of the day was to induce local churches to sponsor
kindergartens, university extension, fresh air funds, holi-
day houses, social settlements, public baths, tenement
house reform, temperance reform, political reform, and
other useful causes.  Such application of Christianity to
the entire life of the community would "prepare men for
the perfect life which all will live when the kingdom of
God is fully come."  The obvious magnitude of such an undertaking required organized cooperation.  But, what should
be the form of such organization?  Dr. Strong discounted
organic union because the need was immediate and such union
could not come for generations.  He thought denominational
federation possible but considered it of little value to

the social mission because it would be as slow as its slowest member.  The answer, in his mind, was cooperation of
local churches or federation-at-the-bottom.  The churches
of a local community, representing as many denominations,
could learn to cooperate concerning advanced social reform
programs when their denominations could not.  Moreover, the
conservatism of one community would not hinder reform of
another.  Such church effort would eventually make apparent the need for statewide organization.  This entire process assumed men may cooperate for practical goals despite
their varying worldviews: "If in essentials there is union,
in nonessentials liberty, and in all things charity, we
shall be able to work for common objects."[74]

        Although these statements anticipated the general
direction of unity in the United States during the next
two decades, they also reflected the kind of nationalist
parochialism which disturbed Bishop Coxe and denied the
internationalist position which Philip Schaff took to the
last.  "The Reunion of Christendom" proved to be the cap-
stone of Schaff's ecumenical thought and one of the high-
lights of the Conference.  This brilliant church historian
testified to the continued existence of church unity, despite schism, since the time of Christ.  Such unity may be
seen in the agreement among the churches, whether they be
Protestant, Greek or Roman Catholic, concerning the essentials of faith and doctrine.  On the other hand, differences in church government and discipline reflect the un-
folding of God's merciful and wise plan for humanity
whereby the peculiar needs of time, place, and people are
met.  The fact that variety in unity is inherent in nature,
history, and God's kingdom, reveals to man that there will
be the greatest variety in the church of the future.  The
virtues of the Greek, Roman, and Protestant forms of Christendom shall eventually win the applause of all the rest
while whatever areas of disagreement which still exist
shall be overcome.  More specifically, Dr. Schaff assessed
carefully recent forms of unity like the individualism of
the Alliance, such confederations as the Presbyterian Alliance, and the organic unity attained by the Methodist
churches of Canada.  His conclusion seemed clear.  Reunion
of Christendom could never be complete until the three
major divisions of the church were brought together.[75]

        This conception, of course, went beyond the pragmat-
ic aspirations of Protestants in America.  The movements
of the day were wending their way toward the fulfillment
of a lesser goal, that of Protestant federation in America.
Nevertheless, Schaff appears prophetic of the Federal Council to both its founders and historians.  This paradox,

that Schaff called for much more, but Americans listened
only to his comments on federal union, indicates somewhat
the single-minded nature of the blossoming federation movement.  Taken out of context, however, his statements on
federalism do suggest the type of union which appealed to
American federationists:

> Federal or confederate union is a volun-
> tary association of different churches in
> their official capacity, each retaining
> its freedom and independence in the manage-
> ment of its internal affairs, but all recog-
> nizing one another as sisters with equal
> rights, and co-operating in general enter-
> prises, such as the spread of the gospel at
> home and abroad, the defense of the faith
> against infidelity, the elevation of the
> poor and neglected classes of society,
> works of philanthrophy and charity, and
> moral reform.

> Such an eccelsiastical confederation
> would resemble the political confederations
> of Switzerland, the United States, and the
> modern German empire.  The beauty and
> strength of these confederate governments
> lie in the union of the general sovereignty
> with the intrinsic independence of the sev-
> eral cantons, or states, or kingdoms and
> duchies.[76]

Philip Schaff died soon after the Chicago Conference
because of the strain attendance placed upon his fragile
health—he knew the risk but the cause of Christ could not
be gainsayed.  His death left Josiah Strong as the most
vocal Alliance spokesman for unity, albeit a cooperative
and national form.  Although Secretary Strong continued to
favor federation-at-the-bottom, his conception of the purposes and nature of such federation altered significantly
by 1895.

In 1893, the Alliance decided to create Interdenominational State Commissions modeled after the Interdenominational Commission of Maine.  The state commissions would
rectify an area relatively neglected by the Alliance by
providing permanent cooperation of the denominational home
missionary societies and rural churches to meet the needs
of the vast neglected rural areas of the nation.  It was
still believed local alliances would be able to channel
the civic patriotism, philanthropy and social scientific

interests of the churches toward bringing the community
and society into tune with Jesus' teachings.

In 1895, disillusioned by the failure of the churches to accept their social mission, General Secretary
Strong initiated a new education program and conception of
Alliance activity designed to achieve broadly based federation-at-the-bottom.  Citing the rise of a new spirit of
civic patriotism and philanthropy, he regretted such well
intentioned activism  wasted resources by duplicating local social reform and ameliorative institutions.  Hopefully, the new form of local Alliance would win all churches and individuals who believed Christ offered salvation
for society as well as for the individual, thus enabling
the Alliance to coordinate the reform movement.  According
to the amended branch constitution, the object of the new
approach "'shall include the aid, in all practical ways,
of such existing organizations as, in its judgment, are
wisely seeking the common wellbeing.'"[77]

> 'The Alliance shall stand in the name
> of Christ on the side of practical religion,
> good citizenship, the enforcement of the law,
> the promotion of sobriety, the prevention of
> cruelty, the alleviation of suffering, the
> correction of injustice, the rescue of the
> unfortunate, the reformation of the depraved,
> and for such kindred ends as pertain to the
> true  social mission of the church; it being
> understood that all activities of the Alli-
> ance shall be subservient to spiritual
> results, which must always be the supreme
> object of the churches.'[78]

The new approach meant "men of all faiths or of no faith"
accepting these goals could participate in the local Alliance and its standing committees, although officers had to
be evangelical to allow that breadth of agreement needed
for cooperative efforts to succeed in a wide range of
problems.[79]

By 1897, Strong added a tractarian campaign to his
program.  Social gospel pamphlets by leading men of the
times such as Washington Gladden, Bishop Frederick Dan
Huntington, John R. Commons, Woodrow Wilson and Carl
Schurz would be carried directly to the homes of the people by Epworth Leagues, Baptist Leagues, Luther Leagues
and other young people's religious groups.  The first
"Truths for the Times" involved two series, foreign language pamphlets aimed at teaching immigrants democratic

principles and requirements of citizenship, and an English
language series designed to remind native Americans of
their citizenship duties. (Although 50,000 citizenship
leaflets were issued, with enthusiastic reception by clergy and youth leaders, the forces leading to reassertion of
an evangelical and internationalist position prevented
further publications.) At the same time, he organized Alliances in 25 Pennsylvania cities, capped by a state committee. The literature campaign and organization of state
alliance systems intended attainment of appropriate social
legislation by means of an educated public opinion. Such
an attempt to instill the democratic elements of the Religion of the Republic among the masses would have been acceptable if its evangelical aspects were emphasized as
well. Strong's new movement however smacked too much of
social mission and too little of traditional Alliance membership requirements and commitment to evangelical spirituality. It raised the inherent tension, within the evangelical version of the Religion of the Republic, between
the ultimate otherworldly evangelical goal of individual
salvation and the worldly goal of sustaining the democratic
Republic. Alliance evangelicals thought they ought to
sponsor both among the masses but believed democratic citizenship and social reform were merely aids towards conversion of the masses for their eternal lives. Emphasis on
citizenship without evangelicalism surely missed the point.
The fissure between Strong and the Alliance dated with
this work.[80]

The Alliance traditionally sought to uphold evangelical identity, thus enabling churches to foster actual
unity of a more concrete sort at the national and international levels. For years it supported "cooperation" in
religious and ideological matters and then, in the 1880s,
telescoped religion's relevance to the practical problems
of the American people. Such an adjustment proved compatible to the Alliance constituency until Josiah Strong,
continuing his evolution towards a more liberal (almost
modernist) stance, desired Alliance acceptance of nonevangelical members as a means to what must have appeared
secular ends. His social gospel position veered increasingly away from the evangelical goal of saving souls to
one of social reform per se. To make matters worse, federation-at-the-bottom began to short-circuit the denominational system by enmeshing local churches in an Alliance
reform structure pyramiding from the local, through state,
to national levels, portending a superchurch. Once they
realized a crisis of allegiance impended, alliancemen
chose to avoid collision entirely by altering their cooperative stress to a denominationally sound form. The

irony of such realization was the Alliance returned to the
older view that Christian unity, comprising fellowship of
an aggregate of the faithful, would *evolve* into interdenominational union of some far off day.  This meant the
Alliance withdrew *official* support both from federation,
although it favored federation-at-the-top because congru-
ent with denominational integrity, and from commitment to
a social gospel movement beginning to neglect the gospel.
This identity crisis worsened when many of the more able
alliancemen either died (Philip Schaff, Morris K. Jessup,
Rev. George R. Crooks), retired (John Jay, Frank Russell,
R. R. McBurney), or became inactive due to ill health
(William E. Dodge, Jr.)  That no bright young men waited
in the wings to replace the old leaders (they had gone off
to the federation movement which the Alliance encouraged
but refused to lead), meant Josiah Strong had less talented people to listen to his plea.  This combination of factors contributed to a deterioration of relations between
the Alliance executive structure and Secretary Strong.
That deterioration accelerated when the depression of 1893
required cutting Alliance overhead.  Financial stringency
led to reduction of Strong's salary (from $5,000 to $4,000)
as well as dismissal of a clerk in early 1897.[81]

    By April 1898, the Board of Managers authorized Ex-
ecutive Committee assessment of the present condition and
future policy of the Alliance.  After listening to Dr.
Strong, the Committee recommended a return to the policy
evident at the time of Alliance incorporation in 1885.
Even though the Board later tabled that recommendation,
the Executive Committee decision precipitated Josiah
Strong's break with the Alliance.  In his letter of resignation, Dr. Strong characterized the post-1886 Alliance as
reflecting a new departure designed to obtain church cooperation in social mission.  Failure of the churches to
cooperate sufficiently inspired successful Alliance efforts to educate them in their duty.  Consequently, "during the last ten years a profound change has taken place
on the part of pastors and churches in their conception of
the mission of the church, due undoubtedly to many causes,
but in no small measure to the efforts of the Alliance."
The tragedy of it all, in Strong's eyes was the Alliance
verged on federation of the churches, only to give up due
to "certain disabilities or limitations," which he never
explains.  Hence, Strong decided some other agency would
better fulfill such work.[82]

    In explaining the situation to its constituency, the
Alliance agreed that Dr. Strong's "special plans for civic
and religious betterment" ought to be fulfilled by an

agency of his own. The Board of Managers believed the
"chartered objects and cherished traditions" of the Alliance, coupled with obvious need, justified a nondenomina-
tional body dedicated to extension of liberty worldwide.
Despite this internationalist stance, Alliance leaders
made clear they still supported cooperation on the national level.[83]

> ...there can be no doubt that the need
> for Christian unity, as embodied in
> Christian co-operation, is greater now
> than ever before...It appears but reas-
> onable that those 'who profess and call
> themselves Christians,' should ally them-
> selves for actual Christian service....
> The rural communities and the cities alike
> demand the united efforts of all the good.
> Home missions and foreign missions, in
> equal degree are dependent on mutual help-
> fulness for their highest success.
>
> This Alliance stands for such united
> Christian effort. It seeks no ends of
> its own. It allows itself no slightest
> meddling with denominational differences.
> It seeks no direct denominational action.
> Its aim is to unite all Christians in co-
> operative labors for the advancement of
> Christ's kingdom.[84]

Although the Alliance stressed cooperation after Strong,
its refusal to interfere with the denominations or to attain cooperation by attempting "results too greatly varied
or too greatly comprehensive," indicates an aversion to
the complicated and overly comprehensive programs which
Strong desired.[85]

Josiah Strong later claimed the Alliance laid the
foundations for the Federal Council of the Churches of
Christ in America (1908) for the wrong reasons; too many
entered the Alliance in America "not to save society but
to save the *church*." The evangelicalism of Alliance constituency meant they lacked, in Strong's judgment, the
breadth of perspective needed to fulfill his conception of
applied Christianity. Indeed, Strong tells us more than
he realized about both Alliance and denominations. In the
words of H. Paul Douglass, institutionalization qualita-
tively altered the mood of the federation movement by
"straining out something of its original genius" and prophetic leadership:[86]

> With the establishment of the Federal
> Council it was transformed to a place
> within the ecclesiastical system and be-
> came an adjunct to the existing denomina-
> tional order.  Shortly before the final
> merging of the Evangelical Alliance in
> the new federation organization, its dis-
> tinguished secretary, Dr. Josiah Strong,
> had withdrawn from its leadership.  His
> primary interest was in the social gospel.
> This could be only a minor part of the
> general cooperative concern as dominated
> by average church-leadership.  He was too
> single-hearted for the transitional years
> through which the movement he had directed
> was getting back upon the main track of
> official acceptability.  In short, the
> adjustment of the cooperative movement to
> a national scheme of federation based
> strictly upon denominational representa-
> tion and a formal delegation of authority,
> implied a radical shifting of mood.  The
> movement was set back to the position, and
> compelled to take the pace, of the slower
> of the denominations and of the regions
> they represented. [87]

These comments are ironic.  They mention the very flaw
which encouraged Strong to oppose federation-at-the-top
and, yet, became the way of federation in America because
evangelicals would not tolerate the undercutting of denominationalism augured by federation-at-the-bottom.  Even
more ironic, Josiah Strong contributed to the rise of the
Federal Council and supported it subsequently.

The Alliance rapidly declined after Strong resigned.
The national Alliance conception of itself no longer allowed it to sponsor *officially* federation of the churches
at the very time when the federation impulse mushroomed
into a movement attracting a large portion of the evangelical leadership of the nation.  This is all the more un-
fortunate in that William E. Dodge, Jr., Josiah Strong,
and Frank Russell contributed to the process leading directly to the Federal Council when they helped to create
the Open and Institutional Church League in 1894.  Indeed,
Dodge was a financial bulwark for both the league and National Federation of Churches and Christian Workers.  Furthermore, the more powerful branch Alliances in Boston and
Philadelphia and the State Alliance of Pennsylvania took
leading parts in the movement which created the Federal

Council, and numerous alliancemen represented their re-
spective denominations at the November 1905 conference
which founded the Federal Council. Among the latter were:
Rev. George U. Wenner, Rev. Robert S. MacArthur, Rev.
James M. Buckley, Rev. Joachim Elmendorf, Hon. Henry Kirke
Porter, Bishop Thomas Bowman, Bishop Edward G. Andrews,
Bishop Cyrus D. Foss, Rev. James King, President Paul Brad-
ford Raymond, President George Edward Reed, Bishop John H.
Vincent, Bishop William T. Sabine, and Rev. George Alex-
ander.[88]

Meeting as an Inter-Church Conference on Federation,
in New York City during November 15-21, 1905, these founders of the Federal Council of Churches thought their new
creation superior to that which came before. Their published proceedings testify generally to a forgetfulness
concerning their real links to the nineteenth century Alliance. The Council rested on that federation-at-the-top
and pragmatic cooperation espoused, unofficially in the
former case, by the Alliance for so very long. And, although it denied any authority to set forth creedal statements even as simple as that of the Alliance Basis, it
assumed the actuality of that evangelical identity and
spiritual unity symbolized for nearly fifty years by the
Evangelical Alliance when it announced: "the time has come
when it seems fitting more fully to manifest the essential
oneness of the Christian Churches of America, in Jesus
Christ as their Divine Lord and Saviour, and to promote
the spirit of fellowship, service and coöperation among
them." Granted this federation of denominations held far
more official prestige and potential power than an organization of individuals, it is still true that the list of
initial member denominations held few churches not represented previously in the Alliance. Indeed, the National
Federation of Churches and Christian Workers intentional-
ly limited its call for an inter-church council to "the
larger Churches, and those which were already in fraternal
relations and in substantial agreement as to fundamental
Christian doctrine," in other words, to the mainline evangelical denominations. No place on the Council existed
for Unitarian, Universalist, Mormon, or Roman Catholic
churches, the very bodies so upsetting to the Alliance.[89]

That the Evangelical Alliance for the United States
of America had been of great importance in its day may be
seen in the judgement of two men most intimately connected
with the creation of the Federal Council, Elias B. Sanford
(the "Father of the Federal Council") and Charles S. Mac-
Farland (its first general secretary). These men testified that the Alliance, whatever its shortcomings, was the

major precurser of the Federal Council.  MacFarland even
suggested that the demise of the Alliance was the result
of its success: "it had itself opened up the way for the
churches to something larger."[90]

As soon as the Federal Council of Churches became a
reality, the social gospel Evangelical Alliance leaders
like Methodist Frank Mason North used Alliance funds to
pay for the formerly Alliance but now Council-sponsored
annual week of prayer and various other programs.  The
overlap of leadership proved ultimately so great that the
Council replaced the Alliance in the forefront of the social gospel.  By 1944, thinking the Alliance had outlived
its usefulness, this interlocking directorate disbanded
the Alliance after turning its assets and archives over
to the Council.[91]

This domination by a liberal directorate related to
the Federal Council meant more conservative evangelicals
desirous of religious unity based on clear and publicly
affirmed doctrinal consensus had to seek elsewhere to re-
gain that part of the Evangelical Alliance tradition.
Bruce Shelly correctly sees the April 7, 1942 St. Louis
"National Conference for United Action Among Evangelicals"
and subsequent "National Association of Evangelicals" as
heir to that tradition.  The constitution of the NAE,
adopted in May of 1943, set forth a doctrinal statement
quite similar to the earlier Alliance:[92]

    1.  We believe the Bible to be the inspired,
    the only infallible, authoritative word of God.

    2.  We believe that there is one God,
    eternally existent in three persons, Father,
    Son, and Holy Ghost.

    3.  We believe in the deity of our Lord
    Jesus Christ, in His virgin birth, in His
    sinless life, in His miracles, in His vicar-
    ious and atoning death through His shed blood,
    in His bodily resurrection, in His ascension
    to the right hand of the Father, and in His
    personal return in power and glory.

    4.  We believe that for the salvation of
    lost and sinful man regeneration by the Holy
    Spirit is absolutely essential.

    5.  We believe in the present ministry of
    the Holy Spirit by whose indwelling the

Christian is enabled to live a godly life.

6. We believe in the resurrection of both
the saved and the lost; they that are saved
unto the resurrection of life and they that
are lost unto the resurrection of damnation.

7. We believe in the spiritual unity of
believers in our Lord Jesus Christ.[93]

Just as clearly, the more liberal Federal Council
wandered from this doctrinal position. Even so, the Evangelical Alliance sponsored simultaneously both evangelical
doctrinal integrity *and* the social gospel. The successive
Councils and the National Association of Evangelicals
therefore each represent one of the two wings of a more
healthy minded earlier movement.

Of course I am deeply aware that nineteenth century
evangelicalism left much to be desired as to its often
limited perception of such things as the role of the woman in society or in its reaction to the treatment of
Indians, blacks, and immigrants by the larger culture.
Still, Alliance evangelicals showed a breadth of faith,
erudite knowledge and social commitment which compares to
the disadvantage of both religious liberalism and conservatism today. In the 1980s, an era of continued evangelical revival and national awakening, I cannot but applaud
the decade long efforts of "new evangelicals" like Donald
W. Dayton, Donald G. Bloesch and Richard J. Coleman to
break from fundamentalist obscurantism by rediscovering
their evangelical heritage and bridging creatively the unwarranted gap between the liberal Protestant and Roman
Catholic traditions with that of more conservative evangelicalism. Rediscovery and restatement of the ties that
bind cannot but help to strengthen Christianity and culture in modern America.[94]

# CONCLUSION

The fifty year saga of the Evangelical Alliance for the United States of America ended for all intents and purposes with the rise of the Federal Council of Churches and the later National Association of Evangelicals on the American landscape. Its hope of formal interdenominational comity, one proposed almost seventy years before by Samuel Simon Schmucker, became fact for some churches in 1908 and others in 1943. Yet the Alliance story involves much more than creation of Christian unity because it took place in a human drama of national and international tensions, church controversy, and personal needs. Above all, it reflects evangelical enthusiasm to transmit their gospel message, church forms, democratic ways, their Religion of the Republic, to mankind.

Dedicated to the voluntaryist principle in religion and civil order, evangelicals were forged by that cultural rejuvenation movement, the Second Great Awakening, into a powerful democratic force operating through all manner of religious and reform associations. These early nineteenth century and Jacksonian Era societies did much good but left evangelicals an even more important legacy. At a time when religion was channeling into denominational forms, cooperation among evangelicals showed their individual identities so interwoven that the faithful began to glimpse the real meaning of Christ's prayer that His followers be one. The potentiality of such inspiring Christian teachings encouraged many evangelical leaders publicly to express their fellowship and common identity. This strong, positive thrust towards Christian union was reinforced by various negative trends threatening evangelical comity. Denominational discord, confessionalist and ritualist claims of adherence to the only church (a small and suffocating one at that), the attacks of rationalists, Unitarians and Universalists who questioned the need for personal salvation and threatened the emotional base of true religion, and the portly face of a cynical materialism that denied meaning to the spiritual realm, all contributed to a context impelling some evangelicals toward organized Christian fellowship and union. Successful revivalist evangelization of the populace as the United States approached its nineteenth century midpoint welded evangelicals both to the nation and its worldwide

gospel mission. In a world generally ruled by monarchy and
assuming an established and often intolerant state church
essential to social stability, American evangelicals knew
they were obliged to convert mankind to separation of religion from civil authority, to civil and religious liberty,
and to the American democratic way of politics and of life.
The providential mission to save the world required the
salvation of man through evangelization and democrati-
zation.

The gropings  for Christian union by men like Samuel
Simon Schmucker, Robert Baird, and George Peck gained new
meaning by the early 1840s when hundreds of thousands of
Irish sought refuge in America. This introduction of vast
numbers of Roman Catholics alienated from the English tradition and contemptuous of Protestantism created an unwanted and fearful pluralism which inflamed the festering
sores of ritualism and confessionalism on the Protestant
body religious, cultural, and political. Immigration of
men and ideas therefore provided a negative which further
precipitated indecision into outright action. The desire
to forge a *visible* identity and unity now became a necessity. Moreover, international religious unity might reduce tensions between the United States and nations like
Britain. Many Americans therefore participated enthusiastically in the ecumenical movement which created the
World Evangelical Alliance in London of 1846 and the American Branch in New York of 1847.

Nevertheless, tragedy stalked Christian union as
well as the American political Union from the beginning.
Just as southerners thought the Federal Union waxed too
strong for the safety of its parts, so the evangelical denominations became anxious with an Alliance potentially
capable of unifying the churches. Just as the nation began to question the quality of its leadership as it approached the Civil War, so the denominations wondered
about the wisdom of those in the forefront of ecumenism.
Of course, the central element of this tragic drama related to the increasing cacophony of collapsing national
institutions, be they national denominations or national
political parties, as the war rose on the horizon. And,
the overwhelming weight crushing the fulcrum of national
balance was slavery. Introduction of the slavery issue at
the London Conference did not prevent evangelical articu-
lation of religious identity in an explicit Basis, but did
condemn the subsequent American Alliance to a life short-
ened by the taint of antislavery sympathies and the sus-
picion of being insufficiently nationalist. The U.S. body
struggled under the dual burden of being in advance

ecumenically of the bulk of the faithful while also having
to defend 'itself against both slavery and antislavery
forces.  Its moderate antislavery stance no longer suited
the increasingly schismatic national temper.

The ensuing Civil War wracked the nation with patri-
otic gore for four agonizing years but, happily, provided
some benefits.  The abhorrent institution of slavery vapo-
rized in the maelstrom, thereby eliminating a prime irri-
tant among northern evangelicals.  Wartime cooperation may
have increased northern evangelical commitment to the
American democratic faith and mission, a religious patriotism favorable to continued search for church unity, but
it also strengthened international respect and recognition
of that common identity which bridged denominational
chasms.  Consequently, evangelical leaders from North and
Midwest began to plan continued cooperation and sought
more complete forms of religious union at war's end.  Sur-
rounded by the rubble of their peculiar institutions and
values, evangelicals in the South persisted in hostility
to all that was northern, including the ecumenical movement, for the next two decades.

From its beginnings, the Evangelical Alliance appealed most fully to the urban educated elites of the middle and upper class among the evangelical churches.  Now,
after the war, concentration of mushrooming industrialization, materialism, rationalism, cultural and religious
pluralism, and population in the cities of the East and
Midwest confronted these urbanites with valid reason for
organized comity and action.  Their confidence still knew
few limits and their inspired regrouping of denominational
families toward reunion reinforced an optimistic grasping
for ecumenical perfection, but confrontations to the evangelical base of American culture added an urgency to evangelical organization.

The U.S. Evangelical Alliance revived in 1866 in
large part to prove that evangelical identity and spiritual unity undergirded religious diversity.  Evangelicals
also desired to show the superiority of a democratic society, inspired by their Religion of the Republic, which
relied on that separation of religion and civil authority
so peculiar to America and so upsetting to the establishment mentality of Europeans.  The American sponsored World
Alliance Conference in New York (1873) succeeded beyond
imagination in terms of national popularity and impressive-
ness to Europe.  Yet the post-1873 American Alliance found
its one-shot program left little to do but expand religious liberty worldwide and defend an evangelicalism

established in public institutions at home.  The contradiction between commitment to religious liberty and separation of religion from civil authority *and* to the defense
of established religion never dawned on Alliancemen like
Robert Baird, Philip Schaff, and Henry B. Smith.  They sincerely thought democracy relied on a citizenry born of the
evangelical perspective.  Roman Catholic attacks on democracy, liberalism and free public education as well as its
concentration of church power in a papal monarchy only reinforced evangelical alienation from this polar opposite.
Consequently, Catholic critiques of American evangelical
culture found even less sympathy than that of rationalists,
Unitarians, and Mormons.  The Alliance defended evangelicalism in public schools and reform institutions with a
tenacity which made it the bane of Catholic attempts at
cultural adjustment.

     Alliance desire for unity beyond its own structure,
that of individuals banding together in fellowship and
spiritual oneness, continued unabated during this period.
By 1883, however, more reflective leaders across the nation began to sense the great gap between the elites and
the masses.  Such divorce of the evangelical bodies from
the class of their origins proved upsetting to leaders
accustomed to thinking their's the religion of democracy's
idol, the ordinary man.  Even more disturbing, these prophets of peril realized accommodation to contemporary individualistic, laissez faire economic and social philoso-
phies may have allowed evangelicals to have worldly success, but only at the cost of poor living conditions and
festering social environment for the masses.  As a result,
a new generation of Alliance leaders like William E. Dodge,
Jr., John Jay, and R. R. McBurney recognized the Alliance
had to adjust its ecumenism to a different kind of work.
Their new departure reflected growing realization that
alienated mass man would remain such until the churches
heeded his physical and emotional as well as spiritual
needs.  Consequently, the U.S. Alliance began aggressively
to sponsor the social gospel after a period of reorganization, recruitment of new supporters, and acquisition of
Josiah Strong as general secretary.  Its education conferences—Washington (1887), Boston (1889), and Chicago
(1893)—succeeded admirably.

     The new social emphasis represented a departure from
the older pattern of cooperation and ecumenism.  The Alliance shifted from stress on identity in fellowship and
union to stress on cooperation in pragmatic action, identity being the assumed basis for such action.  The shift
is even more important because that federal union posed by

Samuel Simon Schmucker and thought too illusory by the Alliance of the 1870s now became a topic of admiration, discussion and potential reality.  From its beginnings, alli-
ancement indulged in an often-unspoken but constant current
of hope that the denominations would federate according to
the principle of diversity in union, that is, according to
some sort of federal union which allowed continued denominational autonomy.  Such federation-at-the-top must be distinguished from the federation-at-the-bottom which Josiah
Strong's determined personality made Alliance policy until
1898.  Undeclared and ill-defined at first, this policy
crystallized as Alliance attempts to encourage denominational social gospel cooperation met only partial success
during the 1880s.  Strong and his Alliance supporters became convinced that such cooperation prospered according
to the pace of the slowest denomination.  Hence, by the
late 1880s federation-at-the-bottom emerged increasingly
as a topic of discussion and became actual Alliance policy
in 1893.

Originally, this conception of federation was expressed in terms which avoided any threat to the traditional denominational polity.  It merely referred to cooperation between local congregations in seeking out, assessing
and solving those urban problems blocking evangelization
of the masses.  As time went on, however, this federation
principle underwent a twofold transformation on the practical level which augured ill for the churches.  First, the
Alliance began to realize more completely that the cultural and religious crisis was so truly national that only
state and national organization could cope with it.  An
energetic program to create state and regional Alliances
began to succeed to the point where the denominational
leaders who ruled the Alliance began to understand the
danger to their respective religious fiefs.  Second,
Strong added a twist to the mushrooming Alliance federation during the mid-1890s by welcoming all reform groups,
both religious and secular, evangelical and other, into
the branch Alliances.

The growing chasm between the Alliance governors and
Strong dates with this work.  Only at this point do the
denominational leaders realize federation-at-the-bottom
might add an unwanted secularism to a heretofore evangelical campaign and ultimately might succeed in creating a
powerful Alliance pyramid paralleling—it would have in
its fold most of the liberal urban congregations irrespective of religious family—but more powerful than the individual denominations themselves.  This sobering prospect
precipitated the break between the Alliance and Strong as

well as Alliance jettisoning of federation-at-the-bottom.
Indeed, the Alliance reacted in such haste (it could have
sponsored federation-at-the-top but was too shocked about
its discovered heresy to do the obvious) that it returned
to the internationalist-nationalist balance of the pre-
1885 era: succoring of religious liberty and separation of
religion and civil authority around the world while also
encouraging cooperation and denominational comity.  Nevertheless, state Alliances and numerous alliancemen guided
to completion the federative impulse formerly spawned by
the American Alliance.  Their federation-at-the-top pro-
tected the denominations from organic union while fulfill-
ing over seventy years of evangelical yearning for concrete and physical expression of that common religious and
democratic identity inherent in their Religion of the Republic.  The Federal Council of the Churches of Christ in
America and later but parallel National Association of
Evangelicals capped the two wings, that of social Christianity and doctrinal integrity, of this conservative
tradition.

# NOTES

## CHAPTER ONE: INTRODUCTION

[1]Charles Clayton Morrison, *The Unfinished Reformation* (New York, 1953); William Nicholls, *Ecumenism and Catholicity* (London, 1952). Even Robert McAfee Brown's insightful book, *The Ecumenical Revolution* (New York, 1967), falls under this stricture.

[2]Gaius Jackson Slosser, *Christian Unity: Its History and Challenge in All Communions, in All Lands* (New York, 1929); John T. McNeill, *Unitive Protestantism: A Study in Our Religious Resources* (New York, 1930). While William Adams Brown realizes the World Evangelical Alliance was important, he treats it only as one of several nineteenth century bodies leading to the World Council of Churches in his *Toward a United Church: Three Decades of Ecumenical Christianity* (New York, 1946).

[3]J. B. A. Kessler, Jr., *A Study of the Evangelical Alliance in Great Britain* (Goes, Netherlands, 1968), p. 33; John Ewing, *Goodly Fellowship: A Centenary Tribute to the Life and Work of the World's Evangelical Alliance, 1846-1946* (London, 1946); Ruth Rouse and Stephen Charles Neill, eds., *A History of the Ecumenical Movement, 1517-1948*, 2nd ed. (Philadelphia, 1968), especially pp. 321-24. For an update on more recent world ecumenism, see Harold E. Fey, ed., *The Ecumenical Advance: A History of the Ecumenical Movement,* vol. 2/1948-1968 (Philadelphia, 1970).

[4]Bruce L. Shelly, *Evangelicalism in America* (Grand Rapids, Mich., 1976), pp. 72-84; Elias B. Sanford, "A History of the Evangelical Alliance for the United States," MSS [1917], Library of the National Council of the Churches of Christ in America, Federal Council Collection. Xerox copy, University of Iowa Library; John A. Hutchison, *We Are Not Divided: A Critical and Historical Study of the Federal Council of the Churches of Christ in America* (New York, 1941); Robert T. Handy, *A Christian America: Protestant Hopes and Historical Realities* (New York, 1971); Henry F. May, "The Recovery of American Religious History," *American Historical Review,* LXX (October, 1964), 79-92. In addition to Sanford's study, Wallace N. Jamison comprehends the importance of the American Alliance in his short Master's thesis, "A History of the Evangelical Alliance for the United States of America" (unpublished S.T.M. thesis,

Union Theological Seminary, 1946). Aside from my own previous articles, which will be cited later, the only other
recent article about the American Alliance was written by
Ernest R. Sandeen. Sandeen argues correctly that American
and British evangelical perspectives and religious organizations were quite similar. But, he shows rather superficial knowledge of the Alliance movement, as well as of
the related original documents and secondary literature,
in his "The Distinctiveness of American Denominationalism:
A Case Study of the 1846 Evangelical Alliance," *Church
History*, 45 (June, 1976), 222-34.

[5]Any quick sampling of current journals and news mag-
azines reveals a complex pattern of response to this controversial issue. It is clear that many Roman Catholics,
liberal Protestants and evangelicals have always advocated
use of government to enforce Sunday store closure laws and
various other "moral" reforms. What is new is the emergence politically of a vast number of religious conversa-
tives and evangelicals who in this century heretofore have
not been active in politics. The balance of power in
politics and the future directions of society may be at
stake, a state of affairs which antagonizes all sorts of
political, social and religious vested interests which
prefer the status quo. Cf.: John Garvey, "Made for Each
Other: the Fundamentalist-Humanist Complex," *Commonweal*,
Jan. 16, 1981, 6-8; "As Religious Right Flexes Its Mus-
cles," *U.S. News and World Report*, Dec. 29, 1980, 69;
"Preachers in Politics: Decisive Force in '80's?," *U.S.
News and World Report*, Sept. 15, 1980, 24-26; L. J. Davis,
"Conservatism in America," *Harpers*, vol. 261 (October,
1980), 21-26.

[6]Clifford S. Griffin, *Their Brother's Keepers: Moral
Stewardship in the United States, 1800-1865* (New Brunswick,
1960), p. x; Charles I. Foster, *An Errand of Mercy: The
Evangelical United Front, 1790-1837* (Chapel Hill, 1960);
John R. Bodo, *The Protestant Clergy and Public Issues,
1812-1848* (Princeton, 1954). Foster most conspicuously
advances the conspiratoral interpretation; Bodo and Griffin are more subtle.

[7]Griffin, *Brother's Keepers*, p. xiv; Lois Banner,
"Religious Benevolence as Social Control; A Critique of
An Interpretation," *Journal of American History*, LX (June,
1973), 23-41.

[8]William G. McLoughlin, *Revivals, Awakenings and Reform: An Essay on Religion and Social Change in America,
1607-1977* (Chicago and London, 1978), pp. xiii-xv.

[9]Ibid.

[10]Ibid., p. 1.

[11]Ibid., p. xiv.

[12]Erik H. Erickson, "The Problem of Ego Identity," in Maurice R. Stein, Arthur J. Vidich, David Manning White, eds., *Identity and Anxiety: Survival of the Person in Mass Society* (Glencoe, Illinois, 1960), p. 38; "Means of Promoting Christian Union," *Christian Advocate and Journal,* Oct. 2, 1844, 1—this journal later changes in title to *Christian Advocate* and henceforth will be cited as *CA.* Also see Charles Y. Glock and Rodney Stark, *Religion and Society in Tension* (Chicago, 1965), pp. 5-6.

[13]For background on early democracy and evangelicalism in the United States, see: Ralph Henry Gabriel, *The Course of American Democratic Thought,* 2nd ed. (New York, 1956), pp. 1-39; Stow Persons, *American Minds: A History of Ideas* (New York, 1975), pp. 176-99; Sidney E. Mead, *The Lively Experiment: The Shaping of Christianity in America* (New York, 1963), pp. 72-133.

[14]Sidney E. Mead, *The Nation with the Soul of a Church* (New York, 1975), pp. 71, 73-74, 18-19.

[15]Gabriel, *The Course,* pp. 14-25.

[16]Cyrus D. Foss "The Mission of Our Country," *CA.* July 6, 1876, 210; George R. Crooks, ed., *Sermons by Bishop Matthew Simpson of the Methodist Episcopal Church* (New York, 1885), p. 82.

## CHAPTER TWO: "PLURALISM," THE SEEDBED OF EVANGELICAL IDENTITY, 1730-1839

[1]Most of the generalizations in the first few pages of this chapter will be validated in the ensuing text but one may glean elements of them, particularly on the colonial awakenings not covered by this study, by comparing the following: Ruth Rouse, "Voluntary Movements," in Rouse and Neill, *Ecumenical Movement,* pp. 309-11, 316-17; Mead, *Lively Experiment,* pp. 29-34; 115-27; William G. McLoughlin, ed., *The American Evangelicals, 1800-1900* (New York, 1968), pp. 1-13; Perry Miller, *The Life of the Mind in America* (New York, 1965), pp. 3-27, 46-57; Winthrop S. Hudson, *Religion in America* (New York, 1965), pp. 78-82, 158-72, 178-80; Persons, *American Minds,* pp. 90-115;

Sydney Ahlstrom, *A Religious History of the American People,* 2 vol. (Garden City, New York, 1975), pp. 182-328.
The observations on the Protestant Reformation rest on a
wide range of reading and research but the general reader
will find hints of this position covered by the Ahlstrom
citation above as well as by A. G. Dickens, *Reformation
and Society in Sixteenth-Century Europe* (London, 1966);
A. G. Dickens, *The English Reformation* (New York, 1964);
Roland H. Bainton, *Here I Stand: A Life of Martin Luther*
(New York, 1950); John T. McNeill, *The History and Character of Calvinism* (New York, 1954).

   [2]Edwin Scott Gaustad, *The Great Awakening in New Eng-
land* (New York, 1957); Wesley M. Gewehr, *The Great Awaken-
ing in Virginia, 1740-1790* (Durham, N.C., 1930); Charles
H. Maxson, *The Great Awakening in the Middle Colonies*
(Chicago, 1920); Alan E. Heimert, *Religion and the American
Mind from the Great Awakening to the Revolution* (Cambridge,
Mass., 1966).

   [3]Ahlstrom, *Religious History,*  I, p. 33.

   [4]Mead, *Lively Experiment,* p. 104.

   [5](New York, 1844), p. 288. The "Chris-tians" are not
to be confused with Alexander Campbell's "Christian" movement leading to the Disciples of Christ.  The former arose
in New England and adhered to Unitarian doctrine, Baptist
ordinances, and Methodist actions.  "The Christian Sect,"
*New-York Evangelist,* Jan. 13, 1848, 6—henceforth cited as
*NYE.*

   [6]Cf.: Timothy L. Smith, *Revivalism and Social Reform:
American Protestantism on the Eve of the Civil War* (New
York, 1957, 1965), pp. 26-35; Hudson, *Religion,* pp. 158-
73; Elwyn A. Smith, "The Forming of a Modern American Denomination," *Church History,*XXXI (March, 1962), 82-89.

   [7]Elwyn A. Smith, "The Forming of a Modern American
Denomination," *Church History,* XXXI (March, 1962), 90-96.
This behavior pattern has occurred often in American religious history.  One of the most recent cases, during the
mid-1970s, involves the casting out of the moderate wing
by the conservatives from the Missouri Synod Lutheran
Church.

   [8]"Christian Union a Testimony for Christian Truth,"
*Christian Union and Religious Memorial,* III (June, 1850),
323—henceforth cited as *CURM.*  It should be noted that
some denominations, such as the Methodists, stressed

denominational voluntary societies almost from the beginning and did not reflect influence from either ritualism or confessionalism.

[9]Cf.: "Theories of the Church," review of *The Unity of the Church* by Henry Manning, *Biblical Repository and Princeton Review,* ser. 2, XVIII (January, 1846), 139; "Evangelical Alliance; Correspondence Between Sir Culling Eardley Smith, and Dr. Cox, of America," *CA,* May 12, 1847, 75. The latter journal focuses heavily on these issues from the fall of 1845 to the fall of 1846, inclusive.

[10]Charles Tiffany, *A History of the Protestant Episcopal Church in the United States of America,* 2nd ed., VII, in Philip Schaff, *et al.,* eds., The American Church History Series (New York, 1895), pp. 460-62. Bishop Charles P. McIlvaine, an evangelical and ecumenical leader, set forth the basic evangelical position within his Episcopalian order in *The Temple of God* (Philadelphia, 1860).

[11]S. D. McConnell, *History of the American Episcopal Church* (New York, 1890), pp. 320-21.

[12]James Hastings Nichols, *Romanticism in American Theology* (Chicago, 1961), pp. 2-4, 66-68; Abdel Ross Wentz, *Pioneer in Christian Unity: Samuel Simon Schmucker* (Philadelphia, 1967), p. 172. One of Nichols' major themes is Nevin drew upon Puritan and European sources while Schaff, a Swiss, was trained in the romantic theological and religious tradition of the Reformed faith in Europe.

[13]Wentz, *Pioneer,* pp. 49-51, 171-74. On Lutheran immigration, refer to E. Clifford Nelson, *The Lutherans* (Philadelphia, 1975), pp. 152-67, 171-72. Schmucker held such an American view of religion that this too caused him no amount of difficulty within his denomination when large numbers of European confessionalists joined the fold. See Kay Irene Kirkpatrick Jordan, "Samuel Simon Schmucker's Conception of A Christian America," (unpublished M.A. Thesis, Western State College, 1973).

[14][Italics mine.] "Means of Promoting Christian Union," *CA,* Oct. 2, 1844, 1; (Editorial), "The Evangelical Alliance," *CA,* Sept. 30, 1846, 30. For an example of the evangelical sense of comity and cooperation spawned by the voluntary societies, see Letter, William Patton and John J. Owen to Samuel Simon Schmucker, May 21, 1834, MSS, Schumucker Collection. Archives, Gettysburg College. See Smith, *Social Reform,* pp. 42-43 for a position similar to mine.

[15]"Means of Promoting Christian Union," *CA*, 1.

[16]Cf.: J. W. Corson, Letter to editor, "Evangelical
Alliance," *CA*, Sept. 3, 1846, 30; B. Hawley, "Rationalism,"
*CA*, Nov. 24, 1847, 185.  For fairly typical Protestant reactions to the dangers that Roman Catholicism posed for
America and its Protestant religion, see: the evangelical
Lyman Beecher's *A Plea For the West*, 2nd ed. (Cincinnati,
1835) and the more liberal Horace Bushnell's *Barbarism, the
First Danger*, in his *Work and Play*, I (New York, 1912),
pp. 227-67.  That evangelicals considered America to be
not only a Christian nation, but a Protestant one as well,
may be seen in Robert Baird's comment concerning the freedom that Roman Catholics experienced in America.

> Rome will find it difficult to contend with
> our free institutions, our free schools, our
> open Bible, and all the other Protestant in-
> fluences which exist among us.  She may send
> us as many Bishops, Archbishops, and even
> Cardinals, as she pleases.  It will require
> something more than all this to make headway
> against the evangelical influences which per-
> vade that Protestant country....I am happy to
> say that our Christian people are beginning to
> understand better the work they have to do in
> relation to Roman Catholics....

*The Progress and Prospects of Christianity in the United
States of America* (London, 1851), p. 38.  Also see Bishop
Bedell's speech as quoted in "This Nation Protestant,"
*New York Observer*, April 20, 1876, 121—henceforth cited
as *NYO*.

[17]All these citations bemoan the sectarian spirit
that reigned to varying extent among the churches.  Cf.:
Rev. Augustus J. Thebaud, S. J., *Forty Years in the United
States of America* (1839-1885), ed. Charles George Herber-
mann (New York, 1904), pp. 162-65; Rev. Thomas H. Skinner,
"Sectarianism and Christian Union," *CURM*, III (April,
1850), 225; [Robert Baird], "Editorial Remarks," *CURM*, III
(January, 1850), 3; [Robert Baird], "Editorial Remarks,"
*CURM*, III (March, 1850), 130; Rev. Thomas DeWitt, "The
Claims of the Cause of Christian Union Upon Every Believ-
er," *CURM*, I (February, 1848), 65-66; "Christian Union,"
*CA*, reprinted in *CURM*, I (February, 1848), 82-83; Rev.
George Peck, "Religious Controversy," *CURM*, I (January,
1848), 16; Rev. Gorham D. Abbott, "The Importance of Chris-
tian Union at the Present Time," *CURM*, I (January, 1848),
17-18; Rev. Nathan Bangs, "Evangelical Alliance," *CURM*,
III (September, 1849), 518.  Also see Ray Allen Billington,

*The Protestant Crusade,* 1800-1860 (Chicago, 1938, 1964),
pp. 3-4.

[18]Hence Rev. Thomas E. Vermilye could utilize evangelical consensus to define what it meant to be Christian.
"A Discourse on Christian Union," *CURM,* I (December, 1848),
710-11. Also see Mead, *Lively Experiment,* pp. 121-27
concerning the impact of revivalism on the denominations.

[19]Tamotso Shibutani, "Reference Groups as Perspectives," *American Journal of Sociology,* LX (May, 1955), 569
quoted in Glock and Stark, *Religion and Society in Tension,*
p. 5; Glock and Stark, Ibid., p. 6.

[20]Billington's sophisticated treatment of American
anti-Catholicism before the Civil War is premised on the
notion that Protestants were involved in an unwarranted
and irrational nativist reaction to the foreigner. *Protestant Crusade;* Baird, *Religion in America,* p. 288. Some
Catholic scholars now realize the Great Awakenings and
subsequent revivals spawned a devout American evangelicalism with a doctrinal basis which made it a bitter opponent
of such polar opposites as Roman Catholicism and Unitarianism. See Robert H. Lord, John E. Sexton, Edward T. Har-
rington, *History of the Archdiocese of Boston,* II (New
York, 1944), pp. 182-85.

[21]Oscar Handlin, *Boston's Immigrants, 1790-1865*
(Cambridge, 1941), p. 146. Concerning the distinction between evil Roman Catholic clergy and misguided laity, see
Samuel Simon Schmucker, *Discourse in Commemoration of the
Glorious Reformation of the Sixteenth Century: Delivered
Before the Evangelical Lutheran Synod of West Pennsylvania*
(New York, 1838), pp. v-vii. Cf.: Thomas F. O'Dea, *Sociology and the Study of Religion: Theory, Research, Interpretation* (New York, 1970), pp. 160-61; Smith, *Social Reform,* p. 168; Clifford S. Griffin, "Converting the Catholics: American Benevolent Societies and the Ante-Bellum
Crusade Against the Church," *Catholic Historical Review,*
XLVII (October, 1961), 325; Robert D. Cross, *The Emergence
of Liberal Catholicism in America* (Chicago, 1958), pp. 22-
26.

[22]Handlin, *Boston's Immigrants,* p. 149. The quotations within the quotations were cited in Ibid., footnote
73, as "Cf.: Brownson, *Works of Brownson,* I, xix; *United
States Catholic Intelligencer,* February 24, July 13, 1832;
*Boston Catholic Observer,* January 10, 1847, January 26,
1848; *Jesuit or Catholic Sentinel,* July 2, 1831; *Boston
Pilot,* October 5, 1828...."

A number of Protestant clergy in Cincinnati were quite upset that Catholic priests purportedly told their congregations Protestants gave "divine honors to John Calvin, John Wesley, and Martin Luther," and that Methodists charged "a shilling a head for their love-feast tickets." "Denominational Statistics," *CURM*, I (March, 1848), 176

²³Brownson, *Works,*I, p. 254, quoted in Handlin, *Boston's Immigrants,* p. 134.

²⁴John Hughes, *The Decline of Protestantism and Its Causes* (New York, 1850), quoted in Billington, *Crusade,* pp. 291, 315. Also see, George Peck's analysis of another Hughes' public lecture in "Decline of Protestantism," *CA,* Dec. 5, 1850, 194.

²⁵Cf.: footnote 16 above; William G. McLoughlin, "Isaac Backus and the Separation of Church and State in America," *American Historical Review,* LXXIII (June, 1968), 1392.

²⁶*Boston Pilot,* Jan. 22, 1853, quoted in Handlin's *Boston's Immigrants,* p. 143. Also see Cross, *Liberal Catholicism,* p. 3.

²⁷Cross, *Liberal Catholicism,* pp. 3-7.

²⁸Ibid., pp. 25, 7-10, 15-16; Josef L. Altholz, *The Churches in the Nineteenth Century* (New York, 1967), pp. 83-85.

²⁹(Editorial). "Civil and Religious Liberty," *CA,* Nov. 6, 1851, 178.

³⁰Thebaud, *Forty Years,* p. 237. Despite his very real insight into this situation, Thebaud could not resist blaming the Protestant reaction on prejudice. Cf.: (Editorial), "The Pope and the Christian Alliance," *CA,* Nov. 27, 1844, 63; "Another Bull of the Pope," *CA,* Aug. 21, 1844, 7; "Address of the Rev. Dr. Cheever, Before the Evangelical Alliance," *CURM,* XI (July, 1849), 402-09; "Evangelical Alliance Anniversary," *CURM,* II (November, 1849), 686-87; "Meeting of the Evangelical Alliance for the United States," *CURM,* II (December, 1849), 742-46; [Robert Baird], "Editorial Remarks," *CURM,* III (September and October, 1850), 481-83; [Robert Baird], "Editorial Remarks," *CURM,* II (May, 1849), 258-59; J. P. Durbin, "Let us Petition the Pope," *CA,* Nov. 6, 1851, 177. A random survey of the *American and Foreign Christian Union,* V (1854), reveals a large number of articles on the inter-

action of evangelical Protestantism and Roman Catholicism
in Europe and foreign lands as well as on Roman Catholicism alone: "France," pp. 3-7; "Central Evangelical Society
of France," pp. 7-9; "Mexico and the Jesuits," p. 16; "Roman Catholic Prayers for the Conversion of Protestant Countries," pp. 51-54; "Letter from Lucca—Miss Cunninghame,"
pp. 67-68; "Foreign Field," primarily covering France, Belgium and Italy, pp. 71-85.  These articles are only from
the January and February issues of the *AFCU*—the heavy concentration on foreign affairs reflects the more than 100
missionaries sent by the American and Foreign Christian
Union to Catholic nations.  This gave the Union direct, if
biased, access to knowledge of Europe and Latin America.
Very many American evangelicals also subscribed to the
British Alliance mouthpiece, *Evangelical Christendom*,
whose scholarly and timely articles and notices made it
the news service for world evangelicalism because its basic principle was to foster ecumenism and provide up-to-
date information on worldwide evangelical affairs.  Also
see Lord, *et al.*, *Archdiocese*, II, pp. 185-91; E. E. Y.
Hales, *The Catholic Church in the Modern World: A Survey
From the French Revolution to the Present* (Garden City,
N.Y., 1958), pp. 163-64.

   The secular press of this period also covered Euro-
pean affairs and the Roman Catholic Church very carefully.
Cf.: Howard R. Marraro, "The Religious Problem of the
Italian Risorgimento as seen by Americans." *Church History*,
XXV (March, 1956), 41-62; Howard R. Marraro, *American
Opinion on the Unification of Italy, 1846-61* (New York,
1932).

   The *Christian Advocate* covered the Italian Revolution
of 1848 with great care in the following issues: Dec. 27,
1848, 204; Jan. 3, 1849, 1; Jan. 11, 1849, 5; Jan. 25,
1849, 13; Feb. 8, 1849, 21; (Editorial), "Rome," June 14,
1849, 94; etc. on through 1850.  On final unification of
Italy (1870), see: "America to Italy," *CA*, Jan. 26, 1871,
28; "Italian Unity—the Pope," *CA*, Jan. 12, 1871, 12.

   [31]Thebaud, *Forty Years,* pp. 165-66, 165-71.

   [32]Ibid., p. 171.

   [33]Albert K. Weinberg, *Manifest Destiny: A Study of
Nationalist Expansionism in American History* (Chicago,
1935, 1963), p. 112.

   [34]Cf.: John S. Stamp, "The Roman Catholic College of
Maynooth," *CA*, July 9, 1845, 191; "Anti-Maynooth Movement

in Ireland," *CA*, July 30, 1845, 202; "Christian Union,"
*CA*, Oct. 29, 1845, 46; (Editorial), "The New Year," *CA*,
Dec. 31, 1845, 82; "The Maynooth Question," *New Englander
and Yale Review*, IV (January, 1846), 146-48; [J. Forsyth],
"The Evangelical Alliance," *Princeton Review*, 18 (October,
1846), 569-71; George Peck, "Evangelical Alliance, No.
II," *CA*, March 24, 1847, 45; George Peck, "Evangelical
Alliance, No. III," *CA*, March 31, 1847, 49; Rev. John
Angell James, "Reasons for Union Among Evangelical Chris-
tians," *CA*, March 26, 1845, 131; "Christian Union a Testi-
mony for Christian Truth," *CURM*, III (June, 1850), 322-23;
Gilbert A. Cahill, "The Protestant Association and the
Anti-Maynooth Agitation of 1845," *Catholic Historical Re-
view*, XLII (October, 1957), 273-308; E. R. Norman, *Anti-
Catholicism in Victorian England* (New York, 1968), pp.
1-20.

   [35]Kessler, *Alliance in Britain*, p. 17; Norman *Anti-
Catholicism*, pp. 25-50.

   [36]Ibid.; Norman, *Anti-Catholicism*, p. 51.


CHAPTER THREE: THE FRATERNAL APPEAL OF WORLD-
            WIDE ECUMENISM, 1839-1865

   [1][Robert Baird], "Editorial Remarks," *CURM*, III
(March, 1850), 132; Samuel Simon Schmucker, *Overture for
Christian Union* (1845) in S. S. Schmucker, *Fraternal Ap-
peal to the American Churches* (1839), ed. Frederick K.
Wentz (Philadelphia, 1965), p. 203; Gaius Jackson Slosser,
*Christian Unity: Its History and Challenge in All Commun-
ions, in All Lands* (New York, 1929), p. 179.  Kessler,
*Alliance in Britain*, pp. 16-18.

   [2]Pastor, etter to James quoted in George Peck, "Evangelical Alliance, No. IV," *CA*, April 7, 1847, 53; Letter,
Andrew Fuller to William Ward, Serampore, December 2,
1806, quoted in Rouse and Neill, *Ecumenical*, p. 315; Baird,
*Progress*, p. 51; London Provisional Committee, *Conference
on Christian Union. Narrative of the Proceedings of the
Meetings held in Liverpool, October 1845* (London, 1845), p.
9.  Rev. J. A. James suggests that the Americans were the
first to broach the idea of an Evangelical Alliance;
[Robert Baird], "Editorial Remarks," *CURM*, III (March,
1850, 132; Slosser, *Christian Unity*, pp. 174-75, 178-79;
Wentz, *Pioneer*, p. 282.  For discussion of the Liverpool
Conference per se, see the following as well: "Christian
Union," *CA*, Oct. 29, 1845, 47; "Conference on Christian
Union," *CA*, Dec. 24, 1845, 77-78; "Conference on Christian

Union," *CA,* Dec. 31, 1845, 82.

[3]N.t., *NYO,* May 18, 1839, quoted in Samuel Simon
Schmucker, *The True Unity of Christ's Church,* 3rd ed.
(New York, 1870), p. 15.

[4]Wentz, *Pioneer,* pp. 276-77; George Peck, "Evangelical Alliance, No. IV," *CA,* April 7, 1847, 53.

[5]Philip Schaff, *What is Church History? A Vindication of the Idea of Historical Development* (Philadelphia,
1846), p. 124. Rev. William Patton later criticized this
approach, although he did not mention Schmucker's name, as
one of the forms of union which the Evangelical Alliance
considered but then rejected. "American Evangelical Alliance," *CURM,* III (September and October, 1850), 537-38.
Cf.: Wentz, *Pioneer,* pp. 270-71, 278; Samuel Simon Schmucker, *The Church of the Redeemer* (Baltimore, 1867), pp.
105-06.

[6]Schmucker, *True Unity,* p. 16; Sanford, "A History,"
p. 24; Wentz, *Pioneer,* p. 282; Frederick K. Wentz, "Introduction," to Schmucker, *Fraternal Appeal,* pp. 21-22.

[7]Schmucker, *Overture,* in Schmucker, *Fraternal Appeal,*
pp. 210-12. For complete text of the circular calling for
the London Conference, see "Evangelical Alliance," *CA,*
June 10, 1846, 175.

[8]Appendix, Evangelical Alliance (British), *Report of
the Proceedings of the Conference Held at Freemason's Hall,
London, From August 19th to September 2nd Inclusive, 1846*
(London, 1847), pp. ixxic-xcvi—henceforth cited as E.A.B.,
*Report....1846.* A breakdown of those Americans whose denominational affiliation I am able to determine reveals
that there were at least the following number of each
present: 26 Presbyterians, 17 Methodists, 11 Congregationalists, 6 Baptists, 4 Dutch Reformed, 4 Lutherans, and
1 Episcopalian. Many of the leading lights of American
denominationalism were there: Lyman Beecher, Robert Baird,
Pharcellus Church, Gorham D. Abbott, T. Dwight, S. H. Cox,
Robert Emory, J. Harper (publisher), Stephen Olin, William
Patton, S. S. Schmucker, George Peck, etc.

[9]From a Convention of Friends of Christian Union Assembled in New York," May 13, 1846, Appendix, E.A.B.,
*Report....1846,* p. xxvi.

[10]E.A.B., *Report....1846,* p. 44.

[11]Ibid., pp. 26, 54, 62, 225, 229.

[12]Ibid., pp. 47, 49; "From a Convention," Ibid., p.
xxviii; E.A.B., *Report....1846*, p. 25. Olin is not the
only American clergyman to claim the character of an official Methodist delegate to the Conference. Rev. George
Peck was also sent by Methodist Conferences totalling over
400 clergymen to represent them in the Alliance. The London Conference however accepted men only in their individual capacity to avoid the controversies that acceptance of
official delegates would have brought down upon it. Ibid.,
p. 213.

[13][J. Forsyth], "The Evangelical Alliance," *Princeton
Review* (October, 1845), 572.

[14]E.A.B., *Report....1846*, pp. 178, 179, 202.

[15]*On the Evangelical Alliance. Its Design, Its Difficulties, Its Proceedings, and Its Prospects: With Practical Suggestions* (Edinburgh, 1846), pp. 17-18.

[16]E.A.B., *Report....1846*, pp. 172-73, 173, 177.

[17]Ibid., p. 179.

[18]Cf.: Bishop Cyrus B. Foss's speech in Elias B. Sanford, ed., *Church Federation: Interchurch Conference on
Federation, New York, November 15-21, 1905* (New York,
1906), pp. 69-71; Charles S. MacFarland, *Christian Unity
in the Making: The First Twenty-Five Years of the Federal
Council of the Churches of Christ in America, 1905-1930*
(New York, 1948), p. 26; Hutchison, *We Are Not Divided*,
pp. 24-29.

[19]E.A.B., *Report....1846*, pp. 77-78——Rev. Bickersteth
for example showed such concern; Ibid., pp. 239-40, 278.

[20]Ibid., p. 189.

[21]"From a Convention," E.A.B., *Report....1846*, p.
xxvi; E.A.B., *Report...1846*, pp. 111-12, 113, 113-14. The
undercurrent of dislike for Unitarianism, the older form
of "infidelity," is never quite stated at the Conference.
It nevertheless existed among members of the American Alliance as late as the 1870s. Cf.: N.t. *Protestant Ecumenical,* May 9, 1870, in Evangelical Alliance, "Miscellany," I, Scrapbooks, Union Theological Seminary Archives
——henceforth cited as E.A., "Miscellany"; n.t., *Independent,* August 11, 1870, E.A., "Miscellany," I; n.t. *Standard-Union,* March 31, 1888, E.A., "Miscellany," VI. For a
lengthy contemporary analysis of Unitarianism, see the

editorial series in the *Christian Advocate:* March 15, 1849, 42; March 22, 1849, 46; March 29, 1849, 50; April 5, 1849, 54; April 12, 1849, 58; April 19, 1849, 62.

[22] E.A.B., *Report....1846,* p. 109.

[23] Ibid., pp. 139-40, 143-45, 163-69.

[24] "From a Convention," E.A.B., *Report....1846,* pp. xxvi-xxvii. See: "The Bull of the Present Pope Against the Bible and 'The Christian Alliance,'" *CA,* Feb. 26, 1845, 114.

[25] "From a Convention," E.A.B., *Report....1846,* p. xxvii. The reference to Apostle Paul rests on the four- teenth and fifteenth chapters of the "Epistle to the Ro- mans." Cf.: "Meeting of the Evangelical Alliance for the United States," *CURM,* II (December, 1849), 743-45; "Chris- tian Union," *CURM,* I (February, 1848), 82-83.

[26] E.A.B., *Report....1846,* pp. 137-38, 77-78, 81.

[27] Ibid., p. 81.

[28] Ibid., pp. 286-87.

[29] Ibid., pp. 288-89; Rouse, "Voluntary Movements," in Rouse and Neill, *Ecumenical Movement,* p. 320. Robert Baird says that a number of Americans wanted general con- ferences alone without any central organization. "Editor- ial Remarks," *CURM,* III (March, 1850), 131.

[30] E.A.B., *Report....1846,* pp. 287-89, 288, 288-89. Please note that this resolution involves more than rheto- ric. The Roman Church forbade Protestantism in the Papal States as well as distribution of scriptures to the laity. Such religious intolerance angered and frightened evangeli- cals worldwide, especially when American Catholics such as Orestes Brownson justified it as the right of the Church to stamp out error within its bounds—the implications appeared obvious if Catholics became the majority in Ameri- ca. Cf.: (Editorial), "The Romish Church A Despotism and an Imposture," *CA,* Jan. 20, 1851, 18; (Editorial), "Romish Impostures," *CA,* Feb. 6, 1851, 22; James Sewall, "On Peti- tioning the Pope," *CA,* Aug. 21, 1851, 133; R. B. Westbrook, "Let Us Petition the Pope," *CA,* Sept. 11, 1851, 145; "The Protestant Movement in Italy," *CA,* June 14, 1866, 185; "Italy and Religious Liberty," *CA,* Feb. 14, 1869, p. 50.

[31] On the splintering of the American denominations over slavery, cf.: William Warren Sweet, *The Story of*

*Religion in America* (New York, 1950), pp. 297-305; Smith,
*Social Reform,* pp. 180-203. With reference to the latter
citation, Smith points out that the Methodist Episcopal
Church (North) continued to quash antislavery temperament
in its fold even during the 1850s, well after its split
with southern Methodism over slavery.

[32]Baird, *Progress,* p. 51.

[33]Ibid., pp. 44, 51; E.A.B., *Report....1846,* 290-91.

[34]E.A.B., *Report....1846,* pp. 291, 294-96.

[35]Ibid., pp. 315-16.

[36]Ibid., p. 371.

[37]Ibid., pp. 389, 390, 395-96. The *Report....1846*
says that Lyman Beecher made these statements but the son
of Robert Baird claims his father as their author. The
latter is probably the case because Baird's published comments say exactly the things attributed mistakenly to
Beecher. Henry M. Baird, *The Life of the Rev. Robert
Baird* (New York, 1866), pp. 233-35; [Robert Baird], "Editorial Remarks," *CURM,* III (March, 1850), 131.

[38]E.A.B., *Report....1846,* pp. 437, 503-04.

[39]The British formed an Evangelical Alliance the
November after the London Conference. Evangelical Alliance, British Organization, *A Concise View of Its Principles, Objects, and Constitution* (London, 1846). The Germans created an Alliance in March of 1849 at Wittenberg—
it comprised many of the leading evangelical theologians
such as Hengstenberg, Julius Muller, Nitzsch, Krummacher,
Otto von Gerlach, Luche, etc. [Robert Baird], "Editorial
Remarks," *CURM,* II (May, 1849), 257.

[40]"Evangelical Alliance for the United States of
America," *CURM,* 1 (January, 1848), 4-8, 6. Other Alliance
governing members of note were: Hon. Joseph C. Hornblower
(ex-Chief Justice of the Supreme Court of New Jersey),
Rev. John McLoed, Rev. Robert Emory, Hon. Cyrus P. Smith,
Charles Butler and John Tappan.

[41]Ibid., p. 9; "Evangelical Alliance for the United
States of America," *CURM,* I (January, 1848), 9. A commonly repeated theme was the enemies of Christianity excused
their unbelief by reference to Christian division and dis-
sention. Even Horace Bushnell cited the London Conference

as "a visible confutation of the outcry of schism, perpetually echoed by the Romish and Anglican priesthood and all the adherents of Church authority," aimed at the evangelicals. "The Evangelical Alliance," *New Englander,* V (January, 1847), 104. Cf.: Rev. Thomas DeWitt, "The Claims of the Cause of Christian Union Upon Every Believer," *CURM,* I (February, 1848), 66-67; Speech by Moses Crow cited in "American Evangelical Alliance," *CURM,* III (September and October, 1850), 539-40.

[42]Evangelical Alliance for the United States of America," *CURM,* I (January, 1848), 9-10; [Robert Baird], "Editorial Remarks," *CURM,* III (March, 1850), 130; "Christian Union," *CURM,* II (February, 1849), 82-83.

[43]Chalmers, *Alliance,* pp. 22-36.

[44]Ibid., p. 39.

[45]Ibid., pp. 23, 28-29; Bushnell, "The Evangelical Alliance," *New Englander,* V (January, 1847), 118-21.

[46]Bushnell, "The Evangelical Alliance," *New Englander,* V (January, 1847), 105-13.

[47]Ibid., pp. 109-15.

[48]Ibid., pp. 118-20.

[49]One of the principle sources for these comments is the *CURM.* This journal began in 1848 as the official Alliance publication although it was sponsored and financed from without. Robert Baird was persuaded to add the editorship of this informative publication to his already onerous duties as the Secretary of the American and Foreign Christian Union. The *CURM* died in 1850 for the same reasons which undercut the Alliance itself.

[50]George Peck, "Evangelical Alliance, No. VIII," *CA,* May 5, 1847, 69; Rev. Thomas Skinner, "Fellowship, Not Uniformity, the True Idea of Christian Union," *CURM,* I (February, 1848), 74.

[51]Peck, "Evangelical Alliance, No. VIII," *CA,* May 5, 1847, 69.

[52]Ibid.

[53]Skinner, "Fellowship, Not Uniformity, the True Idea of Christian Union," *CURM,* I (February, 1848), 74.

[54]Peck, "Evangelical Alliance, No. VIII," *CA*, May 5, 1847, 69.

[55]"Religious Controversy," *CURM*, I (January, 1948), 14, 15.

[56]Ibid., p. 15. See "American Evangelical Alliance," *CURM*, III (September and October, 1850), 537-38.

[57]The Claims of the Cause of Christian Union Upon Every Believer," *CURM*, I (February, 1848), 65-67; Rev. Thomas Skinner, "Sectarianism and Christian Union," *CURM*, III (April, 1850), 225.

[58]Skinner, "Fellowship, Not Uniformity, the True Idea of Christian Union," *CURM*, I (February, 1848), 71.

[59]Ibid., p. 73. S. S. Schmucker did not write specifically about the Alliance at this time but he did allow excerpts of one of his papers to be published in the Alliance journal. Those excerpts present a systematic development of many of the points which Skinner, Peck and DeWitt made concerning Christian union. S. S. Schmucker, "Church Development on Apostolic Principles," *CURM*, III (September and October, 1850), 521-25.

[60]DeWitt, "The Claims of the Cause of Christian Union Upon Every Believer," *CURM*, I (February, 1848), 65-67; Skinner, "Fellowship, Not Uniformity, the True Idea of Christian Union," *CURM*, I (February, 1848), 73; Peck "Religious Controversy," *CURM*, I (January, 1848), 15-16; Rev. Gorham D. Abbott, "The Importance of Christian Union at the Present Time," *CURM*, I (January, 1848), 18, 20; Rev. William Patton, "The Evangelical Alliance: Its Object, and Prayer as the Means of Its Attainment," *CURM*, I (February, 1848), 80-85; [Robert Baird], "Editorial Remarks," *CURM*, III (March, 1850), 130-32.

[61]Cf.: Winthrop S. Hudson on Bushnell as a "mediating" rather than strictly "evangelical" theologian, in *Religion in America*, pp. 175-79; Bushnell, "The Evangelical Alliance," *New Englander*, V (January, 1847), 119-25; Peck, "The Evangelical Alliance, No. VIII," *CA*, May 5, 1847, 69.

[62]Cf.: [Robert Baird], "American Evangelical Alliance," *CURM*, II (May, 1849), 310; Rev. Samuel H. Cox, "The Cause of Union," *CURM*, I (March, 1848), 130-33; Speech by Moses Crow in "American Evangelical Alliance," *CURM*, III (September and October, 1850), 539-40; "Evangelical Alliance," *CA*, August 25, 1847, 34; "The Evangelical Alliance," *NYE*, May 17, 1849, 78.

[63]Evangelical assessment concerning insufficient piety may be seen in: "Christian Union," *CURM*, II (February, 1849), 82; the speech of Rev. Samuel H. Cox in "American Evangelical Alliance," *CURM*, II (November, 1849), 355-57; Abbott, "The Importance of Christian Union at the Present Time," *CURM*, I (January, 1848), 18-20; S. H. Cox, "The Cause of Union," *CURM*, I (March, 1848), 129; Miller, *Life of the Mind*, pp. 85-88.

[64]"Evangelical Alliance," *CA*, Oct. 21, 1846, 41.

[65](Editorial), "Evangelical Alliance," *CA*, Oct. 28, 1846, 46.

[66]"The Evangelical Alliance," *CA*, Dec. 23, 1846, 78; "Evangelical Alliance," *NYE*, Jan. 14, 1847, 6; "The American Evangelical Alliance," *NYE*, Jan. 28, 1847, 14; "Meeting of the American Alliance," *NYE*, March 4, 1847, 34; American and Foreign Anti-Slavery Society, *Remonstrance against the Course Pursued by the Evangelical Alliance on the Subject of Slavery* (New York, 1847); Peck, "Evangelical Alliance, No. VIII," *CA*, May 5, 1847, 69; William B. Gravely, *Gilbert Haven: Methodist Abolitionist* (Nashville and New York, 1973), p. 45. For an English view of the power of prayer see Rev. J. A. James, "Christian Union: What it is, and How it may be Promoted," *CA*, July 5, 1848, 104. For a discussion of the evangelical antislavery movement, see: Bertram Wyatt-Brown, *Lewis Tappan and the Evangelical War Against Slavery* (Cleveland, 1969); Gilbert Hobbs Barnes, *The Antislavery Impulse, 1830-1844* (New York, 1933, 1964).

[67]"Meeting of the American Alliance," *NYE*, March 4, 1847, 34; Peck, "Evangelical Alliance, No. VII," *CA*, April 28, 1847, 65; "Evangelical Alliance: Religious Fellowship With Slaveholders," *Eclectic Review*, 84 (1846), 778-80.

[68]Peck, "Evangelical Alliance, No. VI," *CA*, April 21, 1847, 61.

[69]"The Evangelical Alliance for the United States of America," *CURM*, I (January, 1848), 6-7; "American Evangelical Alliance," *NYE*, May 13, 1847, 73; "Evangelical Alliance," *NYE*, May 13, 1847, 74; "Evangelical Alliance," *CA*, May 19, 1847, 78-79; (Editorial), "The Evangelical Alliance," *CA*, May 26, 1847, 82.

[70]Ibid.

[71]Baird, *Progress,* pp. 40-44.  I already have published a summary of significant aspects of the London Conference, subsequent American Alliance formation, and the
problems which eclipsed the American body in Philip D.
Jordan, "The Evangelical Alliance and American Presbyterians, 1867-1873," *Journal of Presbyterian History,* 51
(Fall, 1973), 311-14.

[72]Ibid., p. 44; "Evangelical Alliance: Religious Fellowship with Slaveholders,"*Eclectic Review,* 84 (1846),
757.

[73](Editorial), "Christian Union," *CA,* Jan. 11, 1849,
6.

[74]Ibid.

[75]"Meeting of the American Branch in New York,"
*Evangelical Christendom,* XIII (January, 1859), 10-14.

## CHAPTER FOUR: AN EVANGELICAL RELIGION OF
## THE REPUBLIC, 1866-1873

[1]Portions of this chapter appeared previously in
Jordan, "The Evangelical Alliance and American Presbyterians, 1867-1873," *Journal of Presbyterian History,* 51
(Fall, 1973), 309-26.  Cf: David Schaff, ed., *The Life of
Philip Schaff* (New York, 1897), pp. 253, 271-73; Evangelical Alliance, "Historical Sketch of the Sixth General Conference of the Evangelical Alliance," *Evangelical Conference, 1873.  History, Essays, Orations...New York, October
2-12, 1873,* ed. Philip Schaff and Samuel Irenaeus Prime
(New York, 1874), p. 45—henceforth cited as E.A., *Conference...1873.*

[2]"Divines in Council: Annual Meeting of the Evangelical Alliance," *New York World,* Jan. 27, 1874, in E.A.,
"Miscellany," III, n.p.; Evangelical Alliance, *Document* IX
(1873), p. 7—henceforth cited as E.A., *Document;* Evangelical Alliance, "Minutes," I, Nov. 17, 1873, p. 286, MSS,
Union Theological Seminary Archives—henceforth cited as
E.A., "Minutes,"

[3]One of the characteristics of this Awakening was the
notion that Christian perfection was possible in this
world.  As Vinson Synan suggests in his *The Holiness-Pentecostal Movement* (Grand Rapids, Mich., 1971), p. 28, "by
1840 perfectionism was becoming one of the central themes
of American social, intellectual, and religious life" to

the point where it inspired not only requisite personal
holiness but social reform and ecumenism as well. Advocates of social perfection and of personal holiness tended
to diverge after the Civil War, first in evangelicalism as
a whole and, then, by the 1880s, in their Methodist bastion. The creation of distinct "come-outer" holiness
churches like Daniel S. Warner's "Church of God" (Indiana,
1880) siphoned off holiness devotees from the mainline denominations, paralleling a flight of similar bedfellows,
the fundamentalists. Perfectionism still flourished in
its social implications among the mainline denominations
so that churches like the Methodists became leaders of the
social gospel, by end-of-century, with all of its postmillennial and ecumenical visions of the Kingdom of God gradually coming to earth and to mankind. Holiness, subsequent pentecostal, and fundamentalist groups, to the contrary, took premillennial ground calling for dramatic
separation of the saved individual from both worldly corruption and an essentially damned mankind. Cf.: Ibid.,
pp. 28-29, 46; Ernest R. Sandeen's excellent book, *The
Roots of Fundamentalism: British and American Millenarian-
ism, 1800-1930* (Grand Rapids, Mich., 1970), pp. 4-5; James
Barr, *Fundamentalism* (Philadelphia, 1978), pp. 190ff;
Philip D. Jordan, "Immigrants, Methodists and a Conservative Social Gospel, 1865-1908," *Methodist History,* XVII
(October, 1978), 16-43.

[4]"Report on the State of Religion in the United
States of America made to the Fifth General Conference of
the Evangelical Alliance at Amsterdam, 1867," E.A., *Document,* I (1867), p. 18—henceforth cited as Smith, "Report."

The following officers of the American Christian Com-
mission became leaders in the Alliance: George H. Stuart,
H. Thane Miller, Rev. Stephen H. Tyng, Bishop Edmund S.
Janes, Bishop Charles P. McIlvaine, Dr. Charles Hodge,
Bishop Matthew Simpson, William E. Dodge, Sr., Rev. Heman
Dyer, John V. Farvell and General Clinton B. Fisk. George
H. Stuart, *The Life of George H. Stuart, Written by Him-
self,* ed. Robert Ellis Thompson (Philadelphia, 1890), pp.
131-32; E. A., *Document,* I-IX (1867-1873).

[5]On general Protestant union and identity as well as
growing Methodist comity at the end of the war, see: (Editorial), "Consolidation," *CA,* June 21, 1866, 196; "The
United Brethren and Evangelical Association," *CA,* June 28,
1866, 205; Philip D. Jordan, "Cooperation Without Incorporation—America and the Presbyterian Alliance, 1870-
1880," *Journal of Presbyterian History,* 55 (Spring, 1977),
13-35.

[6]Cf.: Lefferts A. Loetscher, *The Broadening Church*
(Philadelphia, 1954), pp. 4-8; George M. Marsden, *The
Evangelical Mind and the New School Presbyterian Experi-
ence* (New Haven, 1970), pp. 66-87, 128-44, 212-29; Elwyn
A. Smith, "The Forming of a Modern American Denomination,"
*Church History,* XXXI (March, 1962), 74-99; Robert Ellis
Thompson, *A History of the Presbyterian Churches in the
United States,* American Church History Series, vol. 6
(New York, 1895), pp. 104-28, 138-42, 173; Presbyterian
Church in the USA [New School], General Assembly, *Minutes,*
1863 (New York, 1863), pp. 224-25, 229-30—henceforth
cited as GA, *Minutes [O/NS];* GA, *Minutes [NS],* 1864, pp.
478-80; GA, *Minutes [NS],* 1865, p. 45.

The report of the joint Old-New School committee on
reunion made it quite clear that an "evident increase in
evangelic life and energy" in the towns and cities had
propelled the laity toward organic union:

> *If the hearts of Christian people,* combined already
> throughout the land in Christian work, *should be dis-
> appointed* as to that organic union which they crave,
> and this, *through differences asserted by the clergy,
> which the laity either do not understand or with
> which they have no sympathy,* the certain effect will
> be to lessen the sentiment of respect and confidence
> on their part toward their appointed leaders, and
> weaken the force of their paramount motives.

[Italics mine].  "Report of the Committee on Reunion," GA,
*Minutes [OS],* 1868, p. 669; "Report of the Committee on
Reunion," GA, *Minutes [NS],* 1868, p. 29.

[7][Italics mine.]   "To the Christians of America,"
*NYO,* Sept. 14, 1865, 290; "To Convert the Masses," *NYO*
Oct. 5, 1865, 914.  Also see an example of early ecumenical spirit in the "Christian Union Association," *CA,* May
17, 1866, 153.

[8]GA, *Minutes, [NS],* 1868, pp. 28, 28-29; GA *Minutes
[OS],* 1868, pp. 5, 6.

[9]Henry B. Smith, *Christian Union and Ecclesiastical
Reunion, A Discourse Delivered at the Opening of the General Assembly of the Presbyterian Church in the United
States of America, in Dayton, Ohio, May 19, 1864* (New
York, 1864), pp. 11-12.  Cf. the following for further information on evangelical conceptions of and relations to
infidelity at this time; John F. Hurst, *History of Rationalism Embracing a Survey of the Present State of Protestant*

*Theology* (New York, 1865); "Protestant Mass Meeting," *NYO,*
June 22, 1865, 194; "The Signs of Our Times," *NYO,* July 6,
1865, 210-11; George B. Cheever, "Modern Materialism,"
*NYO,* March 13, 1873, 81; William F. Warren, "Phases of
American Infidelity," *CA,* Oct. 23, 1873, 338; "Rational-
ism," *CA,* Jan. 18, 1866, 20; "M. Renan's New Book," *CA,*
July 19, 1866, 226.

[10]Smith, *Christian Union,* pp. 11-12.

[11]"Protestant Mass Meeting," *NYO,* June 22, 1865, 194;
GA, *Minutes* [*NS*], 1865, p. 47—eight out of the fifteen
clergy on this committee, among them Henry B. Smith, belonged to the Alliance by 1869-1873; "Reformed Dutch General Synod: Second Week," *NYO,* June 22, 1865, 195.

[12]Samuel Irenaeus Prime, *Autobiography and Memorials,*
ed. Wendell Prime (New York, 1888), pp. 17-18; David
Schaff, *The Life,* p. 254; E. A., *Document,* I-XXXV (1867-
1894); Philip Schaff, "The Reunion of Christendom," Evangelical Alliance, *Christianity Practically Applied. The
Discussions of the International Christian Conference Held
in Chicago, October 8-14, 1893. The General Conference*
(New York, 1894), pp. 305-40—conference proceedings
henceforth cited as *Applied. General,* Robert D. Clark,
*The Life of Matthew Simpson* (New York, 1956), pp. 195,
198-201. Schaff wrote a paper for the Berlin Conference
but was unable to attend personally.

[13]D. Stuart Dodge, *Memorials of William E. Dodge* (New
York, 1887), pp. 21-44, 149-260; E.A., *Document,* I-XLI
(1867-1899); GA, *Minutes* [*NS*], 1869, pp. 275-79. For a
discussion of the rise of the laity to power in the
churches see Sweet, *Story of Religion,* pp. 347-52 and
Hutchison, *We Are Not Divided,* p. 16.

[14]E.A., *Document,* I-XXI (1867-1886). Although Prime
was important in the early Alliance, particularly as an
administrator for the 1873 conference, Alliance records
bear little testimony to more than his presence at meetings until it became actively anti-Catholic after 1873.

[15]Alliancemen who were major supporters of and/or
teachers in Union Theological Seminary: Rev. Henry B.
Smith, Rev. Philip Schaff, Rev. William G. Shedd, Rev. G.
L. Prentiss, Rev. William Adams, James Brown, Morris K.
Jessup, D. Willis James, William E. Dodge, Sr. David
Schaff, *The Life,* pp. 284-86; E. A., *Document,* I-X (1867-
1875).

[16]Letter, John Jay to James M. King, Jan. 24, 1885,
E.A., "Minutes," II, pp. 240-42; E.A., *Document,* I-XXXV
(1867-1894).

[17]The Alliance represented neither the Disciples of
Christ, who were viewed as sectarian (they will enter the
Alliance in the 1880s), nor vast conservative elements
among the Baptists and Lutherans. For an example of Al-
liance attitudes towards the Disciples, see Letter, Rev.
R. D. Parker to Philip Schaff, Evangelical Alliance,
"Letters," I, MSS, Union Theological Seminary Archives,
May 6, 1875, n.p.—henceforth cited as E.A., "Letters."
Various aspects of Alliance doctrine and practice alien-
ated the latter groups and Quakers as well. Cf.: Philip
Schaff, *A History of the Creeds of Christendom,* vol. I of
*Creeds of Christendom* (London, 1877), pp. 915-16, 918;
"The Evangelical Alliance," *Independent,* Aug. 11, 1870,
n.p., E.A., *"Miscellany,"* I, n.p.

[18]E.A., "Minutes," I: May 4, 1869, pp. 41-42; May 21,
1869, pp. 44-45; Nov. 5, 1869, p. 53; Nov. 17,1873, pp.
282-87. According to E.A., "Minutes," I, officially recognized auxiliaries were founded in: Cleveland, Baltimore,
Washington, D.C., Boston and Philadelphia, June 3, 1870,
p. 97; Cincinnati, Baltimore, March 25, 1870, p. 84;
Flushing, Long Island, N.Y., June 17, 1870, p. 100; Chicago, June 24, 1870, p. 103; Syracuse and Canton, New York,
and Toledo, Ohio, June 24, 1870, p. 109; Southern Kansas
and Springfield, Ohio, Aug. 5, 1870, p. 128.

By 1870, the national Alliance organizational structure involved a President, a series of honorific Vice-
Presidents, two Corresponding Secretaries, a General Secretary, two Recording Secretaries, a Treasurer, a large
Executive Committee and an extensive Board of Councilors.
The key governing positions were those of President, Corresponding Secretaries and Executive Committee. The General Secretary was merely an administrative aid at this
time (although his will be a powerful position by the
1880s), while the Corresponding Secretaries exercised considerable individual influence over policy decisions. See
Evangelical Alliance, *Document,* IV (1870), pp. 12-15.

For contemporary analysis of the urban scene and related national crisis, see: Notes 4, 7-11 above; (Editorial), "The Republic and the Next Quadrennium—The Commission," *CA,* March 1, 1877, 136.

[19]Draper's position is particularly interesting and
may be partially gleaned from his *History of the Conflict*

*Between Religion and Science* (New York, 1874) but is ex-
plained best historically in my unpublished paper "John
William Draper and the 'Conflict Between Religion and
Science' Revisited, 1830-1860," presented before the Rocky
Mountain-Great Plains Regional Conference of the American
Academy of Religion and Society of Biblical Literature,
Iliff Theological Seminary, Denver, Colorado, on April 3,
1981.

[20]Stephen C. Brush, "Irreversibility and Indetermin-
ism: Fourier to Heisenberg," *Journal of the History of
Ideas,* 37 (1976), 603.

[21]Theodore Dwight Bozeman, *Protestants in an Age of
Science: The Baconian Ideal and Antebellum Religious
Thought* (Chapel Hill, 1977), pp. 3, 49-51, 71-72.  Also
see Herbert Hovenkamp, *Science and Religion in America,
1800-1860* (Philadelphia, 1978), pp. ix-xii, 23-36 and all
of George H. Daniels, *American Science in the Age of
Jackson* (New York, 1968).

[22]Stephen G. Brush, *History of Physical Science from
Newton to Einstein.*  Lecture Notes for HS 402 published
by means of Xerox (College Park, Maryland, 1977), p. 3a-9.

[23]This argument requires complex explanation and justification.  It is developed best in my paper, "The Search for
a Scientific Social Gospel, 1885-1914," presented in March,
1980, before the Missouri Valley History Conference, Omaha,
Nebraska.  For some inkling of the evidences to this position, cf.: Josiah Strong, *The New Era of the Coming Kingdom*
(New York, 1893), pp. 11-12, 18-20, 35-39, 116, 118-22, 129-
30, 235; Josiah Strong, *The Next Great Awakening* (New York,
1902), pp. 102-05; Josiah Strong, *Expansion: Under New World
Conditions* (New York, 1900), pp. 284-87; Dorothea R. Muller,
"The Social Philosophy of Josiah Strong: Social Christianity and American Progressivism," *Church History,* 28 (June,
1959), 186; Richard T. Ely, *Social Aspects of Christianity
and Other Essays* (New York, 1889), pp. 1-4, 8, 10-11, 16-17;
John R. Commons, *Social Reform and the Church* (New York,
1884), pp. 1-28, 75; Chapter V, note 4 of this text.

The distinction implied in my comments about the at-
tractiveness of dispensationalist theology and premillen-
ialism to some evangelicals must be understood.  Ernest
Sandeen correctly argues that there are positive and vital
roots to fundamentalism—it is not simply a negative movement—which began in England and won over a portion of
American evangelicals well before this crisis of science.
*Roots of Fundamentalism,* pp. xiii-xxiii.

[24]Again and again, religious authorities of the 1880s
denounced ecumenical efforts which included Roman Catholics, Unitarians, Universalists and Swedenborgians because
true ecumenism rested on agreement as to essentials of
doctrine and faith. See (Editorial), "Causes of Increased
Unity of Feeling Among Christians," *CA,* June 10, 1886, 359.

As for that "interlocking directorate" mentioned in
the previous textual paragraph on page 81, comparison of
Alliance membership rolls with those voluntary societies
to which Philip Schaff belonged proves quite revealing:

a.   Alliance members of the New York Sabbath Commit-
tee: William E. Dodge, Sr.; J. C. Havemeyer; William A.
Booth; Robert Carter; John Elliot; Jonathan Sturges; James
W. Beckman; Rev. Philip Schaff; Nathan Bishop; Gustav
Schwab; Frederick C. Foster. David Schaff, *The Life,*
footnote I, p. 233; E.A., *Document,* I-X (1867-1875).

b.   Alliance members of the [American] Bible Revision
Committee: Rev. Philip Schaff; Rev. Henry B. Smith; Rev.
Edward A. Washburn; Rev. Howard Osgood; Rev. Talbot W.
Chambers; Rev. Howard Crosby; Rev. John DeWitt; Rev.
Charles Hodge; Rev. Theodore Woolsey. David Schaff, *The
Life,* pp. 362-63; E.A., *Document,* I-X (1867-1875).

c.   Alliance members of the Council of Evangelical
Denominations (1869): Bp. Charles P. McIlvaine; Rev. Gor-
ham D. Abbott; Rev. Samuel Irenaeus Prime; Rev. Joseph
Holdich; Rev. A. C. Wedekind; Rev. Cyrus D. Foss; E. C.
Benedict; Rev. Samuel Simon Schmucker; Rev. Howard Crosby;
Rev. E. S. Porter; A. B. Belknap; Rev. Thomas DeWitt.
Schmucker, *True Unity,* footnote, pp. 42-44; E.A., *Document,*
I-X (1867-1875). Also see notes 4 and 15 above.

[25]"Address of the Southern Bishops," *CA,* May 3, 1866,
138; (Editorial), "The Southern General Conference," *CA,*
May 3, 1866, 140; C. C. Worth, "The Methodist Episcopal
Church, South," *CA,* April 5, 1866, 105; GA, *Minutes*
[South], 1870, II, pp. 529-31, 537-43; Ibid., 1874, III,
pp. 498-511; "The Evangelical Alliance," *Harpers Weekly,*
Oct. 18, 1873, 923.

[26]Schmucker, *True Unity,* pp. 4-41; "National Council
of Evangelical Denominations," GA, *Minutes* [OS] 1869, pp.
908-09. The Synod also approached the Evangelical Alliance to obtain its support for such a conference. The Alliance appointed a committee to meet with Synod representatives but there is no indication as to the outcome of
that meeting. E.A., "Minutes," I: March 31, 1869, p. 37;

April 7, 1869, p. 39; Oct. 15, 1869, p. 50.

[27]"National Council of Evangelical Denominations," GA, *Minutes* [*NS*], 1869, p. 290.

[28]Schmucker, *True Unity*, pp. 40-42; Prime, *Autobiography*, pp. 17-18.

[29]See Chapter Five, pp. 114-16.

[30]GA, *Minutes* [*OS*], 1869, p. 935; Presbyterian Church in the USA, General Assembly, *Minutes*, 1870 (New York, 1870), p. 76; Schmucker, *True Unity*, p. 49; E.A. *Conference...1873*, p. 174; Schaff, *A History of Creeds*, pp. 915-16; "Protestant Union," *CA*, May 8, 1873, 148.

[31]E.A., *Document*, I (1867), pp. 6-7, 7. Methodist editor Daniel Curry says much the same thing concerning evangelical consensus and stresses the necessity of an ecumenical movement consensus to isolate the faithful from the rest: (Editorial), "Unity of the Church," *CA*, January 10, 1867, 12; (Editorial), "Church Union, *CA*, Aug. 29, 1867, 276; (Editorial), "Christian Union," *CA*, January 13, 1870, 12—As Curry stated in this issue, "the essential accord of our chief denominations in all the vital doctrines of the Gospel, is a great and precious truth which is slowly but surely entrenching itself in the religious consciousness of evangelical Christendom." As far as denominational affiliation being a matter of taste and preference, Cf.: Bishop Gregory T. Bedell, "Spiritual Unity Not Organic Union," E.A., *Conference...1873*, p. 152; William Augustus Muhlenberg, "The Lord's Supper in Relation to Christian Union," *Conference...1873*, pp. 180-83. Indeed, the conception of denominational adherence as being of an aesthetic nature finds expression in later Alliance policy statements: E.A., *Document*, XXII (1886), pp. 2-3; E.A., "Minutes," III, Dec. 27, 1886, p. 52.

[32]Bedell, "Spiritual Unity," *Conference...1873*, p. 150.

[33]Ibid., pp. 152, 153.

[34]John W. Nevin, "Apollos: Or the Way of God," *Mercersburg Review*, XXI (January, 1874), 33; Philip Schaff, "Christian Union," *NYO*, Dec. 21, 1871, 401; E.A., *Document*, III (1869), pp. 7-9. Also see W. H. Marsh, "The True Grounds of Christian Union," *Baptist Quarterly*, VII (July, 1873), 293-95.

[35]E.A., "Minutes," I, Jan. 12, 1870, p. 74; E.A.,

*Document*, VII (1872), pp. 10-11, 11.

[36]E.A., *Document*, I (1867), p. 5; E.A., *Document* II
(1869), pp. 6-7; *Press* (Philadelphia), March 8, 1870, in
E.A., "Miscellany," I, n.p.—the Executive Committee expressed the same belief in its instructions to Bishop
Charles P. McIlvaine, E.A., "Minutes," I, May 27, 1870, p.
92; "The Report of Dr. Schaff on the Alliance Mission in
Europe," E.A., *Document*, III (1869), p. 32—henceforth
cited as Schaff, "Report."

[37]Invitations were sent to Alliances in Britain,
Canada, Germany, France, Switzerland, Holland, Belgium,
Sweden, Norway, Denmark, Greece, and India.  E.A., *Docu-
ment*, VIII (1873), p. 8.

[38]Letter, McIlvaine, Oct. 28, 1869, to the Conference
(of 4 and 7 November) which was called to hear Schaff's
"Report," E.A., *Document*, III (1869), p. 4; E.A., "Min-
utes," I, Aug. 5, 1870, pp. 123-24; E.A., *Document*, III
(1869), p. 9—Thompson was pastor of the prestigious
Broadway Tabernacle Church and a founder and editor of
both the *New Englander* and the *Independent*. Cf.: President
McCosh's speech, E.A., *Document*, III (1869), pp. 7-8; Rev.
John Cotton Smith's speech, E.A., *Document*, III (1869),
pp. 18-19; Letter, Philip Schaff to Bishop McIlvaine,
March 21, 1870, quoted in David Schaff, *The Life*, p. 250;
E.A., *Document*, III (1869), p. 9; E.A., "Minutes," I, Aug.
5, 1870, pp. 123-24; E.A., *Conference...1873*, pp. 35; Rev.
B. St. James Fry, "Rome and Austria," *CA*, July 23, 1868
234; (Editorial), "Evangelical Alliance—Postponement of
the General Conference," *CA*, Feb. 25, 1869, 61; "The Council of Trent and the Council of the Vatican," *CA*, Aug. 5,
1869, 241; "The Evangelical Alliance," *CA*, June 23, 1870,
196; "Letter from the Old Catholic Congress, Sept. 12-14,
1873," E.A., *Conference...1873*, pp. 485-86.

[39]"The Evangelical Alliance and the American War,"
*New Englander*, XXII (April, 1863), 288-315; "Evangelical
Alliance: Religious Fellowship with Slaveholders," *Eclectic Review*, 84 (1846), 747-81.  This sounds like strong
language but, as Robert Baird told the London Conference
of 1851, most American evangelicals ceased attending the
annual meetings of British religious and reform societies
because of British interference in the American slavery
controversy.  Also see "The Treaty," *CA*, May 18, 1871, 156.

[40]Smith, "Report," pp. 2-12.  British evangelicals as
well were upset by the poor relations between the two nations.  They saw the proposed New York Conference as a

means of re-establishing transatlantic cordiality. Letter, General Council on the Evangelical Alliance for Great Britain to the Executive Committee of the Evangelical Alliance for the United States of America, July 8, 1868, E.A., *Document,* II (1869), p. 4. The Alliance also noted British concern that Anglo-American cordiality continue despite the tensions resulting from the "Alabama Claims" controversy.

The British government, being less than neutral during the Civil War, allowed two cruisers built by British firms for the Confederacy to escape to the high seas over the protests of American Minister to Britain Charles Francis Adams. The *Florida* and *Alabama* destroyed $15 million worth of northern shipping, an enormous amount at that time, before the Union navy could capture them. Bitterness over other British pro-Southern and anti-Union attitudes and actions, coupled with initial British refusal to compensate Americans for their losses to the *Alabama,* soured Anglo-American relations from the war to the early 1870s. Finally, President Grant's Secretary of State Hamilton Fish negotiated the Treaty of Washington (1871) which settled a number of disputes with the English by means of arbitration and a special international tribunal. That court awarded American grievants $15,500,000 compensation for cruiser depredations. Cf.: E.A., "Minutes," I, March 25, 1872, pp. 206-07; and the following items from the Papers of John William Draper and Family, Manuscript Division, Library of Congress—Letter, S. R. Graves to J. D. Jones, typescript MSS, December 24, 1870, Container 1, I "A Miscellany of Letters"; Letter, J. P. Harris Gastrell to John William Draper, March 22, 1872, Container 3, General Correspondence "G."

[41]Smith, "Report," pp. 16-19, footnote 18. Also see John F. Hurst, "British Branch of the Evangelical Alliance," *CA,* Jan. 3, 1867, 2.

[42]GA, *Minutes* [NS], 1866, p. 263. Cf.: Henry F. May, *Protestant Churches and Industrial America* (New York, 1963), pp. 39, 42; John E. Smylie, "Protestant Clergymen and America's World Role, 1865-1900...." (Unpublished Th.D. dissertation, Princeton Theological Seminary, 1959), pp. 2-4; William Clebsch, "Christian Interpretations of the Civil War," *Church History,* XXX (June, 1961), 212-22; Marsden, *Evangelical Mind,* pp. 198-211.

[43]"Our National Conflict," *New York Daily Tribune,* Nov. 7, 1864, 7; GA, *Minutes* [NS], 1866, p. 264; Schaff, "Report," p. 32.

[44]Schaff, "Report," p. 32; Evangelical Alliance,
British Organization, *Deputation to the American Branch of
the Evangelical Alliance*...(London, 1870), pp. 14-15.
Henry Ward Beecher says much the same thing as Schaff concerning the forthcoming conference: (Editorial), "The
Evangelical Alliance," *Christian Union,* Sept. 24, 1873,
250.

[45]E.A.B., *Deputation to the American Branch*..., pp.
15-16; (Editorial), "Unity of Protestantism," *CA,* Sept.
11, 1873, 292; E.A., *Conference...1873,* pp. 139-200.

Among those present from Europe were: James Davis,
General Secretary of the British Alliance; Rev. R. Payne
Smith, Dean of Canterbury; Charles Read, Esq., M.P., Lon-
don; Rev. Matteo Prochet, Genoa, Italy; Prof. I. A. Dorner,
U. of Berlin; Prof. Theodore Christlieb, U. of Bonn; Rev.
H. Krummacher, Prussia; a paper read in absentia for A.
Tholuck, U. of Halle; and Rev. Antonio Carrasco, Madrid.

Among the American participants were: Rev. Philip
Schaff; Rev. S. I. Prime; William E. Dodge, Sr.; Rev. The-
odore Woolsey, ex-President of Yale; Rev. Noah Hunt
Schenck; Rt. Rev. Gregory T. Bedell, Protestant Episcopal
Bishop of Ohio; Rev. William A. Muhlenberg, Director of
St. Luke's Hospital, N.Y.; Rev. James McCosh, President of
the College of New Jersey; Prof. Arnold H. Guyot, Prince-
ton; Rev. Charles Krauth, Vice-Provost, U. of Pennsylvania;
Rev. Noah Porter, President of Yale; N.B. Anderson, Presi-
dent of U. of Rochester; Cephas Brainerd; Rev. John H.
Vincent and Rev. William Nast.

[46]William Adams, "Address of Welcome," E.A., *Conference...1873,* pp. 65, 67; Rev. R. Payne Smith, Dean of Canterbury, says much the same thing in "Christian Union Consistent with Denominational Distinctions," Ibid., pp. 145-
49. Henry Ward Beecher predicted approvingly that the
Conference would represent a revival of Zwinglian fellowship and the Communion of Saints, "A Spectacle of Christian
Liberty," *Christian Union,* Oct. 10, 1873, 270.

[47]A. A. Hodge, *The Life of Charles Hodge* (New York,
1880), pp. 502-04.

[48]Charles Hodge, "The Unity of the Church Based on
Personal Union with Christ," E.A., *Conference...1873,* pp.
139-42.

[49]Ibid., pp. 143-44. Deeply committed to the Alliance form of unity, Rev. Daniel Curry editorialized that

some splintering into new denominations, the sectarian
tendency, could be quite useful to church health——"The
Sects," *CA*, May 7, 1874, 148.  Also see, J. P. Lacroix,
"The Organic Reunion of the Churches," *Bibliotheca Sacra,*
XXXV (April, 1878), 391-95.

[50]George R. Crooks, "Christian Love the Bond of
Christian Union," F.A., *Conference...1873,* pp. 167-68.
Crooks was editor of the powerful New York *Methodist* and
an Alliance Councilor.

[51]Bedell, "Spiritual Unity," E.A., *Conference...1873,*
pp. 150-53.

[52]Noah Hunt Schenck, "Farewell Address," E.A., *Conference...1873,* p. 708.

[53]Such "union" services were open to all evangelicals
of good standing whatever their denominational affiliation.
Cf.: Rev. D. Stork, "Union Without Communion," n.p., May
16, 1873, E.A., "Miscellany," II, n.p.  E.A., "Letters,"
I: Letter, Henry B. Chapin to Rev. I. S. Butler, May 17,
1873, pp. 1-2——Chapin stated that the Executive Committee
refused to sanction a union Lord's Supper because the Alliance makes no claim to being an ecclesiastical body,
although Chapin did expect that a large number of delegates would hold communion under their own auspices; Letter, Chapin to Samuel Simon Schmucker, May 17, 1873, pp.
6-7——Chapin says the same thing as above; Letter, Chapin
to Rev. J. R. Dimm, May 17, 1873, pp. 4-5——Chapin assured
this representative of the Evangelical Lutheran General
Synod that the General Conference was not setting aside
the Lord's Supper to please the Baptists but because a
voluntary association could not exercise an ecclesiastical
prerogative.  He also assured Dimm that Lutherans were
well represented on Alliance governing bodies, Schmucker
being one of them.  Subsequent evidence shows that the
Evangelical Lutheran Synods were satisfied with these explanations——see note 54 and related text in this chapter.

For a discussion of the controversy concerning Bishop
Cummins and the Dean of Canterbury, see "Resignation of
Bishop Cummins," *NYE,* Nov. 20, 1873, 2.  E.A., "Miscellany," II: Letter to Editor, "A Church Divided Within Itself," *New York Tribune,* Nov. 17, 1873, n.p.; Letter to
Editor, "A Reply to Dr. Tozer by Bishop Cummins of Kentucky," *New York Daily Tribune,* Oct. 14, 1873, n.p. Catho-
licus, Letter to Editor, *New York Daily Tribune,* Nov. 17,
1873, n.p.; Letters to Editor, *New York Daily Tribune,*
Oct. 14, 1873, n.p.; "Reformed Episcopal Church," *CA,* May

21, 1874, 165; "The Evangelical Alliance Meeting in London," *CA,* Jan. 15, 1874, 17.  For a summary of the Cummin's
schism, see Philip Schaff, *A History of the Creeds,* pp.
665-68.

     Concerning reaction to Hodge and Conrad, see the edi-
torial footnote to Hodge's speech, E.A., *Conference...1873,*
p. 144, footnote 154.  Hodge and Conrad were less radically
innovative in their notions of intercommunion and cooperation than contemporary furor might indicate.  In 1845, for
example, the General Synod of the Evangelical Lutheran
Church (Schmucker's church) applauded and approved of the
General Assembly of the Presbyterian Church's desire to
exchange delegates and ex officio representatives at the
governing conferences of each body.  Indeed, the General
Synod resolved that it recognized as valid the ministry
and Christian character of any church witnessing to God's
spirit.  It voted to exchange delegates with the Presbyterians and officially approved of the common practice of
inviting those of good standing in one church to partake
of the Lord's Supper in the other as well as the transfer-
ral of members and clergy in good standing from one denomination to the other.  *Proceedings of the Thirteenth Convention of the General Synod of the Evangelical Lutheran
Church in the United States.  Convened in Philadelphia,
May 16, 1845* (Baltimore, 1845), pp. 29-30.

     Look to the following for an evaluation of Alliance
success: Rev. R. H. Richardson, *Lessons of the Evangelical
Alliance* (Trenton, 1873), pp. 17-19; John Hurst, "Christian Union Necessary for Religious Progress," E.A.B., *The
Religious Conditions of Christendom...Basle, 1879* (London,
1880), p. 420; David Schaff, *The Life,* p. 271.  E.A.,
"Miscellany," II: "The Evangelical Alliance," *New York
Times,* Oct. 10, 1873, n.p.; "The Alliance and Its Opponents: from the Baptist Union," *Echoes of the Press,* n.p.,
n.d., n.p.; "The Sixth Conference of the Evangelical Alliance—What will be the Fruit? *New York Herald,* Oct. 12,
1873, n.p.; [J. M. Hoppin], "The Unity of the Church,"
*New Englander,* 33 (January, 1874), 105-20.

     Failure: E. A., "Miscellany," II: "The Evangelical
Alliance and the Roman Catholic Church—A Field Day for
Sectarianism," *New York Herald,* Oct. 9, 1873, n.p.  This
article argues that Protestant efforts towards union are
too anti-Catholic when they should really see Roman Catholics as allies against the actual enemy, infidelity.  Also
see citations in the first two paragraphs of this note.

     [54]Brown, "The Evangelical Alliance," *Quarterly Review*

*of the Evangelical Lutheran Church,* N.S., IV (April, 1874),
234, 235-37; (Editorial), "The Methodists and the Alliance," *CA,* Oct. 23, 1873, 340.

[55] (Editorial), "The Evangelical Alliance," *CA,* Oct.
23, 1873, 340.

[56] "The Synod of New York," *NYE,* Nov. 6, 1873, 2.  Dr.
Dorner returned to Germany with a decidedly favorable impression of these characteristics of American religion and
society and told his people so—"Dr. Dorner on the American Church," *CA,* Jan. 8, 1874, 12.

CHAPTER FIVE: RELIGIOUS LIBERTY ABROAD AND EVANGELICAL
ESTABLISHMENT AT HOME, 1874-1882

[1] Robert Handy, *The Protestant Quest for a Christian
America* (Philadelphia, 1967), pp. 6-7, 11-17.  Also see
Robert T. Handy, *A History of the Churches in the United
States and Canada,* Oxford History of the Christian Church,
ed. Henry and Owen Chadwick (New York, 1977), pp. 262ff.

[2] Cf. Mead, *Lively Experiment,* pp. 135-39; May,
*Protestant Churches,* pp. 2, 41-42, 64—May cites the three
great labor upheavals of 1877, 1886 and 1892-4 as the impetus behind awakening evangelical concern over social
problems, p. 91ff; Jordan, "Immigrants, Methodists and a
'Conservative' Social Gospel, 1865-1908," *Methodist History,*
XVII (October, 1978), 16-20; William G. McLoughlin, in
*Billy Sunday Was His Real Name* (Chicago, 1955), shows the
strength which watered-down evangelicalism still exercised
among the masses at the end of the century.  For a supurb
study of the general nature of American culture and its
attempts to confront modernity during the late nineteenth
and early twentieth century, see Robert A. Wiebe, *The
Search for Order, 1877-1920* (New York, 1967).

[3] Ibid.

[4] Cf.: James McCosh, "Religious Aspects of the Doctrine of Development," E.A., *Conference...1873,* pp. 264-
71 and "Discoveries in Science and Speculation in Philosophy," Alliance of the Reformed Churches Holding the Presbyterian System, *Report of the Proceedings of the First
General Presbyterian Council Convened at Edinburgh, July
1877,* ed. Rev. J. Thomson (Edinburgh, 1877), pp. 187-94;
Joseph P. Thompson, *Man in Genesis and in Geology: Or, the
Biblical Account of Man's Creation Tested by Scientific
Theories of His Origin and Antiquity* (New York, 1870); Rev.
Cyrus D. Foss, "How Christianity Should Treat Science," *CA,*

March 7, 1872, 73. For a general background on the impact
of science and evolutionary theory in particular, on late
nineteenth century thought, see: Cynthia E. Russett, *Darwin in America: The Intellectual Response* (San Francisco,
1976); Paul F. Boller, *American Thought in Transition: The
Impact of Evolutionary Naturalism, 1865-1900* (Chicago,
1969). See note 24, Chapter Four, for members of the
American Bible Revision Committee who belonged to the Alliance.

[5]Cf.: (Editorial), "The Cure of Socialism," *NYO*, Sept.
30, 1871, 378; (Editorial), "The Communists in New York,"
*NYO*, Aug. 2, 1877, 246; Handy, *Quest*, pp. 10-13.

[6]Sidney Mead makes a similar point about an earlier
era. The churches of the colonial and post-revolutionary
periods accepted, out of practical necessity, both religious freedom and separation of religion and civil authority despite the absence of theological justification for
those principles. *Lively Experiment*, pp. 56, 60-61.

[7]E.A., "Minutes," I, Sept. 8, 1873, pp. 257, 257-
58.

[8]E.A., "Minutes," I, Nov. 17, 1873, pp. 282, 283.

[9]Ibid., pp. 283-84.

[10]Ibid., p. 284; E.A., "Minutes," I, Nov. 24, 1873,
p. 292; E.A., *Document*, IX (1874), pp. 6-13. Adam's resolution became Art. II of the amended Constitution. Ibid.,
p. 32.

[11]Schaff, "Report," p. 32; E.A., "Letterbox," Feb.
17, 1883, n.p. This is the official memorandum referring
to the death of William E. Dodge, Sr., on Feb. 9, 1883.

[12]Schenck, "Farewell Address," E.A., *Conference...
1873*, p. 708; Baird, *The Noblest Freedom; or the Influence
of Christianity upon Civil Liberty: A Discourse Addressed
to the Alumni of Jefferson College, PA.* (New York, 1848),
p. 7. Cf.: Rev. Alvah Hovey (President of Newton Theological Institution, Mass.), "Christian Liberty," E.A.,
*Conference...1873*, p. 481; Rev. Daniel Goodwin, "The Effects of Civil and Religious Liberty on Christianity,"
E.A., *Conference...1873*, p. 566; Philip Schaff's introduction to "Letter from the Old Catholic Congress," September
12-14, 1873, E.A., *Conference...1873*, p. 483.

[13]Baird, "The National Prosperity——A Thanksgiving

Sermon," *American National Preacher,* XXI (December, 1847), 282, 281-86.

[14]Baird, *Noblest Freedom,* pp. 8-12.

[15]Ibid., pp. 30, 13-24. Like many evangelicals, Baird claimed too much for the Reformers. Another example of an ahistorical interpretation may be seen in Baird's assertion that the Puritans escaped oppression in Europe in order to carry out more fully the great principles of civil and religious liberty which they had imbibed in the homeland. The Puritans may have escaped oppression but they in no way intended more civil or religious liberty for others in the new than existed in the old world. Ibid., p. 30.

[16]E.A., *Document,* III (1870), pp. 18, 19.

[17]"Religious Liberty and Church Freedom," *NYO,* July 22, 1869, p. 226. Cf.: Hon. J. L. M. Curry, "Evils of a Union of Church and State," E.A., *Conference...1873,* pp. 545-48; (ex-Pres. Yale) Rev. Theodore Woolsey, "The Relations of Constitution and Government in the United States to Religion," E.A., *Conference...1873,* pp. 525-26; Rev. Daniel R. Goodwin, "The Effects of Civil and Religious Liberty on Christianity," E.A., *Conference...1873,* p. 565; Rev. J. F. Astie, "The Free Churches of the Continent; Or American Ideas in Europe," E.A., *Conference...1873,* pp. 549-57.

[18]Jan. 23, 1873, 26. See Baird, "National Prosperity," *American Preacher,* XXI (December, 1847), 282; James Madison, "A Memorial and Remonstrance on the Religious Rights of Man," may be found in Joseph L. Blau, ed., *Cornerstones of Religious Freedom in America* (Boston, 1949).

[19]Ibid.

[20]Bishop Bedell's speech was covered in "This Nation Protestant," *NYO,* April 20, 1876, 121; Schaff, "Progress of Christianity in the United States of America," *Princeton Review,* IV (September, 1879), 212, 223. See Mead, *Lively Experiment,* pp. 55-59, for the background to American acceptance of religion as one's personal opinion. Cf.: Rev. Daniel Goodwin, "The Effects," E.A., *Conference...1873,* pp. 563, 565-66; Rev. W. H. Campbell, "The Influence of Christianity on Civil and Religious Liberty," E.A., *Conference...1873,* pp. 560-61.

[21]*The Progress of Religious Freedom as Shown in the
History of the Toleration Acts* (New York, 1889), pp. 1, 2.

[22]Ibid., p. 2; "Progress of Christianity," *Princeton
Review*, IV (September, 1879), 223; [Daniel Curry], (Editorial), "Church and State," *CA*, March 23, 1871, 92; Woolsey, "The Relations of the Constitution and Government in
the United States to Religion," E.A., *Conference...1873*,
pp. 527-28. Cf.: Rev. J. A. M. Chapman, "A Christian Republic—Its Grounds, Functions, and Claims," *CA*, Dec. 7,
1876, 385; Rev. James King, E.A., *Document*, XX (1886), pp.
13-15; Bishop A. Cleveland Coxe, "A Christian Alliance
the Demand of Our Times." *Independent*, Feb. 14, 1884, 2.

[23]Schaff, *Progress of Religious Freedom*, pp. 3, 82,
83.

[24]Ibid., p. 3; Schaff, *Church and State*, p. 15.

[25]*Church and State*, p. 15. He saw Francis E. Abbot
and the "Liberal League" as infidels. Ibid., pp. 43-44.

[26]Ibid., pp. 15-16; "Progress of Christianity,"
*Princeton Review*, IV (September, 1879), 214; E.A., *Document*, XIV (1879), p. 10; Schaff, *Church and State*, p. 16.
For a discussion of the earlier Anti-Bigamy Act (1862) as
well as the Edmunds Act (1882), see Klaus J. Hansen's
brilliant application of William G. McLoughlin's theory of
Awakenings to Mormonism, *Mormonism and the American Experience* (Chicago, 1981), p. 144. Hansen has provided us
with the best study of Mormonism as an "American" religious movement.

[27]Rouse, "Voluntary Movements," In Rouse and Neill,
*Ecumenical Movement*, p. 322. For a detailed discussion of
this symbiotic relationship between missions and ecumenism,
see Jordan, "Cooperation Without Incorporation—America
and the Presbyterian Alliance, 1870-1880," *Journal of
Presbyterian History*, 55 (Spring, 1977), 13-35.

[28]E.A., *Document*, IX (1874), pp. 14-19. E.A., "Minutes," I: Feb. 23, 1874, pp. 313-14; July 15, 1870, pp.
105-06; July 21, 1870, pp. 132-33. E.A., "Minutes," II,
Feb. 4, 1878, p. 200; Jan. 29, 1883, pp. 126-27. E.A.,
"Miscellany," III, "Oppression of Protestants by the Spanish Government." (Petition sent to the U.S. Minister to
Spain), Oct. 9, 1876, p. 73; "Oppression of Protestants by
the Spanish Government," *CA*, Nov. 2, 1876, 345; E.A., *Document*, XIII (1877 & 1878), pp. 6-9; Letter, Charles A.
Stoddard, George U. Wenner, Josiah Strong to Hon. Walter Q.

Gresham, Dec. 20, 1894, E.A., "Letters," VI, pp. 175-77;
Letter, Josiah Strong to Hon. John W. Foster, May 13,
1896, E.A., "Letters," VI, pp. 283-84; Memorial from the
Evangelical Alliance for the United States of America,
"*To His Excellency Grover Cleveland, the President of the
United States,*" E.A., "Miscellany," IV, 4 pages, n.p.;
Memorial from the Evangelical Alliance..., "*His Imperial
Majesty, the Sultan,*" E.A., "Miscellany," IV, 3 pages,
n.p.; E.A., *Document,* VI (1871), pp. 3-11; Shanghai and
Hankow Committees of the Evangelical Alliance, *Memorandum
on the Persecution of Christians in China* (Shanghai, 1885),
pp. i, 14-18; [Article], *NYO*, July 20, 1886, E.A., "Miscel-
lany," VI, n.p.; E.A., *Document,* XXI (1886), pp. 3-21.

On March 29, 1875, the American body had missionaries
visiting its meetings from Syria, Chile, and Turkey—the
gentleman from Turkey was a member of the Constantinople
Alliance. This is but one example of missionary attendance at Alliance meetings. E.A., "Minutes," I: March 29,
1875, p. 351; Jan. 31, 1876, p. 366.

For information on the British Alliance attempts to
succor persecuted Christians and expand the sphere of religious liberty, see John W. Ewing, *Goodly Fellowship: A
Centenary Tribute to the Life and Work of the World's
Evangelical Alliance, 1856-1946* (London, 1946), pp. 58-79.

[29]E.A., *Document,* VI (1871), pp. 3, 3-4.

[30]Ibid., pp. 9-10.

[31]Ibid., p. 10.

[32]Some members of the American delegation were unable
to go to Europe: Salmon P. Chase, S. F. B. Morse, Peter
Parker, John Crosby Brown, Norman White and Bp. Matthew
Simpson. Cf.: E.A., "Minutes," I: July 21, 1870, pp. 132-
33; Nov. 2, 1870-April 3, 1871, pp. 151-75; April 28, 1871,
pp. 180-82; July 15, 1870, pp. 104-06; March 25, 1872, p.
206. D. Schaff, *The Life,* pp. 259-60; Sanford, "A History," pp. 55-58; Evangelical Alliance (British), *Report
of the Secretaries of the British Organization of the
Evangelical Alliance, Deputations from European and American Branches of the Evangelical Alliance to the Emperor of
Russia on Behalf of Protestants in the Baltic Provinces*
(London, 1871), pp. 1-10; [Article], *Baptist Examiner &
Chronicle,* n.d., n.p., n.d., (probably 1871), E.A., "Miscellany," II, n.p.; E.A., *Document,* VII (1872), pp. 3-4;
E.A., *Document,* VI (1871), pp. 4-11; "The Evangelical Al-
liance and Prince Gortschakoff," *CA*, Aug. 21, 1871, 268;

"The Evangelical Alliance Deputation Again," *CA,* Sept. 14,
1871, 292; "The Evangelical Alliance——Religious Liberty in
Russia," *CA,* Nov. 30, 1871, 380.

[33]Jamison, "A History of the Evangelical Alliance for
the United States of America" (unpublished M.S.T. Thesis,
Union Theological Seminary, 1946), pp. 37-39.  He also
discusses somewhat the Alliance efforts on behalf of the
persecuted, Ibid., pp. 37-43.  For evidence of Alliance
efforts to aid the persecuted irrespective of their religion, see: "Meetings of the American Branch in New York,"
*Evangelical Christendom,* XIII (January, 1859), 10-14; E.A.,
*Document,* VI (1871), pp. 3, 4-6; "Persecutions in Japan——
Action of the Evangelical Alliance," *CA,* April 21, 1870,
122; E.A., *"His Imperial Majesty, the Sultan,"* March 26,
1896, "Miscellany," IV, n.p.; Letter, Charles A. Stoddard,
George U. Wenner and Josiah Strong to Hon. Walter Q. Gresham
Dec. 20, 1894, E.A.,"Letters," VI, pp. 175-77; E.A., *Document,*
XXXV (1895), pp. 7-9; E.A., *Document Number Four of the Evange
ical Alliance in Protest Against the So-Called "Freedom of
Worship Bill" Now Before the Assembly of the State of New
York* (New York, 1885), p. 11——henceforth cited as *Document Num
ber Four* (1885). E.A., "Minutes," I: June 3, 1870, p. 94;
June 10, 1870, p. 98; April 8, 1870, p. 87; July 21, 1870,
pp. 130-31; Feb. 12, 1872, pp. 198-205; Oct. 9, 1876, pp.
372-73. E.A., "Minutes," II, Jan. 30, 1882, pp. 108-09.

[34]E.A., "Minutes," II, Jan. 26, 1885, p. 238.

[35]"The Signs of Our Times," 210, 211, 210.  Cf.:
Hales, *Catholic Church,* pp. 123-26; Rev. R. Wheatley,
"Romanism in the Nineteenth Century," *CA,* Jan. 16, 1868,
17; Altholz, *Churches in Nineteenth Century,* pp. 83-85.

The *New York Observer* covered the *Syllabus* at least
four other times during the first seven months of 1865
alone: March 9, 1865, 73; March 23, 1865, 93; April 27,
1865, 190; July 6, 1866, 210-11.

[36]Encyclical letter from the Pope to his Bishops,
Feb. 2, 1849, quoted in Schaff, *A History of the Creeds,*
p. 109; also see *ibid.,* pp. 111, 112, 113, 116.

[37]Ibid., pp. 129, 133, 134.  Josiah Strong expressed
the last generalization in the quotation as strongly in
*Our Country: Its Possible Future and its Present Crisis*
(New York, 1891), pp. 84, 79-84.  Also see: E.A., *Document,*
XX (1886), p. 18.

[38]*A History of the Creeds,* pp. 146, 146-47;

(Editorial), "What is the Council Doing? What Will It Do?"
*NYO,* Feb. 10, 1870, 42; (Editorial), "Letter to the President," *NYO,* April 28, 1870, 130. Protestant hostility to
the forthcoming Vatican Council may be seen in "Pastoral
Letter: The General Assemblies of Both Branches of the
Presbyterian Church in the United States of America, to
the Presbyterian Churches Under Their Care," *NYO,* July 15,
1869, 219; Letter from the Council of the British Alliance
to the Evangelical Alliance for the United States of America, quoted in E.A., "Minutes," I, Feb. 12, 1869, pp. 24-
26.

[39]Schaff, *A History of the Creeds,* pp. 164, 165, 165-
88; Philip Schaff, "The Pope's Temporal Power," *NYO,* Sept.
29, 1870, 310. Also see E.A., *Document,* V (1871), pp. 4-5.

[40]Schaff, *A History of the Creeds,* p. 147; "Evangelical Alliance: First Biennial Conference," (Pittsburgh)
*Commercial,* Nov. 2, 1875, E.A., "Miscellany," III, pp. 46-
48. Also see James M. King's extended elaboration of this
type of distinction and his thesis of an ultramontane conspiracy in E.A., *Document,* XX (1886), pp. 3, 1-80; Rev.
James King, "Romanism in Relation to Education," E.A.,
*Vital Questions. Discussions of the General Christian Con-
ference Held in Montreal, Que., Canada, October 2nd to
25th, 1888* (Montreal, 1889), pp. 152-72.

[41]Cross, *Liberal Catholicism,* pp. 1-44—this is the
theme of his entire book but Chapters II-VII are especially germane to this discussion.

[42]Strong, *Our Country,* pp. 83, 79-84. Also see
Strong, *New Era,* p. 26. Cf.: Schaff, *A History of the
Creeds,* p. 134; (Editorial), "Preparations for the General
Conference of the Evangelical Alliance," *NYO,* March 6,
1873, 74; (Editorial), "Political, Not Religious," *NYO,*
Sept. 23, 1875, 298; "The Evangelical Alliance," *New York
Times,* Oct. 10, 1873, E.A., "Miscellany," II, n.p.; Philip
Schaff introduction to "Letter from the Old Catholic Con-
gress," September 12-14, 1873, E.A., *Conference...1873,* pp.
485-86, Speech of Dr. Joseph P. Thompson in E.A., *Document,*
III (1870), p. 9; Roswell D. Hitchcock, "Romanism in the
Light of History," E.A., *Conference...1873,* pp. 436-37;
Bp. Foster's speech in "Evangelical Alliance: First Bien-
nial Conference," (Pittsburgh) *Commercial,* Nov. 2, 1875,
in E.A., "Miscellany," III, p. 38; (Editorial), "The Progress of the Fight," *NYO,* April 8, 1875, 106; Strong, *Our
Country,* pp. 64, 74, 62-91.

[43]"A National or State Church," *Catholic World,* XX

(April, 1874), 31. Cf.: Lord, *et al.*, *Archdiocese*, III, pp. 64-65; Donald L. Kinzer, *An Episode in Anti-Catholicism: The American Protective Association* (Seattle, 1964), pp. 4-5; Aaron I. Abell, *American Catholicism and Social Action: A Search for Social Justice, 1865-1950* (Garden City, N.Y., 1960), p. 19. Please realize that this list of goals is hardly exhaustive. They are important in terms of Roman Catholic religious rights and aspirations but those Catholics who were immigrants, and some of the natives as well, also faced very real and embittering discrimination as to jobs, housing, recreation facilities and other areas of their lives. The burden of their grievance was quite heavy.

[44] "Unification and Education," *Catholic World*, XIII (April, 1871), 1-2, 3-4, 7, 4-5. Cf.: An Evangelical Alliance letter to the public, "A Fatal Choice," *NYO*, March 9, 1871, 74; Robert Michaelsen, "Common School, Common Religion? A Case Study in Church-State Relations, Cincinnati, 1869-79," *Church History*, XXXVIII (June, 1969), 214-17, 201-07; James King, *Sectarian Indian Schools, or the Relation of the Churches to the General Government in the Education of the Indian Races* (New York, 1890); [James King], The National League for the Protection of American Institutions, *Document No. Twenty-One: To Protect in New York State the Free Common Schools and to Prohibit All Sectarian Appropriations. An Address to the Citizens* (New York, 1894), pp. 1-11.

[45] "Evangelical Alliance: First Biennial Conference," (Pittsburgh) *Commercial*, Nov. 2, 1875, E.A., "Miscellany," III, p. 47; "Unification and Education," *Catholic World*, 5. See [James King], E.A., *Document*, XX (1886), pp. 9, 67; Abel Stevens, "Romanism and the Common School System," *Methodist Quarterly Review*, LII (April, 1870), 204-20.

[46] "Unification and Education," *Catholic World*, p. 6. D. A. Whedon is one evangelical who approved fully of a national education system, "Senator Wilson on National Education," *CA*, Jan. 12, 1871, 9.

[47] "Unification and Education," *Catholic World*, 6. On King, see: E.A., *Document*, XX (1886), pp. 25, 32, 41-42, 47; E.A., *Document*, XXII (1887), pp. 11-12. That Protestants thought the American conservative Catholic view of education typical of the papal hierarchy as well found support from Americans who examined the school systems of the city of Rome during Papal rule. Hence, Dexter A. Hawkins visited the Roman schools as an official commissioner of an American state. Noting that Roman public schools

taught only catechism, and pointing out the inferiority of training thereby engendered, Papal Secretary of State Cardinal Antonelli replied to Hawkins that the Roman was far preferable to the American school system because it was far better to be ignorant but properly catechized. Hawkins thought this meant the conservative Catholic was attuned to papal goals and thereby posed a real threat to America. "The Roman Catholic Church in New York City, and the Public Money and Public Property of the People," *CA,* Jan. 1, 1880, 1.

⁴⁸"Unification and Education," *Catholic World,* XIII (April, 1871), p. 9. E.A., *Document,* XX (1886), pp. 9, 20-23, 28, 32. Anson Phelps Stokes quotes the official Jesuit organ in Rome in 1949 to the effect that wherever the Church is able to use legitimate (i.e., nonrevolutionary) means, it will assert its authority over all religious aspects of civilization at the expense of all other forms of religion because there can be religious freedom only within the Catholic Church, the source of divine truth. *Church and State in the United States* in 3 vols., I (New York, 1950), p. 18.

⁴⁹"Unification and Education," *Catholic World,* pp. 13, 10-13.

⁵⁰E.A., *Document,* XIV (1879), pp. 41, 42; E.A., *Document,* V (1871), pp. 4-5. Also see Hon. J. T. Headley, "Manifest Destiny," *NYO,* April 21, 1870, 125.

⁵¹Lord, *et al, Archdiocese,* III, pp. 65, 4-65. Cf.: Abell, *American Catholicism,* pp. 15-19, 24-25; Kinzer, *Episode in Anti-Catholicism,* pp. 4-5. For contemporary examples of this interpretation of Catholic actions and expectations, see: John Jay, *Rome in America: An Address Before the Bible Society at Mount Kisco, New York, September 21, 1868* (New York, 1869), pp. 1-26; (Editorial), "The Romish Revival in England," *NYO,* June 22, 1865, 194; "Political Reform," *NYO,* April 21, 1870, 125; (Editorial), "The City Frauds," *NYO,* Nov. 2, 1871, 350; An Evangelical Alliance Letter to the Public, "A Fatal Choice," *NYO,* March 9, 1871, 74; J. T. Headley, "Manifest Destiny," *NYO,* April 21, 1870, 125.

⁵²Lord, *et al., Archdiocese,* III, p. 65; Pratt, *Religion, Politics and Diversity* (Ithaca, N.Y., 1967), pp. 195-218, 233-35. Cf.: (Editorial), "The Sectarian School Fund, $171,630.40," *NYO,* Nov. 18, 1869, 366; (Editorial), "Outrageous Appropriations," *NYO,* April 21, 1870, 126; (Editorial), "Sectarian Appropriations," *NYO,* April 14, 1870,

118; (Editorial), "Sectarian Appropriations," *NYO*, Dec. 7, 1871, 386; E.A., *Document*, XIX (1885), p. 4; "State Aid to Roman Catholics," *CA*, June 20, 1867, 197; (Editorial), "Conspiracy Against the School System," *CA*, Nov. 25, 1869, 372; (Editorial), "Church and State," *CA*, March 23, 1871, 92; (Editorial), "Church and State—Charities," *CA*, March 30, 1871, 100.

[53]John Higham, *Strangers in the Land: Patterns of American Nativism, 1860-1925* (New York, 1963), p. 4. Examples of the very complicated social gosepl reaction by Protestants to the immigrant and especially to the "new immigration" may be seen in my article on Methodism as well as Lawrence B. Davis's supurb study of *Immigrants, Baptists, and the Protestant Mind in America* (Urbana, Ill., 1973). For information concerning immigration in general, see: Maldwyn Allen Jones, *American Immigration* (Chicago, 1960); Marcus Lee Hansen, *The Atlantic Migration, 1607-1860* (Cambridge, Mass., 1940); Oscar Handlin, *The Uprooted* (New York, 1951). Finally, some very good recent studies of the religious identity, life and trials of primarily Roman Catholic immigrants in America are: Jay Dolan, *The Immigrant Church: New York's Irish and German Catholics, 1815-1865* (Baltimore, Maryland, 1975); Randall M. Miller and Thomas D. Marzik, *Immigrants and Religion in Urban America* (Philadelphia, 1977). Jay Dolan has also done an exceptional assessment of the nature of American Catholicism and its parallels with evangelical Protestantism in *Catholic Revivalism: The American Experience, 1830-1900* (Notre Dame and London, 1978). Those interested in the Italian experience in America ought to start with Slivano M. Tomasi and Edward C. Stibili, ed., *Italian-Americans and Religion: An Annotated Bibliography* (New York, 1978).

[54]Cf.: Report of Samuel I. Prime to the Executive Committee, E.A., "Minutes," I, Nov. 17, 1873, p. 284; E.A., *Document*, X (1875), pp. 8-12; E.A., "Minutes," I, 340 ff; E.A., "Minutes," II, pp. 1-122.

[55]E.A., "Minutes," I, Oct. 2, 1883, p. 155; E.A., *Document*, XVII (1883). Josiah Strong's *Our Country* was one of the most popular expressions of contemporary evangelical malaise.

[56]E.A., "Minutes," I: March 25, 1870, p. 85; April 8, 1870, pp. 87-88; Pratt, *Religion, Politics and Diversity*, pp. 216-20.

[57](Editorial); "Church and State," *CA*, March 23, 1871, 92. Also see (Editorial), "Sectarian Schools," *CA*, Dec.

21, 1871, 404; "The Public School Controversy," *CA,* Dec. 21, 1871, 412; "State Aid," *CA,* Dec. 21, 1871, 412.

[58](Editorial), "Church and State—Charities," *CA,* March 30, 1871, 100.

[59]E.A., *Document,* XI (1876), Appendix, "Protest and Memorial," pp. 15, 16, 15-16; E.A., "Minutes," I, March 29, 1875, pp. 352-53.

[60]E.A., *Document,* XI, "Protest and Memorial," pp. 16-17. Once the Ohio State Supreme Court (1873) allowed local option as to choice of scripture in the public schools, thereby opening the way to Catholic, Jewish, or even Mormon bibles, Daniel Curry decided solely secular public education superior to such polyglot approach. He, again, was well ahead of many evangelical contemporaries and, in this, was not representative of the Alliance. (Editorial), "The Bible-in-Schools Question in Ohio," *CA,* July 17, 1873, 228. Also see [Daniel Curry], "Our Schools," *CA,* Dec. 18, 1873, 402.

[61]Pratt, *Religion, Politics and Diversity,* pp. 170-71; Cross, *Liberal Catholicism,* pp. 131-45. Cf.: *CA,* 1878-1880, for dozens of articles on the crisis precipitated by Catholics; Dexter A. Hawkins, "The Roman Catholic Church in New York City, and the Public Money and Public Property of the People," *CA,* Jan. 1, 1880, 1; (Editorial), "Our Established Church," *CA,* Jan. 1, 1880, 8. Abel Stevens blamed this contemporary crisis of government and schools in the cities on insufficient democratic patriotism. See Abel Stevens, "Republics and Patriotism," *CA,* Jan. 8, 1880, 17.

[62]E.A., *Document,* XVI (1883), pp. 8-18 or Evangelical Alliance, *Protest of the Evangelical Alliance of the United States Against the Bill Entitled 'An Act to Secure to Inmates of Institutions for the Care of the Poor Freedom of Worship,' (In Senate #136, In Assembly #131 & 133)* (New York, 1883), pp. 1-12—henceforth cited as *Protest... Against* (1883); Jay Letter, E.A., "Minutes," II, April 28, 1883, pp. 143, 143-44. On the death of William E. Dodge, Sr., see: E.A., "Minutes," II: Feb. 17, 1883, p. 133; April 7, 1883, pp. 138-39; E.A., *Document,* XVI (1883), pp. 6-7.

[63]E.A., *Document,* XIX (1885), pp. 17-18; E.A., *Document,* XXI (1886); pp. 25-35; E.A., *Document,* XXV (1887), pp. 24-39. E.A., "Minutes," II: Feb. 25, 1884, p. 192; April 21, 1884, p. 199; Dec. 29, 1884, p. 223; Oct. 24, 1884, p. 215; Nov. 26, 1884, pp. 217-18; Feb. 25, 1884, p.

192; Sept. 29, 1884, p. 210; Jan. 26, 1885, p. 239; June
8, 1885, pp. 258-63.

[64]Cf.: E.A., *Document,* XIX (1885), pp. 3, 8-9, 11.
E.A., "Minutes," II: July 27, 1885, p. 382; Sept. 18,
1885, p. 284; June 8, 1885, pp. 258-59; Nov. 21, 1885, p.
303; Oct. 29, 1885, pp. 289-90; E.A., *Document Number Four*
(1885), p. 8.

[65]*London Times,* April 11, 1879, quoted in E.A., *Document,* XVI (1883), pp. 12, 10; E.A., *Protest...Against,*
(1883), p. 5; E.A., *Document Number Four*(1885), p. 10.
See State Sen. Esty's speech in defense of the nonsectarian character of the Refuge against the charges of the
Catholic Union.  He saw the Union as a party of "radicals
and extremists" not representative of the Catholic Church
but still a threat to the nonsectarian character of reform
institutions, and the public schools by implication,
through means "worthy of the palmiest days of Jesuitical
sophistry."  "Legislature of New York," (Albany) *Argus,*
March 17, 1885, E.A., "Miscellany," VI, n.p.

[66]State Sen. McCarthy claimed a previous investigation of the House of Refuge by the Senate finance committee, of which he was a member, elicited the unabashed admission from the director of the Refuge that the bulk of
the clergy training the youth were Presbyterian and that
Baptist clergy, for example, were inadmissible because of
their "'peculiar doctrines of immersion.'"  Yet the director, Mr. Agnew, still considered such instruction to be
nonsectarian—the implications for the Roman Catholic
clergy seemed obvious.  "Legislature of New York," (Albany)
*Argus,* March 17, 1885, E.A., "Miscellany," VI, n.p.

For the evangelical view, see: note 65 above; Letter,
Rev. R. H. Wilkinson to Rev. H. B. Chapin, Oct. 24, 1885,
E.A., "Letterbox," n.p.; E.A., *Document,* XX (1886), p. 7.

[67]E.A., *Protest...Against* (1883), p. 7; E.A., *Document,* XVI (1883), pp. 12, 13.

[68]E.A., *Protest...Against* (1883), pp. 10, 7-11; E.A.,
*Document,* XVI (1883), pp. 13-18; E.A., *Document,* XX (1886),
pp. 10, 18; E.A., *Document,* XVII (1883), pp. 11-12—the
bill was defeated.  See [Rev. Augustus J. Thebaud, S.J.],
"Freedom of Worship in the United States," *American Catholic Quarterly Review,* X (April, 1885), pp. 293-311 for a
discussion of the general context and specific implications of the House of Refuge practices as well as a justification for the Freedom of Worship Bills.

[69]E.A., *Protest...Against* (1883), pp. 5-6; E.A., *Document*, XVI (1883), p. 11. Cf.: "Freedom of Worship," *Baptist Monthly*, April 24, 1884, E.A., "Miscellany," VI, n.p.; debate between State Sens. Esty, Murphy, Gibbs and McCarthy. "Legislature of New York," (Albany), *Argus*, March 17, 1885, "Miscellany," VI, n.p.

[70]E.A., *Protest...Against* (1883), pp. 5-6; E.A., *Document*, XVI (1883), p. 11.

[71]E.A., *Document Number Four* (1885), pp. "Preface," 7, Letter, John Jay to Chairman of the Executive Committee, Rev. James King, Jan. 24, 1885, E.A., "Minutes," II, Jan. 26, 1885, pp. 239-43.

[72]E.A., *Document Number Four* (1885), pp. 7, 8, 9; E.A., *Protest of the Evangelical Alliance of the United States, Against the Senate Bill Introduced Jan. 6, 1885, by Senator Gibbs and Senator Murphy Entitled 'An Act to Secure to Inmates of Institutions for the Care of the Poor Freedom of Worship'* (New York, 1885), p. 3—henceforth cited as *Protest...Entitled* (1885).

[73]E.A., *Document Number Four* (1885), pp. 14, 19, 10-24; E.A., "Minutes," II, May 27, 1885, pp. 254-56; E.A., *Document*, XIX (1885), p. 15; Letter, William E. Dodge to John Jay, Jan. 21, 1894, E.A., "Letters," III, n.p.; The National League for the Protection of American Institutions, *Document No. Twenty-One*, pp. 1-11. The Alliance later decided that such an amendment was also needed for the federal constitution, E.A., *Document*, XXXIV (1894), p. 4.

[74]E.A., *Document Number Four* (1885), p. 22; E.A., *Protest...Entitled* (1885), pp. 15, 7-9; E.A., *Document*, XX (1886), pp. 7, 15, 1-7, 15-18, 43; E.A., *Document*, XIX (1885). See James M. Buckley's editorial supportive of *Document* XX—"Ultramontanism and Its Roman Catholic opposition in the United States," *CA*, Jan. 28, 1886, 10. For further evangelical reaction to the Roman Catholic threat to public institutions, see: James M. King, "Protestants Awake," *CA*, Feb. 17, 1887, 104; "The Jesuit Assault Upon the School Fund," *CA*, March 3, 1887, p. 133; (Editorial), "The New Work of Dr. King," *CA*, June 12, 1890, 373.

[75]Cf.: Lord, *et al.*, *Archdiocese*, III, pp. 78-79; the Methodist State Conference call for a state constitutional amendment, in (Editorial), "Sectarian Schools," *CA*, Dec. 21, 1871, 404; "Unanimous Protest Against the Bill 894," Annual Conference of the Methodist Episcopal Church, E.A.,

*Document,* XXVII (1889), pp. 15-20; E.A., *Document,* XXXIV
(1893), pp. 4-5; (Editorial), "The New Work of Dr. King,"
*CA,* June 12, 1890, 373; James M. King, *Facing the Twentieth Century* (New York, 1899), especially pp. 519-42.

[76]Ibid.; William E. Aikin, "The War of the Bishops:
Catholic Controversy on the School Question in New York
State in 1894," *New York Historical Society Quarterly,* L
(January, 1966), 41-61; notes 44 and 73 above.

Among the League members were John Jay, Bishop E. G.
Andrews, Bishop Arthur G. Coxe (A Cleveland Coxe?), Howard
Crosby, John Hall, General Clinton B. Fiske, William E.
Dodge, Jr., William Fellowes Morgan, Churchill H. Cutting,
Peter Donald, A. A. Low, Cornelius Vanderbilt, Abraham S.
Hewitt, and numerous others of high prominence from within
and without the Alliance.  (Editorial), "The New Work of
Dr. King," *CA,* June 12, 1890, 373.

As late as 1889, Philip Schaff still insisted that
Christian beliefs be inherent in American education but
his high regard for Sunday Schools and other church means
as a separate channel for Christianizing the people may be
seen in *Church and State,* pp. 77-78.

CHAPTER SIX: ECUMENISM, NATIONALISM AND AN EVAN-
          GELICAL SOCIAL GOSPEL, 1883-1900

[1]McLoughlin, *Revivals, Awakenings,* p. 152.

[2]C. Howard Hopkins, *The Rise of the Social Gospel in
American Protestantism* (New Haven, 1940); May, *Protestant
Churches;* Aaron I. Abell, *The Urban Impact on American
Protestantism, 1865-1900* (London, 1962).  My selection may
be found in Ronald C. White, Jr. and C. Howard Hopkins,
*The Social Gospel: Religion and Reform in Changing America*
(Philadelphia, 1976), pp. 202-05.  Also see Frank Szasz's
excellent article on the conservative and liberal Protes-
tant cooperation behind the social gospel and Progressive
Reform in "The Progressive Clergy and the Kingdom of God,"
*Mid-America,* 55 (January, 1973), 3-20 as well as his article on "The Scopes Trial in Perspective," *Tennessee Historical Quarterly* (Fall, 1971), 288-98.

[3]Jordan, "Immigrants, Methodists and a 'Conservative'
Social Gospel, 1865-1908," *Methodist History,* XVII (October, 1978), 16-43.

[4]Cf.: Hutchison, *We Are Not Divided,* p. 19; James A.

Smylie, "Philip Schaff: Ecumenist. The Reunion of Protestantism and Roman Catholicism," *Encounter,* XVIII (Winter,
1967), 3-16; MacFarland, *Christian Unity in the Making,* p.
19; H. Paul Douglass, *Protestant Cooperation in American
Cities* (New York, 1930), pp. 44-45. Also see, E.A., "Minutes," II: Jan. 27, 1879, p. 56; Nov. 21, 1883, p. 165;
Dec. 19, 1883, p. 169; April 28, 1884, pp. 202-03. E.A.,
"Minutes," II, April 1, 1886, p. 15; E.A., *Document,* XXX
(1891), p. 31.

    [5]E.A., *Document,* XVIII (1884), pp. 27, 21-27—hence-
forth cited as Schaff, "Discord."

    [6]Ibid., pp. 28-29, 27-29. For a careful elaboration
of the unique qualities of each division and of the necessity for the survival of Roman Catholicism in an evangelical form, see Philip Schaff, "The Renaissance and the Reformation," a speech before the Florence Conference, E.A.,
*Document,* XXX (1891), pp. 17-31.

    [7]Schaff, "Discord," pp. 32, 30-32.

    [8]Philip Schaff, *Christ and Christianity* (New York,
1885), pp. 20, 15-20; Schaff, "Discord," pp. 32-38.

    [9]Schaff, *Christ and Christianity,* pp. 148, 146-48.
Most themes in this paragraph may be found in Schaff's
earlier work. Also see Philip Schaff, "Denominationalism
and Sectarianism," *Christian Literature and Review of the
Churches,* X (n.d., 1894), 144-46.

    [10]E.A., "Minutes," III: April 28, 1887, pp. 90, 87-
90; April 1, 1886, p. 15; April 28, 1887, p. 89. Also
see, E.A., "Minutes," II, Dec. 28, 1885, pp. 307-08.

    [11]J. H. Ward, "The Evangelical Alliance in Boston,"
*Churchman* (American), Dec. 21, 1889, 771; E.A., "Minutes,"
III, April 28, 1887, pp. 86-87; Letter, Josiah Strong to
Edouard Naville, President of the International Committee,
n.d., 1887, E.A., "Letter," V, p. 141; Letter, Josiah
Strong to Count Bernstoff and Dr. Baumann, March 27, 1888,
"Letters," V, p. 144; E.A., *Document,* XXX (1891), pp. 4-
10.

    [12]Rev. E. O. Haven, "The Proposed Ecumenical Confer-
ence," *CA,* Nov. 14, 1878, 726. Cf.: William G. Blaikie,
"Introductory Narrative," in Alliance of the Reformed
Churches Holding the Presbyterian System, *Presbyterian
Council...Edinburgh,* pp. 2-4; "More Union Proposed," *NYO,*
Aug. 3, 1875, 242; Philip Schaff, "The Reunion of

Christendom," E.A., *Applied. General,* pp. 318-19.

    [13]N.a., n.t., *NYE,* Aug. 28, 1884, n.p., E.A., "Mis-
cellany," VI, n.p.

    [14]Coxe, "A Christian Alliance the Demand of Our
Times," *Independent,* Feb. 14, 1884, 2, 1-2.  Coxe found
the American Congress of Churches more congenial because
it dealt with doctrinal issues and espoused union essentially from the Episcopalian perspective as set forth by the
Lambeth proposals (absorption of the churches by the Episcopalian Church)—the Congress proved short-lived (1883-
1886).  See Julius H. Ward, "The New Movement Toward Unity," *Andover Review,* IV (October, 1885), 376-83.

    [15]E.A., "Minutes," II: Jan. 29, 1883, p. 131; April
28, 1883, p. 145; June 5, 1883, pp. 148-51; Dec. 19, 1883,
p. 172.

    [16]E.A., "Minutes," III, April 1, 1886, p. 16.  Cf.:
E.A., "Minutes," II: June 8, 1885, pp. 248-63; June 15,
1885, pp. 265-73; June 22, 1885, pp. 274-75; June 29, 1885,
p. 276; July 6, 1885, p. 277; Sept. 18, 1885, p. 285; Oct.
19, 1885, p. 286; Nov. 21, 1885, pp. 301-02.  E.A., "Minutes," III: April 1, 1886, p. 16; March 19, 1887, p. 76;
May 12, 1890, p. 243.  E.A., "Minutes," IV: April 24, 1891,
pp. 1-2; April 30, 1891, p. 6.  E.A., *Document,* XX (1886), p. 29;
E.A., *Document,* XXI (1886), pp. 29-31.  Philip Schaff was accorded the honor of being the first to affix his name to the
otherwise alphabetical list of signatories to the certifica-
of incorporation. E.A., "Minutes," II, June 8, 1885, p. 263.

    [17][Lyman Abbott], "The Evangelical Alliance to be Re-
vised and Enlarged," *Christian Union,* April 15, 1886, 20;
E.A., "Minutes," III, April 29, 1886, p. 19 and June 4,
1886, pp. 23-24; E.A., *Document,* XXI (1886), pp. 9-10.
Aaron I. Abell is in error when he states Josiah Strong
and Frank Russell were appointed to their offices at this
meeting. *Urban Impact,* p. 91.

    [18]Letter, G. B. Safford to Rev. David A. Reed, July
28, 1886, E.A., "Letters," III, pp. 10-11; Letter, G. B.
Safford to Rev. Henrick Johnson, Aug. 30, 1886, E.A.,
"Letters," III, pp. 60-61.

    [19]"Report of the Committee on the Proposed Washington
Conference, to the Executive Committee of the Evangelical
Alliance for the United States of America," October 23,
1886, pp. 1-2, 3, E.A., "Miscellany," IV, n.p.—published
for private circulation among the Board of Managers on Oct.

23, 1886, E.A., "Minutes," III, Oct. 22, 1886, p. 43.
Henceforth cited as "October Report," "Miscellany."

[20] Ibid. For evangelical reactions to Mormonism see:
J. H. Vincent, "The Great Danger," *CA*, June 24, 1886, 393;
(Editorial), "Mormonism," *CA*, April 5, 1877, 216; and the
weekly series of articles and editorials in *CA* starting
with January 23, 1879, 49 and continuing for the ensuing
months of the year. Also see the *NYO* for the same period.

[21] "October Report," "Miscellany," pp. 4-5, 5, 6, 7.

[22] Ahlstrom, *Religious History*, II, pp. 265-66.

[23] Strong, *Our Country*, pp. 179-94, 228-67; Letter,
Lyman Abbott to Mr. Mornay Williams, May 3, 1916, MSS,
Josiah Strong Collection, Box #1, Special Collections,
Union Theological Seminary.

[24] E.A., "Minutes," III, Oct. 29, 1886, pp. 46, 49, 48;
Oct. 22, 1886, p. 43.

[25] Letter, William E. Dodge, Jr., to Josiah Strong,
Oct. 29, 1886, Xerox copy of MSS, Union Theological Seminary Archives, Josiah Strong Collection (this citation
comes from the collection when it was in the organization
phase and cannot be cited as to box, file, etc.). For
Robert S. MacArthur's complimentary analysis of the Alliance and its Washington Conference, see (Editorial), "The
Late Washington Conference," *Baptist Quarterly Review*, X
(1888), 94-96.

[26] Letter, Dodge to Strong, Oct. 29, 1886.

[27] Ibid.

[28] E.A., "Minutes," III: Oct. 29, 1886, p. 49; Dec.
27, 1886, pp. 51-57.

[29] "October Report," "Miscellany," p. 7.

[30] "Report of the Committee on National Conferences to
the Board of Managers of the Evangelical Alliance for the
United States," pp. 2, 3, 1-3 of the 8-page printed version, Dec. 21, 1886, E.A., "Miscellany," IV, n.p.—henceforth cited as "December Report," Miscellany," and pagi-
nated according to the printed version; E.A., "Minutes,"
III, Dec. 27, 1886, pp. 52, 50-57 and Dec. 30, 1886, p.
60; E.A., *Document*, XXV (1887), pp. 6-19.

[31] "December Report," "Miscellany," pp. 4, 2-7; E.A.,

"Minutes," III, Dec. 27, 1886, pp. 54, 52-55; E.A., *Document,* XXII (1886), pp. 3, 2-3; Interdenominational Congress, *Discussions of the Interdenominational Congress in the Interest of City Evangelization, Held in Cincinnati, December 7-11, 1885* (Cincinnati, 1886), pp. 191-97; "The Christian Conference at Cincinnati," *Advance,* Dec. 17, 1885, 818-19; Rev. Frank Russell, *A Method of Christian Co-operation for Reaching the Non-church-going Class* (New York, 1887), pp. 1-10—Russell states on page 2 that he used this method successfully in both Mansfield, Ohio, and Oswego, N.Y.

For an extensive discussion of the railroad strikes and Haymarket Riot as affecting Protestant opinion, see May, *Protestant Churches,* pp. 91ff.

[32] "December Report," "Miscellany," pp. 5-6; E.A., "Minutes," III, Dec. 27, 1886, pp. 54-55; E.A., *Document,* XXII (1886), pp. 4-5.

[33] "December Report," "Miscellany," p. 8; E.A., "Minutes," III, Dec. 27, 1886, pp. 56, 57 and Dec. 30, 1886, p. 60; E.A., *Document,* XXII (1886), p. 6.

[34] Letter, Anson D. Phelps to William E. Dodge, Jr., Dec. 7, 1889, typewritten copy courtesy of Cleveland E. Dodge; Ward, "The Evangelical Alliance in Boston," *Churchman,* Dec. 21, 1889, 771. Note that young Theodore Roosevelt implicitly accepted this kind of position when he wrote he would shoot the Haymarket rioters in the street. See Henry David, *The History of the Haymarket Affair* (New York, 1963), p. 334.

[35] Letter, Phelps to Dodge, Dec. 7, 1889.

[36] *We Are Not Divided,* pp. 16-17.

[37] Edward Talmage Root, "Josiah Strong, A Modern Prophet of the Kingdom of God," *New-Church Review,* XXIX (n.d., 1922), 47-54; Dorothea Muller, "Josiah Strong and the Challenge of the City" (unpublished Ph.D. dissertation, New York University, 1956), pp. 9-10; E.A., "Minutes," II: Jan. 21, 1887, p. 64; Feb. 26, 1887, pp. 70-71; Jan. 10, 1888, p. 127; Jan. 31, 1888, p. 136; E.A., *Document,* XXVI (1889), pp. 5-7; Sanford, "A History," p. 83; Josiah Strong, "Progress of Christian Co-operation Since the Washington Conference," E.A., *National Needs and Remedies: The Discussions of the General Christian Conference Held in Boston, Mass., December 4th, 5th, and 6th, 1889* (New York, 1890), p. 12—henceforth cited as *National Needs;*

Rev. Frank Russell, *A Method of Christian Co-operation,*
pp. 1-10.

To compare Strong's *Our Country* with the earlier literature, see: American Home Missionary Society, *Our Country: Number Two, A Plea for Home Missions* (New York, 1858);
Bushnell, *Barbarism, the First Danger;* Beecher, *A Plea For
the West.*

[38] E.A., "Minutes," III: March 28, 1887, pp. 81, 79-81
and March 19, 1887, p. 76—Hutchison, in *We Are Not Divided,* p. 15, calls the Basis a theological strait jacket on
the movement but these actions belie his judgment; Letter,
William E. Dodge to Bishop Alonzo Potter, May 28, 1887,
E.A., "Letters," VI, pp. 27-28; "The Lord Help Them,"
March 31, 1888, *Standard-Union* (Brooklyn), E.A., "Miscellany," VI, n.p. For a definition of evangelical as applied to the Alliance in the 1890s, see Letter, Josiah
Strong to Dr. [James] Buckley, Feb. 1, 1894, E.A., "Letters," III, n.p.

[39] Letter, Josiah Strong to the editor of *Kingdom,*
E.A., "Miscellany," IV, n.d., 1895, n.p.; Henry F. May, in
*Protestant Churches,* p. 255, suggests the Alliance wanted
Strong to break with the *Kingdom* because of George D.
Herron's connection with it—Herron seemed too radical.

[40] William E. Dodge letters, E.A., "Letters," VI, May,
1887, pp. 18-31; Appendix, "Call for the Washington Conference," E.A., *Document,* XXV (1887), pp. 26-30. These
names were compared to the Alliance membership rolls of
1870, 1874, and 1886, to ascertain those who belonged to
the Alliance previous to the "Call." Cf.: E.A., *Document,*
IV (1870), pp. 12-15; E.A., *Document,* IX (1873), pp. 34-35;
E.A., *Document,* XXI (1886), pp. 32-35.

[41] E.A., *National Perils and Opportunities. The Discussions of the General Christian Conference Held in Washington, D.C., December 7th, 8th and 9th, 1887* (New York,
1887), p. v.—henceforth cited as *National Perils.*

[42] Ibid., pp. v-vi.

[43] Hutchison, *We Are Not Divided,* p. 18; William E.
Dodge, Jr., "Opening Address," E.A., *National Perils,* pp.
2, 2-8. For similar views, cf.: Rev. Richard S. Storrs,
"Necessity of Co-operation in Christian Work," E.A., *National Perils,* pp. 290-91; Bishop Edward G. Andrews, "Address of Welcome," E.A., *National Perils,* pp. 14-15; Rev.
A. J. Gordon, "Address of Welcome," E.A., *National Needs,*

pp. 8-9.

[44]Dodge, "Address of Welcome," E.A., *National Perils,*
pp. 13, 14, 16, 13-16; Andrews, "Address of Welcome," E.A.,
*National Perils,* pp. 16-17.   Cf.: Storrs, "Necessity,"
E.A., *National Perils,* pp. 289-99; Bishop Samuel Harris,
"Necessity of Co-operation in Christian Work," E.A., *Na-
tional Perils,* p. 309.

[45]"Necessity," E.A., *National Perils,* pp. 301, 299-
302.

[46]"Necessity of Co-operation in Christian Work," E.A.,
*National Perils,* pp. 313, 304-13.

[47]"Necessity of Co-operation in Christian Work," E.A.,
*National Perils,* pp. 317, 315-26.

[48]"General Discussion," E.A., *National Perils,* pp.
332-35.

[49]E.A., *National Perils,* pp. 345, 345-46, 346.

[50]Ibid.

[51]Ibid., pp. 348-51.   Also see Josiah Strong, "Circular Letter," E.A., "Minutes," III, March 28, 1887, p. 81,
for further elaboration on the merits of the canvass.
Various suggested forms for Alliance constitutions also
provide a detailed statement of goals and steps to the
visitation method.   For example, see: "*Constitution and
Bylaws*—of—The Branch Evangelical Alliance of Greencastle
and Vicinity," 1888, E.A., "Miscellany," IV, n.p.   These
suggestions met widespread approval—(Editorial), "Denominational Co-operation," *CA,* Jan. 17, 1889, 33.

[52]"Methods," E.A., *National Perils,* pp. 347, 352-55.

[53]Ibid., pp. 356-63.   At the Florence Conference,
Russell gave ultimate credit to Thomas Chalmers for being
the first to devise a full-fledged visitation system in
Glasgow, Scotland.   E.A., *Document,* XXX (1891), pp. 67-68.

[54]"National Christian Conference," *CA,* Dec. 15, 1887,
817, E.A., "Minutes," III, Dec. 20, 1887, pp. 123-24;
"Call for the Syracuse Conference," E.A., "Minutes," III,
Nov. 1, 1888, pp. 162-64; E.A., *Document,* XXVI (1889), pp.
5-7; Josiah Strong, "The Progress of Christian Co-operation Since the Washington Conference," E.A., *National
Needs,* pp. 12-13.

[55]E.A., *Document,* XXVI (1889), p. 8; E.A., "Minutes," III, March 7, 1889, p. 186.

[56]Ward, "The Evangelical Alliance in Boston," *Churchman,* Dec. 21, 1889, 772.

[57]"Introduction," E.A., *National Needs,* pp. xi-xiii.

[58]"Opening Address," E.A., *National Needs,* pp. 3, 1-5.

[59]Strong, "The Progress of Christian Co-operation Since the Washington Conference," E.A., *National Needs,* pp. 11-13; E.A., *Document,* XXVI (1889), pp. 5-12.

[60]Strong, "Progress of Christian Co-operation Since the Washington Conference," E.A., *National Needs,* pp. 21, 12-21. Cf.: R. Fulton Cutting," Co-operative Religious Work in New York State," E.A., *National Needs,* pp. 22-24; "Reports from Local Alliances," E.A., *National Needs,* pp. 31-42; E.A., *Document,* XXIX (1890), pp. 5-11

[61]Strong, "The Needs of the City," E.A., *National Needs,* pp. 57-66. In "The Alliance Methods," E.A., *National Needs,* Russell quotes from Ephesians 4:16, Romans 12:5, and John 17 on pp. 101-02, and analyzes the visitation system on pp. 108-11.

[62][Lyman Abbott], "The Church and the Masses," *Christian Union,* Dec. 12, 1889, 757; [Lyman Abbott], "The New Departure of the Evangelical Alliance," *Christian Union,* Jan. 16, 1890, 78. Also see National Council of the Congregational Churches of the United States, *Minutes,* 1889, p. 252.

[63]"Christianity and Social Questions," E.A., *Document,* XXX (1891), pp. 36, 36-37.

[64]E.A., "Minutes," III: "Confidential Circular," and related decisions, April 22, 1890, pp. 236-40; May 12, 1890, pp. 243-45; Sept. 16, 1890, pp. 260-64; Oct. 30, 1890, pp. 273-75. E.A., *Document,* XXVIII (1890), pp. 9-11; E.A., *Document,* XXIX (1890), pp. 5-9; E.A., *Document,* XXXI (1891), pp. 7-13; E.A., *Document,* XXXII (1892), pp. 5-9.

[65]Strong, *New Era,* pp. v, 11-12, 18; E.A., *Document,* XXXIV (1893), p. 10.

[66]Strong, *New Era,* pp. 19-20, 116, 6-27; E.A., *Document,* XXXIV (1893), p. 10.

[67]Strong, *New Era,* pp. 39, 130, 115-30.

[68]Ibid.

[69]Ibid., pp. 115-26, 130-31, 260-320, 362-63.

[70]E.A., *Document,* XXXI (1891), p. 6; E.A., "Minutes,"
IV: April 30, 1891, p. 6; July 8, 1891, p. 12; "Introduction," E.A., *Applied. General,* pp. iii-iv.

[71]*We Are Not Divided,* p. 18; William E. Dodge, Jr.,
"Chairman's Address," E.A., *Applied. General,* pp. 22-23,
21-25; Charles C. Bonney, "Greetings and Responses," E.A.,
*Applied. General,* pp. 2-3.

[72]*Applied. General,* pp. 31, 31-33.

[73]"Organic Union: Its Reasons and Prospects," E.A.,
*Applied. General,* pp. 225, 221-225.

[74]Strong, "The Aims of the Evangelical Alliance for
the United States," E.A., *Applied. General,* pp. 257, 258-
59; James McCosh, "The Federation of Churches," E.A.,
*Applied. General,* pp. 230-33.

[75]E.A., *Applied. General,* pp. 305-40. Cf.: Hutchison,
*We Are Not Divided,* p. 19; Sanford, "A History," pp. 90-92.

[76]Schaff, "Reunion of Christendom," E.A., *Applied.*
*General,* p. 316. See: Elias B. Sanford, *Origin and His-*
*tory of the Federal Council of the Churches of Christ in*
*America* (Hartford, 1916), pp. 96-99; Charles S. MacFarland,
*Christian Unity in Practice and Prophecy* (New York, 1933),
p. 36; Hutchison, *We Are Not Divided,* p. 19.

[77]Josiah Strong, "A Federation of Churches," *Chris-*
*tian Work,* Jan. 9, 1896, 56, 55-56. For public response
to the program, cf.: (Editorial), "Christian Co-operation,"
*NYO,* Dec. 26, 1895, 998-99; Editorial comment, p. 1, concerning Josiah Strong, "The Churches and Reforms," *CA,* Dec.
26, 1895, 4; (Editorial), "An Important Federation Movement," *Christian Work,* Jan. 9, 1896, 48-49. The last
cited work interpreted this new Alliance program as in-
tending to organize all reform and ameliorative agencies
of the local community irrespective of religious connections and beliefs.

For the planning behind this program, see: E.A.,
"Minutes," IV: April 28, 1893, pp. 107-08; Feb. 9, 1894,
p. 149. E.A., *Document,* XXXIV (1893), pp. 11-12; E.A.,

*Document,* XXXV (1894), pp. 5-7; E.A., *Document,* XXXVII (1895), pp. 5-7. E.A., "Letters," III: Letter, Josiah Strong to L. T. Chamberlain, April 28, 1894, pp. 487-89; Letter, Josiah Strong to William E. Dodge, Jr., May 16, 1894, pp. 493-94.

[78]Strong, "A Federation of Churches," *Christian Work,* Jan. 9, 1896, 55-56.

[79]Josiah Strong, "Local Alliances," *American Journal of Sociology,* I (September, 1895), 178-80.

[80]E.A., *Document,* XXXIX (1897), pp. 4-8; "A New and Important Movement." E.A., "Miscellany," IV, n.p.; Printed letter form, May 5 [1898], E.A., "Miscellany," IV, n.p. E.A., "Minutes," IV: Dec. 31, 1897, p. 312; Feb. 11, 1898, p. 313. (Editorial), "An Important Federation Movement," *Christian Work,* Jan. 9, 1896, 48-49.

[81]Schaff: E.A., "Minutes," IV: Nov. 9, 1893, pp. 126-27; Nov. 17, 1893, pp. 129-30. Russell: E.A., "Minutes," IV, Feb. 10, 1893, p. 95. Jessup and Crooks: E.A., "Minutes," IV, Feb. 11, 1898, pp. 318-19. Jay: E.A., "Minutes," III, Dec. 10, 1890, p. 288. McBurney: E.A., "Minutes," V, April 22, 1898, pp. 5-6. Also see: E.A., "Minutes," IV, Feb. 10, 1893, p. 95; May 27, 1897, p. 300; June 17, 1897, pp. 302-03. E.A., "Minutes," V, March 25, 1898, p. 1.

[82]Letter, Letter of Resignation from Josiah Strong to the Board of Managers, E.A., "Letters," V, May 19, 1898, pp. 15, 14-15. E.A., "Minutes," V: April 22, 1898, pp. 7-8; May 6, 1898, pp. 9-10; May 19, 1898, pp. 14-16.

[83]E.A., *Document,* XL (1898), pp. 3, 4-5. Cf.: "Dr. Strong Resigns," *New York Times,* June 11, 1898, 5; "The Rev. Dr. Josiah Strong Resigns," *New York Daily Tribune,* June 11, 1898, 5.

[84]E.A., *Document,* XL (1898), pp. 4-5.

[85]E.A., *Document,* XL (1898), p. 5.

[86]Josiah Strong, *Our World, The New World Religion* (New York, 1915), p. 463; Douglass, *Protestant Cooperation,* pp. 48-49.

[87]Strong, *Our World,* p. 463.

[88]Sanford, *Origin and History of the Federal Council,*

pp. 34-52, 93-112, 146-67; Sanford, *Church Federation,* pp.
43, 647-67; and Alliance membership lists of late century,
especially E.A., *Document,* XXXIX (1898), pp. 28-30 and
E.A., *Document,* XL (1898), pp. 18-21.  Also see Abell,
*Urban Impact,* pp. 161-63; Hopkins, *Rise of the Social Gospel,* p. 303.

[89]Sanford, *Church Federation,* pp. 33, 43.

[90]MacFarland, *Christian Unity in Practice,* pp. 41,
25-44; Sanford, "A History," p. 95; Douglass, *Protestant
Cooperation,* pp. 41, 43-45.

[91]See note 88.

[92]Shelly, *Evangelicalism,* p. 69.

[93]Ibid., pp. 72-73.

[94]Donald W. Dayton, *Discovering an Evangelical Heritage* (New York, 1976): Donald G. Bloesch, *The Evangelical
Renaissance* (Grand Rapids, Mich., 1973); Richard J.
Coleman, *Issues of Theological Conflict,* rev. ed. (Grand
Rapids, Mich., 1980).

# BIBLIOGRAPHY

The only extant records known to me concerning the
United States body are located at Union Theological Seminary of New York City, and the Wisconsin State Historical
Society—the latter has a very small collection of local
Alliance documents pertinent to the early 1870s and is
relatively useless. Union became the depository of all
U.S. Alliance archives covering the period from 1868-1940
and has: a very valuable and comprehensive set of MSS
"Minutes," Vols. I-V (1868-1940); three disorganized boxes
of MSS Letters; "Letterbox"; six volumes of MSS "Letters";
and six volumes of newspaper clippings, printouts, pamphlets, etc., "Miscellany." The Union collection contains
nearly all Alliance published *Documents*, I-XLIX (1867-
1907), while the Union library itself is a goldmine of
nineteenth century church and ecumenical literature as
well as manuscript materials. A letter campaign to the
major libraries of regions where branch Alliances once
existed netted nothing of value. Absence of other docu-
mentary evidence required the piecing together of ecumenical and Alliance history through research in Alliance
spokesmen letter collections, publications, etc. The
Samuel Simon Schmucker Collections, MSS, Gettysburg College and Gettysburg Lutheran Seminary are very useful for
study of this prominent Lutheran. The Philip Schaff hold-
ings at Union, and the William E. Dodge, Sr., business
papers at the New York Public Library were of little help
in understanding their efforts on behalf of Christian
union. Indeed, the bulk of the Dodge private papers appear to be in family hands. I received some typed copies
of letters which the family thought relevant, courtesy of
Cleveland E. Dodge, New York City. Subsequent perusal of
Union Theological Seminary's Josiah Strong Collection,
papers put into order after the bulk of this book was re-
searched and written, merely substantiated the generalizations I made about Strong and is useful especially concerning Strong's interest in social science. The Papers of
John William Draper and Family, Manuscript Division, Library of Congress, are a major resource concerning science
in the nineteenth century as well as the Civil War and related *Alabama* claims.

No extant records exist concerning the antebellum U.S.
Alliance. The *Christian Union and Religious Memorial*

[*CURM*] (New York, 1848-1850), Methodist *Christian Advocate*
[*CA*] (New York, 1835-1900), *New York Observer* [*NYO*] (New
York, 1835-1900), and *New York Evangelist* [*NYE*] (New York,
1835-1900), proved crucial to reconstructing its beginnings.  The *Observer* and the *Evangelist* were printed on
such fragile newsprint that they fell apart with use and,
consequently, do not exist in full.  Newberry Library of
Chicago and the New York Public Library together have much
of the *Observer*, while New York Public holds large portions of the *Evangelist*.  Such periodical literature aided
understanding of the postwar Alliance as well.  Both prewar and postwar ecumenism involved so very many personal-
ities that perusal of contemporary published comments
helped to place them in proper context.

     Finally, the following bibliography represents only
that small portion of research material directly cited in
footnotes and not already mentioned in these bibliographi-
cal comments.  The dates after each periodical citation
indicate the years relied upon.

## I. PERIODICAL LITERATURE

*Advance.*  New York (1877-1886).

*American Catholic Quarterly Review.*  Philadelphia
     (1876-1900)

*American and Foreign Christian Union.*  New York (1854).

*American Historical Review.*  New York (1968).

*American Journal of Sociology.*  Chicago (1895-1915).

*American National Preacher.*  New York (1847).

*Andover Review.*  Boston (1884-1893).

*Baptist Quarterly.*  Philadelphia (1867-1877).

*Baptist Quarterly Review.*  New York (1879-1892).

*Bibliotheca Sacra.*  Andover (1844-1900).

*Catholic Historical Review.*  Washington (1961).

*Catholic World.*  New York (1865-1896).

*Christian Literature and Review of the Churches*. New York (1893-1899).

*Christian Union*. New York (1870-1893).

*Christian Work*. New York (1896).

*Church History*. Hartford; Mill Road, Pa. (1940-1980).

*Churchman*. Hartford (1899).

*Commonweal*. New York (1981).

*Eclectic Review*. London (1835-1868).

*Encounter*. Indianapolis (1967).

*Evangelical Christendom*. London (1847-1900).

*Harpers*. New York (1980).

*Harpers Weekly*. New York (1857-1900).

*Independent*. New York (1848-1900).

*Journal of American History*. Bloomington, Ind. (1973).

*Journal of the History of Ideas*. Philadelphia (1976).

*Journal of Presbyterian History*. Philadelphia (1973-1977).

*Mercersburg Review*. Lancaster, Pa. (1849-1875).

*Methodist History*. Lake Junaluska, N.C. (1978).

*Methodist Quarterly Review*. New York (1835-1900).

*Mid-America*. Chicago (1973).

*New-Church Review*. Boston (1922).

*New Englander*. New Haven (1843-1892).

*New York Daily Tribune*. (1864, 1898).

*New York Historical Society Quarterly*. (1966).

*New York Times*. (1870-1900).

*Princeton Review*. New York (1835-1888).

*Quarterly Review of the Evangelical Lutheran Church.*
Gettysburg (1871-1898).

*Tennessee Historical Quarterly.* (1971).

*U.S. News and World Report.* Washington, D.C. (1980).


## II. VOLUNTARY SOCIETY AND CHURCH PUBLICATIONS

Alliance of the Reformed Churches Holding the Presbyterian
System. *Report of the Proceedings of the First Gener-*
*al Presbyterian Council Convened at Edinburgh, 1877,*
*July 1877.* Edited by Rev. J. Thomson. Edinburgh:
Thomas and Archibald Constable, 1877.

American and Foreign Anti-Slavery Society. *Remonstrance*
*Against the Course Pursued by the Evangelical Alli-*
*ance on the Subject of Slavery.* New York: W. Harned,
1847.

American Home Missionary Society. *Our Country: Number Two,*
*A Plea for Home Missions.* New York: American Home
Missionary Society, 1858.

Evangelical Alliance. British Organization. *A Concise*
*View of its Principles, Objects, and Constitution.*
Southern Division. London: Blackburn & Pardon,
Printers, 1846.

_____. *Deputation to the American Branch of the Evan-*
*gelical Alliance: Report of the Official Secretary of*
*the British Organization.* London: Wm. Bowden, 1870.

_____. *The Religious Condition of Christendom, De-*
*scribed in a Series of Papers Presented to the*
*Seventh General Conference of the Evangelical Alli-*
*ance, Held in Basle, 1879.* Edited by J. Murray Mit-
chell. London: Hodder & Stoughton, 1880.

_____. *Report of the Proceedings of the Conference*
*Held at Freemason's Hall, London, from August 19th to*
*September 2nd Inclusive, 1846.* London: Partridge and
Oakey, 1847.

_____. *Report of the Secretaries of the British Organi-*
*zation of the Alliance, Deputations from European and*
*American Branches of the Evangelical Alliance to the*
*Emperor or Russia, on Behalf of Protestants in the*
*Baltic Provinces.* London: [Evangelical Alliance of

Britain], 1871.

Evangelical Alliance. Canadian Organization. *Vital Questions. Discussions of the General Christian Conference Held in Montreal, Que., Canada, October 2nd to 25th, 1888.* Montreal: William Drysdale and Co., 1889.

Evangelical Alliance for the United States of America. *Christianity Practically Applied. The Discussions of the International Christian Conference Held in Chicago, October 8-14, 1893.* 2 vols. *The General Conference, I. The Section Conference, II.* New York: The Baker and Taylor Co., 1894.

_____. *Document Number Four of the Evangelical Alliance in Protest Against the So-Called 'Freedom of Worship Bill' Now before the Assembly of the State of New York. April 25, 1885.* New York: Trow's Printing and Bookbinding Co., 1885.

_____. *Evangelical Alliance Conference, 1873. History, Essays, Orations, and Other Documents of the Sixth General Conference of the Evangelical Alliance held in New York, October 2-12, 1873.* Edited by Philip Schaff and Samuel Irenaeus Prime. New York: Harper & Brothers, 1874.

_____. *National Needs and Remedies. The Discussions of the General Christian Conference, Held in Boston, Mass., December 4th, 5th and 6th, 1889.* New York: The Baker & Taylor Co., 1890.

_____. *National Perils and Opportunities. The Discussions of the General Christian Conference, Held in Washington, D.C., December 7th, 8th and 9th, 1887.* New York: The Baker & Taylor Co., 1887.

_____. *Protest of the Evangelical Alliance of the United States Against the Bill Entitled An Act to Secure to the Inmates of Institutions for the Care of the Poor Freedom of Worship. (In Senate #136, in Assembly #131 & 133).* New York: Trow's Printing and Bookbinding Co., 1883.

_____. *Protest of the Evangelical Alliance of the United States Against the Senate Bill Introduced Jan. 6, 1885, by Senator Gibbs and Senator Murphy Entitled 'An Act to Secure to Inmates of Institutions for the Care of the Poor Freedom of Worship.'* New York: Office of the Evangelical Alliance, 1885.

_____. Evangelical Lutheran Church. *Proceedings of the Thirteenth Convention of the General Synod of the Evangelical Lutheran Church in the United States. Convened in Philadelphia, May 16, 1845.* Baltimore: Publication Rooms of the Evangelical Lutheran Church, 1845.

Federal Council of the Churches of Christ in America. *Federal Council Yearbook: Covering the Year of 1915.* Edited by H. K. Carroll. New York: Missionary Education Movement of the United States and Canada, 1916.

Interdenominational Congress. *Discussions of the Interdenominational Congress in the Interest of City Evangelization, Held in Cincinnati, December 7-11, 1885.* Cincinnati: Interdenominational Congress, 1886.

[James King]. The National League for the Protection of American Institutions. *Document No. Twenty-One: To Protect in New York State the Free Common Schools and to Prohibit all Sectarian Appropriations. An Address to the Citizens.* New York: The National League for the Protection of American Institutions, 1894.

London Provisional Committee. *Conference on Christian Union. Narrative of the Proceedings of the Meetings held in Liverpool, October, 1845.* London: James Nisbit and Co., 1845.

National Council of the Congregational Churches of the United States. *Minutes.*

Presbyterian Church in the United States of America. General Assembly. *Minutes.*

Presbyterian Church in the United States of America. General Assembly (New School). *Minutes.*

Presbyterian Church in the United States of America. General Assembly (Old School). *Minutes.*

Presbyterian Church in the United States of America (South). General Assembly. *Minutes.*


III. PRIMARY SOURCES
_____

Baird, Henry M. *The Life of the Rev. Robert Baird.* New York: Anson D. F. Randolph, 1866.

Baird, Robert. *The Noblest Freedom; or the Influence of Christianity upon Civil Liberty: A Discourse Addressed to the Alumni of Jefferson College, Pa.* New York: C. W. Benedict, 1948.

_____. *The Progress and Prospects of Christianity in the United States of America.* London: Partridge and Oakey, 1851.

_____. *Religion in America: Or, an Account of the Origin, Progress, Relation to the State, and Present Condition of the Evangelical Churches in the United States.* New York: Harper & Brothers, 1844.

Beecher, Lyman. *A Plea for the West.* 2nd ed. Cincinnati: Truman & Smith, 1835.

Bushnell, Horace. *Barbarism, the First Danger.* Vol. I. *Work and Play.* New York: Charles Scribner's Sons, 1912.

Chalmers, Rev. Dr. Thomas. *On the Evangelical Alliance: Its Design, Its Difficulties, Its Proceedings, and Its Prospects; with Practical Suggestions.* Edinburgh: Oliver & Boyd, 1846.

Crooks, George D., ed. *Sermons by Bishop Matthew Simpson of the Methodist Episcopal Church.* New York: Harper & Brothers, 1885.

Hurst, John F. *History of Rationalism Embracing a Survey of the Present State of Protestant Theology.* New York: Phillips & Hunt, 1865.

Jay, John. *Rome in America: An Address Before the Bible Society at Mount Kisco, New York, September 21, 1868.* New York: Charles Scribner & Co., 1869.

King, James M. *Sectarian Indian Schools, or the Relation of the Churches to the General Government in the Education of the Races.* New York: Office of the National League for the Protection of American Institutions, 1890.

McIlvaine, Charles P. *The Temple of God.* Philadelphia: Protestant Episcopal Book Society, 1860.

Prime, Samuel Irenaeus. *Autobiography and Memorials.* Edited by Wendell Prime. New York: Anson D. F. Randolph & Co., 1888.

Richardson, R. H.  *Lessons of the Evangelical Alliance.*
     Trenton: Sharps Book and Publishing House, 1873.

Russell, Rev. Frank.  *A Method of Christian Co-operation*
     *for Reaching the Non-Church-Going Class.*  New York:
     Evangelical Alliance for the United States, 1887.

Sanford, Elias B., ed.  *Church Federation: Inter-Church*
     *Conference on Federation, New York, November 15-21,*
     *1905.*  New York: Fleming H. Revell Co., 1906.

Schaff, David S., ed.  *The Life of Philip Schaff: In Part*
     *Autobiographical.*  New York: Charles Scribner's Sons,
     1897.

Schaff, Philip.  *Christ and Christianity.*  New York:
     Charles Scribner's Sons, 1885.

_____.  *Church and State in the United States, or the*
     *American Idea of Religious Liberty and its Practical*
     *Effects.*  New York: Charles Scribner's Sons, 1889.

_____.  *A History of the Creeds of Christendom.*  Vol.
     I.  *Creeds of Christendom.*  3 vols.  London: Hodder
     and Stoughton, 1877.

_____.  *The Progress of Religious Freedom as Shown in*
     *the History of the Toleration Acts.*  New York:
     Charles Scribner's Sons, 1889.

_____.  *What is Church History?  A Vindication of the*
     *Idea of Historical Development.*  Philadelphia: J. B.
     Lippincott and Co., 1846.

Schmucker, Samuel Simon.  *The Church of the Redeemer, as*
     *Developed within the General Synod of the Lutheran*
     *Church in America.*  Baltimore: T. Newton Kuntz, 1867.

_____.  *Discourse in Commemoration of the Glorious Ref-*
     *ormation of the Sixteenth Century: Delivered Before*
     *the Evangelical Lutheran Synod of West Pennsylvania.*
     New York: Gould and Newman, 1838.

_____.  *Fraternal Appeal to the American Churches with*
     *a Plan for Catholic Union on Apostolic Principles.*
     Edited by Frederick K. Wentz.  Seminar Editions.
     Philadelphia: Fortress Press, 1965.

_____.  *The True Unity of Christ's Church: Being a Re-*
     *newed Appeal to the Friends of the Redeemer, on*

*Primitive Christian Union, and the History of its
Corruption, to Which is Now Added a Modified Plan for
the Re-Union of All Evangelical Churches; Embracing
as Integral Parts the World's Evangelical Alliance
with all its National Branches.* 3rd ed. New York:
Anson D. F. Randolph & Co., 1870.

Shangai and Hankow Committees of the Evangelical Alliance.
*Memorandum on the Persecution of Christians in China.*
Shanghai: American Presbyterian Mission Press, 1885.

Smith, Henry B. *Christian Union and Ecclesiastical Reunion, a Discourse Delivered at the Opening of the General Assembly of the Presbyterian Church in the
United States of America, in Dayton, Ohio, May 19,
1864.* New York: J. M. Sherwood, 1864.

Strong, Josiah. *The New Era or the Coming Kingdom.* New
York: The Baker & Taylor Co., 1893.

_____. *Our Country: Its Possible Future and Its Pres-
ent Crisis.* New York: The Baker & Taylor Co., 1891.

_____. *Our World: The New World Religion.* New York:
Doubleday, Page & Co., 1915.

Stuart, George H. *The Life of George H. Stuart, Written
by Himself.* Ed. Robert Ellis Thompson. Philadelphia:
J. M. Stoddard & Co., 1890.

Thebaud, Rev. Augustus J., S. J. *Forty Years in the
United States of America (1839-1885).* Edited by
Charles George Herbermann. New York: The United
States Catholic Historical Society, 1904.

Tiffany, Charles C. *A History of the Protestant Episcopal
Church in the United States of America.* 2nd ed. Vol.
VII. The American Church History Series. 13 vols.
Edited by Philip Schaff, *et al.* New York: Charles
Scribner's Sons, 1895.

Thompson, Joseph P. *Man in Genesis and in Geology: Or,
The Biblical Account of Man's Creation Tested by
Scientific Theories of His Origin and Antiquity.* New
York: S. R. Wells, 1870.

Thompson, Robert Ellis. *A History of the Presbyterian
Churches in the United States.* Vol. VI. American
Church History Series. New York: Charles Scribner's
Sons, 1895.

## IV. SECONDARY SOURCES

Abell, Aaron Ignatious. *American Catholicism and Social
    Action: A Search for Social Justice, 1865-1950.*
    Garden City, N.Y.: Hanover House, 1960.

_____. *The Urban Impact on American Protestantism,
    1865-1900.* London: Archon, 1962.

Ahlstrom, Sydney. *A Religious History of the American
    People.* 2 vols. Garden City, N.Y.: Image Books, 1975.

Altholz, Josef L. *The Churches in the Nineteenth Century.*
    New York: The Bobbs-Merrill Co., 1967.

Bainton, Roland H. *Here I Stand: A Life of Martin Luther.*
    New York: Abingdon-Cokesbury Press, 1950.

Barnes, Gilbert Hobbs. *The Antislavery Impulse, 1830-1844.*
    New York: Harcourt, Brace & World, 1933, 1964.

Barr, James. *Fundamentalism.* Philadelphia: Westminster
    Press, 1978.

Billington, Ray Allen. *The Protestant Crusade, 1800-1860.*
    Quadrangle Paperbacks. Chicago: Quadrangle Books,
    1938, 1964.

Blau, Joseph, ed. *Cornerstones of Religious Freedom in
    America.* Boston: Beacon Press, 1949.

Bloesch, Donald G. *The Evangelical Renaissance.* Grand
    Rapids, Mich.: William B. Eerdmans Publishing Co.,
    1973.

Bodo, John R. *The Protestant Clergy and Public Issues,
    1812-1848.* Princeton , N.J.: Princeton University
    Press, 1954.

Boller, Paul F. *American Thought in Transition: The Im-
    pact of Evolutionary Naturalism, 1865-1900.* Rand
    McNally Series on the History of American Thought
    and Culture. Chicago: Rand McNally, 1969.

Bozeman, Theodore Dwight. *Protestants in An Age of Sci-
    ence: The Baconian Ideal and Antebellum Religious
    Thought.* Chapel Hill: University of North Carolina
    Press, 1977.

Brown, Robert McAffee. *The Ecumenical Revolution.* New

York: Doubleday and Co., 1967.

Brown, William Adams. *Toward a United Church: Three Decades of Ecumenical Christianity*. New York: Charles Scribner's Sons, 1946.

Brush, Stephen G. *History of Physical Science from Newton to Einstein*. Xerox. College Park, Maryland: 1977.

Cavert, Sameul McCrea. *The American Churches in the Ecumenical Movement, 1900-1968*. New York: Association Press, 1968.

Clark, Robert D. *The Life of Matthew Simpson*. New York: The Macmillan Co., 1956.

Coleman, Richard J. *Issues of Theological Conflict*. Rev. ed. Grand Rapids, Mich.: William B. Eerdmans Publishing Co., 1980.

Cross, Robert D. *The Emergence of Liberal Catholicism in America*. Quadrangle Paperbacks. Chicago: Quadrangle Books, 1958.

Daniels, George H. *American Science in the Age of Jackson*. New York: Columbia University Press, 1968.

David, Henry. *The History of the Haymarket Affair*. New York: Collier Books, 1963.

Davis, Lawrence B. *Immigrants, Baptists, and the Protestant Mind in America*. Urbana: University of Illinois Press, 1973.

Dayton, Donald W. *Discovering an Evangelical Heritage*. New York: Harper & Row, Publishers, 1976.

Dickens, A. G. *The English Reformation*. New York: Schocken Books, 1964.

_____. *Reformation and Society in Sixteenth-Century Europe*. London: Harcourt, Brace and World, 1966.

Dodge, D. Stuart. *Memorials of William E. Dodge*. New York: Anson D. F. Randolph and Co., 1887.

Dolan, Jay. *Catholic Revivalism: The American Experience, 1830-1900*. Notre Dame and London: University of Notre Dame Press, 1978.

_____. *The Immigrant Church: New York's Irish and Ger-
     man Catholics, 1815-1865.* Baltimore and London:   The
     Johns Hopkins University Press, 1975.

Douglass, H. Paul. *Protestant Cooperation in American
     Cities.* New York: Institute of Social and Religious
     Research, 1930.

Draper, John William. *History of the Conflict Between
     Religion and Science.* New York: D. Appleton & Co.,
     1874.

Ewing, John. *Goodly Fellowship: A Centenary Tribute to
     the Life and Work of the World's Evangelical Alliance,
     1846-1946.* London: Marshall, Morgan, and Scott, 1946.

Fey, Harold E., ed. *The Ecumenical Advance:  A History of
     the Ecumenical Movement.* Vol. 2/1948-1968.  Phila-
     delphia: Westminster Press, 1970.

Foster, Charles I. *An Errand of Mercy: The Evangelical
     United Front, 1790-1837.* Chapel Hill: University of
     North Carolina Press, 1960.

Gabriel, Ralph Henry. *The Course of American Democratic
     Thought.* 2nd ed.  New York: The Ronald Press Co.,
     1956.

Gaustad, Edwin Scott. *The Great Awakening in New England.*
     New York: Harper & Row, 1957.

Gewehr, Wesley M. *The Great Awakening in Virginia, 1740-
     1790.* Durham: The University of North Carolina Press,
     1930.

Glock, Charles Y. and Stark, Rodney. *Religion and Society
     in Tension.* Rand McNally Sociology Series.  Chicago:
     Rand McNally, 1956.

Gravely, William B. *Gilbert Haven: Methodist Abolitionist.*
     Nashville, Abingdon Press, 1973.

Griffin, Clifford S. *Their Brother's Keepers: Moral Stew-
     ardship in the United States, 1800-1865.* New Bruns-
     wick, N.J.: Rutgers University Press, 1960.

Hales, E. E. Y. *The Catholic Church in the Modern World:
     A Survey from the French Revolution to the Present.*
     Image Books.  Garden City, New York: Doubleday &
     Co., 1958.

Handlin, Oscar. *Boston's Immigrants: 1790-1865.* Cam-
    bridge, Mass.: Harvard University Press, 1941.

_____. *The Uprooted.* New York: Grosset and Dunlap,
    1951.

Handy, Robert T. *A Christian America: Protestant Hopes
    and Historical Realities.* New York: Oxford Univer-
    sity Press, 1971.

_____. *A History of the Churches in the United States
    and Canada.* Oxford History of the Christian Church.
    Edited by Henry and Owen Chadwick. New York: Oxford
    University Press, 1977.

_____. *The Protestant Quest for a Christian America,
    1830-1930.* Facet Books Historical Series. Phila-
    delphia: Fortress Press, 1967.

Hansen, Klaus J. *Mormonism and the American Experience.*
    Chicago and London: University of Chicago Press, 1981.

Hansen, Marcus Lee. *The Atlantic Migration, 1607-1860.*
    Cambridge, Mass.: Harvard University Press, 1940.

Heimert, Alan E. *Religion and the American Mind from the
    Great Awakening to the Revolution.* Cambridge, Mass.:
    Harvard University Press, 1966.

Higham, John. *Strangers in the Land: Patterns of American
    Nativism, 1860-1925.* College Edition. New York:
    Atheneum, 1963.

Hodge, A. A., ed. *The Life of Charles Hodge.* New York:
    Charles Scribner's Sons, 1880.

Hopkins, Charles Howard. *The Rise of the Social Gospel.*
    New Haven: Yale University Press, 1940.

Hovenkamp, Herbert. *Science and Religion in America,
    1800-1860.* Philadelphia: University of Pennsylvania
    Press, 1978.

Hudson, Winthrop S. *Religion in America.* New York:
    Charles Scribner's Sons, 1965.

Hutchison, John A. *We Are Not Divided: A Critical and
    Historical Study of the Federal Council of the Chur-
    ches of Christ in America.* New York: Round Table
    Press, 1941.

Jamison, Wallace N.  "A History of the Evangelical Alli-
    ance for the United States of America."  Unpublished
    S.T.M. Thesis, Union Theological Seminary, 1941.

Jones, Maldwyn Allen.  *American Immigration.*  Chicago:
    University of Chicago Press, 1960.

Jordan, Kay Irene Kirkpatrick.  "Samuel Simon Schmucker's
    Conception of a Christian America."  Unpublished M.A.
    Thesis, Western State College of Colorado, 1973.

Kessler, J. B. A., Jr.  *A Study of the Evangelical Alli-
    ance in Great Britain.*  Goes, Netherlands: Osterbaan
    & Le Contre, 1968.

Kinzer, Donald L.  *An Episode in Anti-Catholicism: The
    American Protective Association.*  Seattle: University
    of Washington Press, 1964.

Loetscher, Lefferts A. *The Broadening Church.*  Philadel-
    phia: University of Pennsylvania Press, 1954.

Lord, Robert H.; Sexton, John E.; and Harrignton, Edward
    T.  *History of the Archdiocese of Boston.*  3 vols.
    New York: Sheed & Ward, 1944.

MacFarland, Charles S.  *Christian Unity in the Making: The
    First Twenty-Five Years of the Federal Council of the
    Churches of Christ in America, 1905-1930.*  New York:
    The Federal Council of the Churches of Christ in
    America, 1948.

_____.  *Christian Unity in Practice and Prophecy.* New
    York: The MacMillan Co., 1933.

McConnell, S. D.  *History of the American Episcopal Church.*
    New York: Thomas Whittaker, 1890.

McLoughlin, William G., ed.  *The American Evangelicals,
    1800-1900.*  Harper Torchbooks.  New York: Harper &
    Row, 1955.

_____.  *Billy Sunday was His Real Name.*  Chicago: Uni-
    versity of Chicago Press, 1955.

_____.  *Revivals, Awakenings and Reform:  An Essay on
    Religion and Social Change in America, 1607-1977.*
    Chicago and London: University of Chicago Press, 1978.

McNeill, John T.  *The History and Character of Calvinism.*

New York: Oxford University Press, 1954.

_____. *Unitive Protestantism: A Study in Our Religious Resources*. New York: Abingdon Press, 1930.

Marraro, Howard R. *American Opinion on the Unification of Italy, 1846-1861*. New York: Columbia University Press, 1932.

Marty, Martin E. *Righteous Empire: The Protestant Experience in America*. New York: The Dial Press, 1970.

Maxson, Charles H. *The Great Awakening in the Middle Colonies*. Chicago: The University of Chicago Press, 1920.

May, Henry F. *Protestant Churches and Industrial America*. New York: Octagon Books, 1963.

Mead, Sidney E. *The Lively Experiment: The Shaping of Christianity in America*. New York: Harper & Row, 1963.

_____. *The Nation with the Soul of a Church*. New York: Harper & Row, 1975.

Miller, Perry. *The Life of the Mind in America: From the Revolution to the Civil War*. New York: Harcourt Brace, Inc., 1965.

Miller, Randall M. and Marzik, Thomas D. *Immigrants and Religion in Urban America*. Philadelphia: Temple University Press, 1977.

Morrison, Charles Clayton. *The Unfinished Reformation*. New York: Harper & Brothers, 1953.

Muller, Dorothea Rosalie. "Josiah Strong and the Challenge of the City." Unpublished Ph.D. dissertation, New York University, 1956.

Nelson, E. Clifford. *The Lutherans in North America*. Philadelphia: Fortress Press, 1975.

Nicholls, William. *Ecumenism and Catholicity*. London: S C M Press, Ltd., 1952.

Nichols, James Hastings. *Romanticism in American Theology*. Chicago: University of Chicago Press, 1961.

Norman, E. R.  *Anti-Catholicism in Victorian England*.  New
    York: Barnes & Noble, 1968.

O'Dea, Thomas F.  *Sociology and the Study of Religion:
    Theory, Research, Interpretation*.  New York: Basic
    Books, Inc. 1970.

Persons, Stow.  *American Minds: A History of Ideas*.  Rev.
    ed. Huntington, N.Y.: Robert E. Krieger Publishing
    Co., 1975.

Pratt, John Webb.  *Religion, Politics, and Diversity: The
    Church-State Theme in New York History*.  Ithaca,
    New York: Cornell University Press, 1967.

Rouse, Ruth and Neill, Stephen Charles, ed.  *A History of
    the Ecumenical Movement, 1517-1948*.  2nd ed.  Phila-
    delphia: Westminster Press, 1968.

Russett, Cynthia.  *Darwin in America: The Intellectual
    Response*.  San Francisco: W. H. Freeman and Company,
    1976.

Sandeen, Ernst R.  *The Roots of Fundamentalism: British and
    American Millenarianism, 1800-1930*.  Grand Rapids,
    Mich.: Baker Book House, 1970.

Sanford, Elias B.  "A History of the Evangelical Alliance
    for the United States."  MSS [1917] Library of the
    National Council of the Churches of Christ in America,
    Federal Council Collection.  Xerox copy, University
    of Iowa Libraries, Iowa City.

_____.  *Origin and History of the Federal Council of
    the Churches of Christ in America*.  Hartford: The
    S. S. Scranton Co., 1916.

Shelly, Bruce L.  *Evangelicalism in America*.  Grand Rapids,
    Mich.: William B. Eerdmans Publishing Co., 1967.

Slosser, Gaius Jackson.  *Christian Unity: Its History and
    Challenge in All Communions, In All Lands*.  New York:
    E. P. Dutton, 1929.

Smith, Timothy L.  *Revivalism and Social Reform: American
    Protestants on the Eve of the Civil War*.  Harper
    Torchbooks.  New York: Harper & Row, 1957, 1965.

Smylie, John Edwin.  "Protestant Clergymen and America's
    World Role, 1865-1900: A Study of Christianity,

Nationality, and International Relations." Unpublished Th.D. dissertation, Princeton Theological Seminary, 1959.

Stein, Maurice R.; Vidich, Arthur J.; and White, David Manning, eds. *Identity and Anxiety: Survival of the Person in Mass Society.* Glencoe, Illinois: The Free Press of Glencoe, 1960.

Stokes, Anson Phelps. *Church and State in the United States.* Vol. I. 3 vols. New York: Harper & Bros., 1950.

Sweet, William Warren. *The Story of Religion in America.* Rev. ed. New York: Harper & Bros., 1950.

Synan, Vincent. *The Holiness-Pentecostal Movement.* Grand Rapids, Mich.: William B. Eerdmans Publishing Co., 1971.

Tomasi, Silvano M. and Stibili, Edward C., ed. *Italian-Americans and Religion: An Annotated Bibliography.* New York: Center for Immigration Studies, 1978.

Weinberg, Albert K. *Manifest Destiny: A Study of Nationalist Expansionism in American History.* Chicago: Quadrangle Paperbacks, 1935, 1963.

Wentz, Abdel Ross. *Pioneer in Christian Unity: Samuel Simon Schmucker.* Philadelphia: Fortress Press, 1967.

White, Ronald C., Jr. and Hopkins, C. Howard. *The Social Gospel: Religion and Reform in Changing America.* Philadelphia: Temple University Press, 1976.

Wiebe, Robert H. *The Search for Order, 1877-1920.* New York: Hill and Wang, 1967.

Wyatt-Brown, Bertram. *Lewis Tappan and the Evangelical War Against Slavery.* Cleveland: The Press of Case Western Reserve University, 1969.

# INDEX

STUDIES IN AMERICAN RELIGION

Philip Jordan is professor of history at Western State College of Colorado

FOR A COMPLETE LIST OF TITLES AND PRICES
PLEASE WRITE:
**The Edwin Mellen Press**
**P.O. Box 450**
**Lewiston, New York   14092**